COLLINS COBUILD

KEY WORDS IN THE MEDIA

Bill Mascull

THE UNIVERSITY
OF BIRMINGHAM

COLLINS
COBUILD

HarperCollins*Publishers*

HarperCollins Publishers
77-85 Fulham Palace Road
London W6 8JB

COBUILD is a trademark of William Collins Sons & Co. Ltd.

ISBN 0 00 370951 5

Design and typesetting by
eMC Design, 3 Grange Lane, Bromham,
Bedfordshire MK43 8NP

Printed in Great Britain by
HarperCollins Manufacturing, Glasgow

Corpus Acknowledgements

We would like to thank those authors and publishers
who kindly gave permission for copyright material
to be used in the Bank of English. We would also
like to thank Times Newspapers Ltd. and the
BBC World Service for providing valuable data.

Contents

Introduction

Key Words in the Media is designed to help unlock the English of newspapers, radio and television.

It systematically covers wórds and expressions that frequently occur and recur in the news media. Some of these words and expressions appear much more frequently there than elsewhere. Others occur more generally, but are used in the media in a particular way.

This book shows what these words and expressions mean, how they are used and how they relate to each other.

The book covers eight main subject areas. You look at the meanings of frequently occurring words in these areas in the context of real examples from broadcasting and newspapers.

You then go on to apply and develop your knowledge of the meanings and use of these words in specially devised language activities.

Key Words in the Media has been written so that each chapter can be read sequentially from beginning to end. Or you may just want to dip and browse, looking at things that interest you.

Who is *Key Words in the Media* for?

Key Words in the Media is designed for:

Learners of English: upper intermediate and advanced learners of English working on their own who read English-language newspapers and listen to radio with the objective of improving their English by following the news.

The book can also be used as a complement to language classes where newspapers and radio news are frequently used as input and discussion material.

Media studies course participants at secondary and university level, to develop awareness of how language is used in the media.

Structure

Each chapter consists of a logical sequence of topic sections. Each topic section contains these parts:

◆ **Key words and commentary.** The key words in a specific area are listed, explained and defined in relation to each other and in their grammatical context.

◆ **Examples** from broadcasting and newspapers illustrate the meanings of these key words in context. Most of these extracts are at least one sentence or longer so as to give a good sense of overall context. The examples have been chosen for their intrinsic interest, and for their illustrative and explanatory power.

◆ **Language activities** further refine understanding of how the key words are used, relate to each other and to other words, develop awareness of grammatical context, and show how the key words fit into overall patterns of meaning.

Section content

Key words and commentary

Each commentary brings together a number of related key words, explaining and defining them in a continuous text. The key words are indicated in bold in the commentary itself and are also listed in logical groups in the left hand column.

viewer couch potato zap zapper remote control	People watching TV are **viewers**. Viewers who watch a lot of television without caring what they watch are **couch potatoes**. If you **zap** between channels, you use your **remote control** or **zapper** to change channels a lot, perhaps looking for something interesting to watch, and perhaps not succeeding. A zapper is also a person who zaps.
tube box telly	Informal words for television are the **tube** in the US, and the **box** or the **telly** in Britain.

Language notes

Where relevant, the commentary is followed by language notes providing grammatical information about key words in the commentary (where this information is not given in the commentary itself) and giving variations in spelling and hyphenation.

broadcast
 	
programme
show
  host a programme
  host a show
 	
disc jockey
DJ
host
	Programmes on radio and television may be referred to formally as **broadcasts**; and they may be referred to informally as **shows**, specially in American English.
	
	Programmes or shows on radio and television are often presented or **hosted** by a programme host. Popular music programmes are presented by **disc jockeys** or **DJs**.
		show 184 ⇓

◆ **LANGUAGE NOTE**

Programme is spelt **program** in American English.
Broadcast is a noun and a verb.
Disc jockey is spelt **disk jockey** in American English and can be spelt with a hyphen.

Examples

The examples have been chosen to provide interesting illustrations of how the key words are used. They are in *italics*, and the first occurrence of a key word is *underlined*.

Do you think there are a lot of high powered lawyers, doctors, educators out there who say they don't watch TV and secretly go home at night and turn the <u>tube</u> on and play <u>couch potato</u>?

Language activities, and hints on how to do them

Each activity gets you to do one of these things, or a combination of them:

◆ **Think about words and their meanings by putting them into an overall context.** Where a list of words is given for gap completion of sentences or a text, read the instructions carefully: some of the words may be used more than once, and some not at all.

◆ **Match words to their definitions.** Look through all the items before completing the exercise: don't jump to conclusions.

◆ **Match sentences or sentence-parts** to take meaning, context and grammar into account. Look specially for clues to help you combine sentence-parts not only meaningfully but grammatically.

◆ **Re-order sentences and paragraphs** to build logically developed articles and broadcasts, sometimes sorting out extracts from different sources.
Read the instructions carefully for clues on which part comes first. Again, look specially for clues to help you combine sections not only meaningfully but grammatically so as to build up logically developed texts.

◆ **Read articles and programme scripts** and answer questions designed not only to *test* understanding of key words but also to *develop* this understanding in wider contexts.
Look at networks of meaning, reusing the key vocabulary of the chapter, relating it to what you already know. You may need to look up some words in the dictionary. Preferably use the *Collins Cobuild English Language Dictionary*.

◆ **Test your knowledge of meaning and spelling of words** in crosswords and word games.

Conventions

Language activities

Where language activities require missing words to be given, a continuous line indicates that the word may be of any length, as here:

Virgin Atlantic is more concerned with using technology to improve _____ entertainment. Last year, Virgin became the first airline with individual colour seatback screens for every passenger on its wide bodied aircraft.

Answer: in-flight

Where spaces are indicated like this, each underlining indicates one missing letter:

Senegal and Mauritania have agreed in principle to _ _ _ _ _ _ diplomatic relations, broken off two years ago after bloody clashes along the Senegal river which forms their common frontier.

Answer: resume

'Gift' letters may sometimes be given, like this:

Here, if a businessman started suggesting to his s _ _ r _ h _ _ d _ r _ that he read poetry, everyone would rush out and sell his shares.

Answer: shareholders

Cross-referencing

An arrow in the right-hand margin indicates that a key word in the text occurs in another chapter of the book. The numbers given are the page numbers of the other occurrences. (Key words occurring elsewhere in the same chapter are not indicated in this way.)

The downturn in sales at the group, which includes Ernest Jones and H Samuel, is due more to recession than to Mr Ratner's remarks. Business in America is believed to have benefited from the upturn in the economy there.

5 'The downturn in sales is due more to the recession than to Mr Ratner's remarks.' Do you believe this?

downturn *89* ⇑
recession *89* ⇑
upturn *89* ⇑

The right hand column may also indicate key words related to key words in the text that are dealt with in another chapter of the book:

own goal

If you make an unforced mistake that gives an advantage to an opponent, you score an **own goal**.

gaffe *35* ⇑

The cross-reference system is designed to encourage you to browse, following your own routes through the book.

Note on sources

Key Words in the Media has been developed using a computer database containing nearly 60 million words of text from a variety of newspaper and broadcast sources. This database is part of the Collins Cobuild Bank of English: the examples and most of the material for the language activities have been taken from it.

Radio

BBC World Service. Best known for its authoritative news and current affairs programmes. Estimated worldwide audience of 130 million.

National Public Radio based in Washington DC. News and current affairs. Audience of 147 million.

Newspapers

Today. Tabloid format daily. Circulation 600,000.

The Times. Sometimes perceived, perhaps wrongly, as the voice of the British establishment. Circulation 550,000.

The Independent. Daily, founded in 1987 to compete in the British quality market, consisting until then of *The Times*, *The Guardian* and the *Daily Telegraph*. Circulation 275,000.

The Economist. Weekly. Focus not exclusively economic, but also political and cultural. Circulation 500,000, half in the United States.

The book contains additional material from:

Newsweek. Weekly American-based international news magazine. Circulation 4 million.

The Sunday Times. British Sunday paper, sister to *The Times*. Circulation 1,247,364

Independent on Sunday. British Sunday paper, sister to *The Independent*. Circulation 400,000.

Types of media

> media
>   mass media
>   print media
>   electronic media
>   news media

News and entertainment are communicated in a number of different ways, using different **media**. The media include **print media** such as newspapers and magazines, and **electronic media** such as radio and television.

entertainment *182* ⇓

The word media is most often used to refer to the communication of news, and in this context means the same as **news media**.

Media and **mass media** are often used when discussing the power of modern communications.

◆ **LANGUAGE NOTE**

Media can be singular or plural.
Mass media is also spelt with a hyphen.

It is difficult for the media *to cover the growing number of crises throughout the world.*

You in the media *are all part of a powerful industry. That power can be used destructively or constructively.*

…impersonal contact through print media *and television.*

For the book's main character, withdrawal is the only means of escape from the crowd, from group-think, from the mass media*.*

The documentary should be required study for all students of mass-media *communications, because it illustrates to perfection the way in which illustrations of man's inhumanity to man can mislead public opinion.*

The White House has announced that they normally will not let any member of the news media *report on what is going to be in the speech until the president actually delivers it.*

Belief systems and older cultures expire under a weight of more or less trivial information conveyed by an all-pervasive electronic media*.*

1 Media partners ı. Look at the extracts and then complete the tasks by combining the word 'media' with the other words in the box below the numbered questions.

After waiting weeks for a day when it would get maximum media exposure*, the Labour Party launched its new policies for industry on February 25th – just as the Gulf War got going.*

The trial of Bruno Hauptmann for the 1932 kidnapping of aviator Charles Lindbergh's baby attracted media attention *unlike any seen before.*

The government has been particularly annoyed at the involvement of the French state in what they are calling a hostile <u>media campaign</u>.

Black had set his heart on the 'News', which he saw as a key part of his plan to build a worldwide <u>media empire</u>.

The thought of a quiet ceremony and a small dinner party to follow is becoming more attractive to stars as they watch publicised marriages like Elizabeth Taylor's being transformed into a <u>media circus</u>.

The director of the campaign for the homeless said yesterday's government announcement is no substitute for a proper national housing policy. 'We were quite upset about the amount of attention this announcement was given, and the amount of <u>media hype</u> that went on around it. Actually there was no new money and it was not a new initiative.'

Those people ought to be our priority. I don't think they would be best pleased to hear this domestic squabble about the leadership of the Conservative Party being <u>hyped up by the media</u> at this sort of time.

Reporters were kept away from the group when they arrived from Nairobi amid fears that any <u>media coverage</u> of the event might compromise their safety.

1 Find three expressions referring to what the media give or show if they talk about something.

2 Find one expression for a very big media organisation, perhaps one containing newspapers and TV stations.

3 Find one expression meaning excitement generated by the media not justified by reality.

4 Find one expression meaning a period of coverage in different media organised to change people's opinions about something or someone.

5 Find one expression showing disapproval describing an event dominated by the presence of the media.

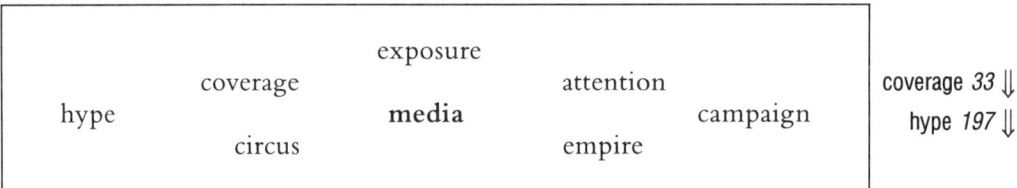

	exposure			coverage *33* ⇓
coverage		attention		hype *197* ⇓
hype	**media**		campaign	
circus	empire			

◆ **LANGUAGE NOTE**

The verbs corresponding to the noun **hype** are **hype** or **hype up**.
Events can be **hyped** or **hyped up** by the media.

2 Media partners II. Make combinations with 'media' from the box below and use them to complete the extracts. (In extract c, it's not possible to find the exact word.)

1 Find one expression meaning an expert on using the media.

2 Find one expression for an expert on the media as a business.

3 Find one expression meaning someone who gives their opinions using the media.

4 Find one expression for someone who reports on the media in the media.

5 Find three expressions for the head of a media organisation.

correspondent

analyst   guru

tycoon   **media**   mogul

pundit   magnate

a Estimates by Browen Maddox, media _____ at Kleinwort Benson Securities are that the company will lose more than £330 million this year.

b But it is not the economists and media _____ who matter. The people who have been driven to fury by the finance minister are those who have lost their livelihoods.

c ...another satellite network, Sky Television, owned by the media _____ Mr Rupert Murdoch.

d The Palace had claimed that Fergie had hired top media _____ Sir Tim Bell to handle publicity on her behalf.

e For the past three years he had been chairman of Thames Television and had been due to retire shortly because of his ill-health. Our media _____ , Torin Douglas, looks back at his career.

Programmes and people

broadcast

programme
show
  host a programme
  host a show

disc jockey
DJ
host

Programmes on radio and television may be referred to formally as **broadcasts**; and they may be referred to informally as **shows**, specially in American English.

Programmes or shows on radio and television are often presented or **hosted** by a programme **host**. Popular music programmes are presented by **disc jockeys** or **DJs**.

show *184* ⇓

3

◆ **LANGUAGE NOTE**

Programme is spelt **program** in American English.
Broadcast is a noun and a verb.
Disc jockey is spelt **disk jockey** in American English and can be spelt with a hyphen.

In an unsportsmanlike and provocative move, they have chosen to <u>broadcast</u> on the same frequency that we have been using for the past five years.

No lawyer representing the tobacco companies would be interviewed for this <u>broadcast</u>.

Groucho flourished in situations with no script at all. One enormous success was his <u>hosting</u> of a show called 'You Bet Your Life' which began in 1947 and ran for four years on radio and 11 on television.

An obsessed fan who sent poison-pen letters to TV presenter Michaela Strachan was yesterday found guilty of threatening to kill her. Clifford Jones, 42, sent 2,000 letters over a two-year period to the children's programme <u>host</u>, a Liverpool court was told.

Top <u>DJs</u> have taken over much of the ground that pop stars used to occupy.

anchor
  anchorman
  anchorwoman
  anchorperson
	News programmes may be hosted, **fronted**, or **anchored** by anchors famous in their own right, sometimes more famous than the people in the news. Variations of the noun **anchor** are shown on the left. anchorman *36* ⇓

anchor a news
  programme
front a news
  programme
	In more traditional news programmes, the news is read by a **newsreader** or **newscaster**: newscaster is now a rather old-fashioned word.

newsreader newscaster	**Reporters** and **correspondents**, or television journalists, make **reports**. They and the camera operators who go with them are **news gatherers**. Together they form **TV crews**.
report reporter correspondent	**Broadcasters** are TV and radio organisations, the people working for them, or, more specifically, the professional media people who actually participate in programmes.
TV crew news gatherer	
broadcaster	

To me, <u>newsreaders</u> are just people who read the news. I've never believed in the TV personality cult.

On the BBC World Service the news men present the news as it is, and not the <u>newscasters'</u> view of it.

Sissons, solid performer, would make an excellent 'Newsnight' <u>anchorman</u>. Though he has <u>fronted</u> live television studio debates for Channel 4 in the past, he seems lost at the BBC.

We have just had this report from our <u>correspondent</u> in Belgrade, Jim Fish.

Television <u>reporters</u> would put on their gas masks on screen to point live at missile streaks in the sky.

The BBC has produced two hard-hitting videos in a bid to cut down the growing number of <u>news gatherers</u> killed or injured while on duty.

His temper finally cracked when he turned on a <u>TV crew</u> and shouted, 'Leave me alone.'

Buerk said, 'Reporters, correspondents and newscasters are not part of the mainstream which flows towards management. So none of our senior managers have been <u>broadcasters</u>, which is like having nobody at the top of the Royal Air Force who can fly.'

3 People in the media jungle. Find eight key words from this section referring to people who work in the news media hidden in the square, in addition to the example. The words go from left to right, from top to bottom or diagonally downwards.

Q	N	E	W	S	R	E	A	D	E	R	X	P	V
W	X	E	H	G	Q	Z	B	N	K	L	M	R	A
E	Z	G	W	W	Q	S	D	F	G	J	K	L	M
R	N	E	W	S	G	A	T	H	E	R	E	R	A
T	X	D	I	S	C	J	O	C	K	E	Y	D	F
Y	C	V	B	R	O	A	D	C	A	S	T	E	R
A	Z	E	R	T	Y	U	S	O	P	Y	T	R	F
S	W	A	C	V	B	F	C	T	W	X	C	B	B
X	E	N	V	C	A	D	R	S	E	X	C	N	O
S	Q	C	C	V	W	R	E	P	O	R	T	E	R
A	X	H	O	S	T	O	P	D	S	C	M	L	E
Z	Q	O	D	F	G	H	J	K	L	M	P	X	E
C	O	R	R	E	S	P	O	N	D	E	N	T	R

News programmes

broadcast
  live broadcast

recording
recorded

footage
  dramatic footage

clip

vox-pop
  interview

talking heads

Programmes and reports are transmitted or **broadcast live** in a **live broadcast**, with events seen or heard as they happen, or **recorded** for broadcast later. A **recording** of an event can be referred to as **footage** of that event.

A news programme might include:

dramatic footage of events such as war or disasters   footage *204* ⇓

interviews and studio discussions: pictures of people participating in these are often referred to as **talking heads**, an informal expression used to show disapproval of what can be a boring form of television

vox-pop interviews, or **vox-pops** getting the reactions of ordinary people, often in the street

or **clips**, or extracts, of any of these things.

◆ **LANGUAGE NOTE**
  Vox-pop is also spelt as two words.

We showed the Channel 4 bosses this four-minute clip of me interviewing Nelson Mandela and they really liked it, you know, particularly the fact that we were doing it all live.

The programme will feature dramatic footage of the Chernobyl disaster, some not released before, as well as live performances by international artists.

Even worse, I discovered the New Year awards show was pre-recorded, so it was probably just a bit of old Big Ben footage filmed one summer's evening to set the scene.

Our Eastern European correspondent, Diana Goodman in Prague, has recorded vox pops with Czech voters who say they are supporting Civic Forum.

It was also the evening of talking heads interviewing talking heads. Studio presenters spoke to giant TV screens worldwide.

4 **All the news that fits.** Match the two parts of these extracts.

1 Down the coast the town of Alasio has an average of 400,000 visitors a year,

2 'I am becoming Death, a destroyer of worlds,' said Robert Oppenheimer in an old clip,

3 The BBC does make mistakes and the reaction story it broadcast after the Conservatives' health debate was one of them.

4 The old footage was fascinating enough,

5 The pope's blessing 'Urbi et Orbi' to the City of Rome and to the world

6 South African writer Nadine Gordimer reading from her novel *A Sport of Nature* about being a writer in a repressive society.

7 The Rugby Football Union was asked to study a video

a without the help of talking heads.

b That clip was from an interview recorded in 1987 for National Public Radio.

c was broadcast live in 50 countries.

d adding sadly, 'I guess we all felt that, at one time or another.'

e recording of events leading up to the punch of the season.

f It consisted of vox-pop interviews of health workers who disliked government policy.

g and TV-footage of black waves can only spell disaster.

The sound-bite and the photo-opportunity

photo-
  opportunity
sound-bite
photogenic
telegenic

When someone, usually a politician, gives a speech or an interview, news editors look for short, interesting sequences that can be used on their own. These sequences are called **sound-bites**, and some people say that this has influenced the way politicians speak, because they hope to get a sound-bite into the day's news programmes.

sound-bite *36* ⇓

A related phenomenon is the **photo-opportunity**, where people, again often politicians, arrange for pictures to be taken of themselves in favourable or picturesque situations. People and things that look good on television are **telegenic**, in the same way that people who look good in photographs are **photogenic**.

telegenic *36* ⇓

Sound-bite and **photo-opportunity** are often used showing disapproval.

◆ **LANGUAGE NOTE**

Sound-bite can be spelt as one or two words.
Photo-opportunity is also spelt as two words.

The shrinking of the average sound-bite (extract from presidential candidate's speech) used in TV news may already have stopped. Studies show that sound-bites shrank from 45 seconds in 1968 to 15 in 1984 and 9.8 in 1988. At that rate they will have disappeared altogether before the election in 2000.

In the general state of unreality which we have entered, it is now thought that you can solve everything by photo-opportunity – that if the president signs a transportation bill standing on a road in Texas, it's better than signing it in the White House because it denotes something.

Elizabeth Taylor was not just a photogenic face but also had strengths as a dramatic actress.

In determining the choice of candidates, was it a case of the more telegenic they were, the more chance they had of success?

5 **Age of the Sound-Bite.** Read this article from *The Times* and answer the questions. (The Beltway is an area outside Washington where many people involved in politics live).

Blaming the Beltway

American campaign politics remains, to the European observer, curiously old-fashioned. The big rally, the visits to every state, the glad-handing and the baby-kissing, the silly hats and balloons all seem to hark back to the days when candidates bellowed their promises from the backs of railway carriages.

To this more recently has been added the photo-opportunity and the sound-bite, both attuned to the needs of television and the press. Both are easily stage-managed. The scene can be visited in advance and the one-liner prepared in advance, to be parroted at every stop.

Even the most risky encounters, studio interviews and debates, are pre-packaged, with 'hosts', chairmen and journalists set to cross-examine the candidates on subjects agreed in advance. The topics are those in common currency. The result is bland and unappetising. Like watching grand-prix racing, the thrill lies in the possibility of an accident.

1 Given the context, if one thing harks back to another, is it
  a) similar to it or
  b) different from it?

        campaign *32* ⇓
        rally *35* ⇓
        glad-handing *35* ⇓

2 If you bellow, do you
  a) shout very loud, or
  b) whisper?

3 If something is attuned to the needs of something else, does it answer those needs?

4 What can be stage-managed, apart from sound-bites and photo-opportunities?

5 What expression is used here instead of sound-bite to mean the same thing?

6 If you parrot something, do you sound as if you believe it?

7 Is bland food tasty?

8 Does thrill mean a) boredom or b) excitement?

The TV diet

documentary
entertainment

docudrama
infotainment

People sometimes say that today's news programmes are **infotainment**, a mixture of information, and entertainment, something that people watch or listen to for pleasure. Another example of infotainment is **docudrama** where real events are dramatised and re-enacted by actors. This is a combination of documentary and drama: a **documentary** is a serious factual radio or TV programme.

entertainment *182* ⇓

infotainment *205* ⇓
docudrama *205* ⇓

What we need is <u>entertainment</u>, variety shows with comedians, singers, pianists, jugglers and acrobats.

We have a <u>documentary</u> on the social issues, like the housing problem and the public policies on education, health and the social policies of the government.

An interview with Ron Brown, the Democratic party chairman, was edited to 40 seconds and transformed with Sonic Youth soundtrack and zappy special video-effects. Slotted between the visual gymnastics of Madonna and McHammer videos, Tabitha Soren is part of an '<u>infotainment</u>' revolution in which the Republicans have sought no part.

That thin line between fact and fantasy has never looked thinner than in this ABC <u>docudrama</u> movie, provisionally titled 'Charles and Diana'.

6 **TV diet exercise.** Look at the extracts and match the types of programmes to their definitions.

His fiction was derived from 'Dallas' and other glossy <u>soap</u> operas which are consumed abroad.

By combining the <u>phone-in</u> with the <u>talk-show</u>, he was able to convey his reaction to the 'concerns of the average American' more immediately than by any other form.

Being a good <u>game-show</u> host means getting to know your contestants.

On my first appearance, interviewing a priest in the <u>God slot</u>, I tripped headlong over some wires – and the programme was live.

The whole point of <u>quiz shows</u> is that, sitting at home you can shout out the answers.

Good <u>sitcom</u> comes out of painful situations, and there doesn't have to be a happy ending every time.

		a	contest of skill, intelligence or knowledge. The term includes quiz shows.
1	**chat-show** or **talk-show**	b	series about the lives of a group of people
2	**game show**	c	short for situation comedy. Comedy series based around a character or group of characters, often an 'ordinary' family
3	**God slot**		
4	**phone-in**	d	a well-known host invites guests to talk, often about something they are trying to sell or promote, like their latest book
5	**quiz show**		
6	**sitcom**		
7	**soap opera** or **soap**	e	a host invites people to phone in and put questions to a studio guest, or just give their opinions about something
		f	religious programme
		g	contest involving answering questions

soap opera *199* ⇓

◆ **LANGUAGE NOTE**

Chat-show, talk-show, quiz-show and **game-show** are also spelt as two words.
The noun **phone-in** is also spelt as two words.
Sitcom is also spelt with a hyphen.

The ratings battle

audience
network
advertising commercial commercial break spot
peak-time prime-time
ratings   ratings battle   ratings war
slot

There is, of course, a lot of competition between broadcasting organisations. Most TV and radio **networks** want to increase the size of their **audience**, or their **ratings**, at the expense of other networks.

Good ratings are especially important during **prime-time** or **peak-time**, the time of day, or **slot**, when most people watch TV. Slot also means any short period in broadcasting reserved for a specific purpose.

High audience figures attract more **advertising** or **commercials** to be shown in **commercial breaks** between programmes. Commercials are also known as **spots**.

advertising *36* ⇓

The media often talk about **ratings battles** or **ratings wars** between networks when discussing competition in the industry.

ratings *46* ⇓

◆ **LANGUAGE NOTE**

Prime-time and peak-time are also spelt as two words.

Mr Akiyama's space mission was paid for by the Tokyo Broadcasting System at a cost of more than $12 million in an effort to gain <u>audiences</u> from rival <u>networks</u>.

Another problem is sleeping habits. The Germans eat dinner and go to bed earlier, so the French are starting on their first aperitif when the Arte channel is into <u>prime time</u>.

At present adverts run for two and a half minutes in the centre breaks, with a maximum of seven and a half minutes in <u>peak time</u> between 6 pm and 11 pm, when most of the <u>advertising</u> revenue is generated.

John Suchet has spent three years hosting ITN's lunchtime <u>slot</u> and is very popular with viewers.

The perfume was marketed with a blitz of TV <u>commercials</u>.

…the important American news programmes, with <u>commercial breaks</u> about every five minutes.

Last week, the Army released the second of two national television <u>spots</u>, an effort to ensure that its battle for American hearts and minds would translate into improved recruitment figures.

Television's top soaps are battling it out in the vital Christmas <u>ratings war</u>.

Marcus Plantin has landed the job of leading ITV's £500 million <u>ratings battle</u> with the BBC.

7 **Decline and fall of the networks.** Read this book review from *The Economist* and answer the questions.

THREE BLIND MICE
by Ken Auletta

For years ABC, CBS and NBC have been the most powerful institutions in the American media, perhaps in all of American life.

But in 1985-6, with their profits falling as viewers turn increasingly to the smorgasbord of choice offered by cable television and VCRs, the networks were taken over by Wall Street dealmakers who thought they could be run more efficiently. The clash of cultures was as dramatic as any in business history. Mr Auletta was allowed to witness all this from a rare angle and he produces some stunning reporting.

He recounts how Mr Tisch craftily took over CBS without its board noticing; and of his, and the other owners' draconian attacks on spending. So frugal is the 'evil dwarf' as he is nicknamed by his colleagues that he tells the head of CBS's record company, which has just made a $160 million profit, that he cannot have a bagel at the Beverly Hills Hotel because it costs too much. With its descriptions of such lunacy, its huge cast of characters and its vivid portraits of the egomania of some in the television industry, Mr Auletta's tale has strong hints of Balzac and Dickens.

It is a story told in numbers that reveal the long, slow, inexorable death-march of the networks: the networks' declining audience share, from 92 per cent in 1976 to 75 per cent in 1984 to 60 per cent today; their profits falling from $800 million in 1984 to (probably) zero this year; the number of channels quadrupling since the mid-1970s; VCRs in 70 per cent of all homes. Mr Tisch and his peers may not like television, and may not even watch it; but to number-crunchers such as themselves the data are pretty plain.

1 Does a smorgasbord restaurant give you a lot of choice?

2 What does VCR stand for?
a) variable channel receiver, or
b) video cassette recorder

3 A clash is a conflict. Which two cultures is there a clash between?

4 Is stunning reporting impressive?

5 If you do something craftily, you do it in a clever way, perhaps without people
n _ _ _ _ i n g.

6 Is a draconian attack
a) a strong one, or b) a weak one?

7 'Evil dwarf.' A dwarf is a very short person. Is someone's   board 93 ⇓
nickname their real name?

8 Do frugal people spend a lot of money?

9 Lunacy is mad behaviour. What example of lunacy does Auletta give?

10 If something is inexorable, will it continue?

11 Which three networks is Auletta talking about in his book?

12 If a figure quadruples, does it get
a) twice as big, b) four times as big,
c) six times as big?

13 Are Tisch's peers a) other TV bosses,
b) his employees, c) members of the British House of Lords?

14 What do number-   number-cruncher 92 ⇓
crunchers do?

15 The data are plain to them. Are the figures a) clear, b) unclear?

Zapping

viewer
couch potato
zap
zapper
remote control
tube
box
telly

People watching TV are **viewers**. Viewers who watch a lot of television without caring what they watch are **couch potatoes**.

If you **zap** between channels, you use your **remote control** or **zapper** to change channels a lot, perhaps looking for something interesting to watch, and perhaps not succeeding. A zapper is also a person who zaps.

Informal words for television are the **tube** in the US, and the **box** or the **telly** in Britain.

Even if the set is on, there is no guarantee that viewers are giving it their full attention. 45 per cent say they read during programmes, 27 per cent talk on the phone and 26 per cent do housework.

Do you think there are a lot of high-powered lawyers, doctors, educators out there who say they don't watch TV and secretly go home at night and turn the tube on and play couch potato?

People think that because you're on the box and act like a fool, you must be like that all the time.

Despite its claims to superiority, the BBC is likely to start as the 56th button on an American viewer's zapper.

Whatever they pay, customers are left with a remote-control zapper that looks as if it could land a spaceship.

Zap through the television channels in a big American city. You will naturally get at least one Spanish-language channel beaming in news of Latin America and lurid Spanish-language soap operas.

8 **Sorting out the channels.** Two articles about zapping, one from *The Times* and one from *Today*, have been mixed up. There are six sections in the first article and five in the second.

1) Say which headlines and sections make up each article. (a is the first section of the first article and b is the first section of the second.)

2) Find all the expressions in both articles that mean 'change channels'.

Kambiz, Switzerland – Cartoonists & Writers Syndicate

Going for the Big Break / Shouting at the box

a Pity the poor television advertiser. He fights for our attention, but it is an unequal fight. We turn on our TV sets to watch programmes; he would rather we watched his adverts. And these days the advertiser has something else to contend with: the zapper, the remote control. The moment a programme is finished or even half-way finished bip! the selfish viewer turns the telly off, or over.

b Remember the time when there was no such thing as a remote control for the telly and you had to haul yourself out of the armchair to change channels? Now everything is about to change again with a new voice-activated method.

c The idea is that instead of pressing buttons, we will be able to channel-hop simply by shouting commands at the set, which will react using "voice recognition". "Channel One, you 'orrible little telly", gets you BBC 1, and so on.

d This is the problem tackled by The Zapper and The Advertiser, a new study from the Billett Consultancy. The consultancy looked at 1,000 households. You could have worked out most of the findings yourself, but there are a couple of surprises.

e The first is that quality is appreciated. Billett found that more people are likely to get bored with a one-hour LA Law than a one-hour Maigret. Eight per cent of people do not stay on after the break in News at Ten, but 42 per cent of live football watchers flip over during half-time, never to return. People change over half as often during weekends.

f Perhaps now is the time to remove programme credits, Billett say, their logic being that most people switch off when the credits come on, anyway.

g This is a bit like a biscuit manufacturer announcing that it will no longer make the first and last biscuits in a pack because they always get broken. Billett believes that ITV could increase the number of viewers aged 16 to 24 if it stopped end-credits and end-break advertising.

h Can you imagine the chaos throughout the living rooms of Britain if this thing catches on?

i 'We also wonder whether a sensible change would be to increase the advertising minutage for centre-breaks during peak hours and a reduction in end-break minutage.' So, this could be the future: a brief pause for breath between programmes, but a massive slice of advertising during them. The advertisers will get you yet.

j At least with the zapper there is only one person in charge of the set at a time. As far as I can make out, using this technique, ... whoever shouts the quickest wins. There'll be my husband bellowing 'three, three, three,' for the news, the kids screaming 'six, six, six' for Sky, and me shouting at it to switch itself off.

k At which point the set will probably have a breakdown. Life was so much simpler when the set stayed on the same channel for three days because no one could be bothered to get up and change it.

TV violence

mayhem
gore
gory

TV is often accused of showing too much violence or **mayhem**: scenes of fights, assault, murder and so on. Violence on TV and in films is often referred to as **gore**, especially when blood is visible. A film with a lot of violence and blood in it is **gory**.

assault *141* ⇓

murder *136* ⇓

gory *188* ⇓

All the available evidence suggests a huge public appetite for lust and <u>gore</u>.

It's not a family film as it's a bit messy in parts and some scenes are very <u>gory</u>.

Hans, played by Hans Hirschmuller, has taken to beating up his young wife Irmgard (Irm Hermann). This tale of domestic <u>mayhem</u> contains many of the usual Fassbinder traits.

'Terminator 2: Judgment Day'. <u>Mayhem</u> and stunning effects as Arnie tackles a killer robot.

Bill Schorr, USA – United Features Syndicate

"He's been watching violent cave drawings again …"

Glancing through the television programmes for the week I was struck by the number of films advertised containing violence, murder and <u>mayhem</u>.

9 **TV gore.** Look at the table about TV violence from *Newsweek* and then read the extracts from the article and answer the questions.

US NETWORKS UNDER THE GUN
THE MAYHEM IS KIDS' STUFF

A study of the 1991-92 television season shows that children's programming actually features more violence than prime time.

	Children's programs	Prime-time
Violent acts per hour	32	4
Violent characters	56%	34%
Characters who are victims of violence	74%	34%
Characters who are killers or get killed	3.3%	5.7%
Characters involved in violence as perpetrators or victims	79%	47%

1 Overall, is there less violence on children's television than during prime-time?

Broadcasters have promised to clean up their act. Critics say don't believe the hype.

Seeing the heads of all four networks gathered in the same room last week was extraordinary enough. Even more intriguing, however were the downcast eyes and somber expressions. No wonder: after 40 years of denial, despite more than 3,000 damning studies, the TV industry's moguls tacitly conceded that violence on television can indeed lead to violence in real life. But the remedy they so proudly unveiled ... generated almost as much heat as the malady it's supposed to help cure.

Beginning this fall, the networks will broadcast parental advisories before excessively violent programs and similar warnings to newspapers and magazines that carry TV listings. ... As a pre-emptive strike, the announcement accomplished its mission. Many in congress, roused by the soaring tide of prime-time gore, have been threatening federally-imposed reforms.

Some of these restrictions, however, would surely raise howls from First Amendment guardians, which may explain the almost palpable relief with which law-makers greeted the networks' voluntary action ...

... In selling their own reform package, the networks provided another reminder of just how unstaunchable TV's blood flow remains. 'This problem will get worse because people will think something has been done about it,' says Dr Carole Lieberman, a psychiatrist who heads the National Coalition on Television Violence. 'But all they're doing is applying a Band-Aid. It's just a sham.'

For openers, the networks will decide for themselves which shows require warning flags. The plan also assumes the presence of a parent to switch the channel. That ignores the millions of children of working parents who watch TV unsupervised, not to mention the nearly 50 per cent between 6 and 17 who own bedroom sets ...

'The advisories are just a faster road map to the violent material,' says Terry Rakolta, founder of Americans for Responsible Television. Kids channel-surfing will stop immediately and say, 'Hey, this is it! We don't even have to look for it.'

2 If your eyes are downcast, in which direction are you looking?

3 If you deny something, you say that it isn't true. What do you do if you concede something?

4 An advisory is a form of w _ _ _ i n g.

5 The pre-emptive strike by the TV moguls was carried out to pre-empt f _ _ _ _ _ _ _ _ - i _ _ _ _ _ r _ _ _ _ _ .

6 Restrictions would raise howls of p r o _ _ _ _ from defenders of free speech.

7 If something is palpable, it is obvious and visible. Relief is what you feel when you stop worrying about something. Why did the law-makers feel relieved?

8 If the flow of blood is unstaunchable, can it be stopped?

9 If you apply a Band-Aid to a problem, do you attack the real causes of the problem?

10 How many objections to the networks' plans are there in this paragraph?

11 Channel-surfing is another expression for z _ _ _ _ _ _ .

Multimedia and virtual reality

multimedia

interact
interaction
interactive
interactivity

virtual reality

Multimedia is the combining of TV, computers and telecommunications to provide information and entertainment services that will be **interactive**. Users will be able to **interact** with the programmes and influence what they see. Programmes such as these will possess **interactivity**.

Virtual reality also provides **interaction** with scenes and people simulated by computer. Special clothing allows users to manipulate this simulated world and experience it with the same intensity as real life.

THE FUTURE OF INTERACTIVE TV

Stayskal, USA – Tampa Tribune

By combining TV and computers, Frox has its toe in the much-hyped multimedia market, the holy grail of the electronics industry.

Lights, camera, interaction. Artists have always tried to involve audiences intimately in their art, but few have gone so far as to offer them creative partnership. Even if it was wanted, such co-authorship was usually technically impossible. Now a generation of young, computer-literate film makers are trying to use the new technologies to make the mass media 'interactive.'

Interactivity in information media entails both the ability on the part of the receiver to choose the programme transmitted to him or her, but also the ability to control changes of direction in a programme. There is a pioneering Canadian cable company, for example, called Videotron, which runs a service that enables viewers to choose the camera angles of the shots in a football match and make the camera focus on particular players.

The physical world is a thing that you perceive with your eyes, your ears, your skin and your other sense organs. Now what we do in virtual reality is we have computerized clothing that you wear over your sense organs and this computerized clothing cuts off the physical world and stimulates your sense organs with exactly the stimulus they would get if you were inside an alternate reality.

10 **Primitive exchanges?** These sections from two articles are in random order. One is from *The Economist* and about multimedia in general; the other, from *The Independent*, is about virtual reality. Put together the two articles. ('The Promise of Multimedia' contains four sections: a is the first section of this article. 'A Step through the Looking Glass' is made up of five sections and begins with b.)

The Promise of Multimedia
A Step through the Looking Glass

a In a loft apartment in New York's Tribeca district, Kenny Miller is having a multimedia interaction. On cable television, he is watching a live programme produced by his friend, David Levitt; over the telephone he is asking Mr Levitt 'to perform for us'. Instantly the picture changes and Mr Levitt's falsetto bubbles from the box, singing an ode to Mr Miller. The camcorders, audio mixers and Macintosh computers strewn around the room look on in mute fascination.

b The heart surgeon is about to perform the most delicate part of the operation when the blade slips and slices through a vital artery. An aircraft pilot is about to land in thick fog, but misses the runway and crashes. Fortunately, neither of these scenarios is real. They exist in the memory of a computer that is simulating the event in what has become known as virtual reality.

c Computer simulators have been used to train pilots since the seventies. Since then, computer simulation has made significant advances, and researchers are now talking seriously of using simulators in more complex situations, such as the training of heart surgeons. The great advantage of working in virtual reality is that the patient never stays dead.

d If the 1980s were a time for media tycoons, the 1990s are for self-styled visionaries like Mr Miller and Mr Levitt. These gurus see a dawning digital age in which the humble television will mutate into two-way medium for a plethora of information and entertainment: movies-on-demand, video games, databases, educational programming, home shopping, telebanking, teleconferencing, even the complex situations of virtual reality. It will, says Time Warner, the world's largest media group, let consumers tune in to 'anything, anywhere, anytime'.

e If the exchange between Mr Miller and Mr Levitt was primitive, it was at least tangible – and thus rare. The most extraordinary thing about the multimedia boom is that so many moguls are spending so vast sums of money to deliver programmes that are still hypothetical. The talk is of fibre-optic networks broadcasting 500 channels; of 'teleputers' that will change the way commerce is pursued and leisure enjoyed; of a global information industry that Apple Computer reckons will one day be worth $3.5 trillion.

f An important part of this concept has been the development of electronic gloves that are wired to be sensitive to the movement of the wearer's fingers. By flexing an index finger or bending a thumb, the wearer can begin to manipulate images of the virtual reality world of the computer. NASA scientists envisage, for instance, that astronauts will wear a virtual reality helmet and see exactly what a robot outside a spacecraft is seeing. By manipulating electronic gloves, the astronaut can manipulate the robot's limbs and perform an otherwise dangerous task in relative safety.

g Is this the future of television? In an embryonic form, it is. Mr Miller is the technical director of the 'new mead' division at Viacom, a cable-TV firm. Mr Levitt used to teach at the Massachusetts Institute of Technology's Media Lab.

h It does not take too much imagination to realise that the image need not be routine and boring. It could be Meryl Streep or Arnold Schwarzenegger, and the room could be anything from an opium den in China to a chalet in the Swiss Alps.

i At the moment, virtual reality in civilian use is still at the stage of creating simple situations, such as a room full of objects. Wearing the virtual reality helmet puts you in this room. Sensors in the helmet follow head movements, and the computer permanently revises the interior of the room, so whichever way your head is moved, appropriate images appear on the two screens. It is all done so quickly that to all intents and purposes, you are actually inside.

The press

press
quality press
popular press
tabloid press
gutter press
tabloid
broadsheet
circulation
readership

The **press** usually refers just to newspapers, but the term can be extended to include magazines. Newspapers are either **tabloid**, a format usually associated in the English-speaking world with the **popular press**, or **broadsheet**, associated with **quality** journalism. Tabloids are sometimes referred to as the **gutter press** by people who disapprove of them.

tabloid *42, 195* ⇓

Tabloids often have very large **circulations** (numbers sold) and even bigger **readerships** (total number of people reading them). Papers such as these are often referred to as **mass circulation** papers.

circulation *224* ⇓

Yet reports in the so-called quality press and on television have blamed tabloid newspapers. Strange that. The broadsheets fill acres of pages with Royal stories and television never misses a chance to show royal footage.

The tabloid newspapers – or gutter press as they're known in Britain – have always been a source of fascination to media watchers.

I wonder whether attacking our popular press is the liberal elite's way of acting out its own fear of the common people.

There are other stories in the papers – the mass circulation tabloids displaying their usual interest in sex and sensation.

Friday night television audiences and Saturday newspaper readerships are, apparently, lower than mid-week's.

With the Easter holiday upon us, the mass circulation paper, 'The Sun', focusses on a strike by French air traffic controllers. In typically robust fashion 'The Sun' headlines the story: FILTHY FRENCH SINK OUR HOLS.

11 **Shock Horror Headlines.** Some papers, especially tabloids, are famous for their headlines. Match these headline words to their meanings and then use them to complete the headlines below.

1 **BID**	a	unpleasant experience, usually lasting some time	
2 **BOOST**	b	argument	
3 **DASH**	c	attempt	
4 **ORDEAL**	d	inquiry	
5 *PLEA*	e	questioning by police or at an enquiry	ordeal *204* ⇓
6 **PLEDGE**	f	fast journey, often with an uncertain outcome	
7 **PROBE**	g	emotional request	
8 *QUIZ*	h	a period of waiting, perhaps by an ill person's bedside or in protest at something	
9 **ROW**	i	promise	
10 **VIGIL**	j	increase in numbers or in confidence, morale or prospects	vigil *123* ⇓

i **GLENDA KEEPS _____ AT INJURED SON'S BEDSIDE**.
Actress Glenda Jackson left hospital last night after spending the day at her son's bedside, and spoke of her relief that he was still alive.

ii **LIVERPOOL'S EURO _____** . Liverpool last night received a European lift when UEFA confirmed that Welsh international Ian Rush will no longer be classified as a foreign player.

iii **MAN FACES _____ ON WIFE DEATH**. Detectives were waiting by the hospital bedside of a man to question him about the death of his wife.

iv **NIGEL'S _____** . World champion Nigel Mansell took a lingering look across the Portuguese Grand Prix track which has caused him both heartache and joy yesterday before declaring: 'I will never come back here again – I'm finished forever with Formula One.'

v *OLYMPIC BOSS IN BRIBE _____* . The head of the Olympics is threatening legal action over a TV documentary alleging his officials are corrupt.

vi **PILOT IN BRITISH PLANE _____** . A British airliner has made an emergency landing in southern England after a cockpit window shattered and the pilot was almost sucked out.

vii **_____ TO 'DIVORCE' BID GIRL**. The mother of a teenager who has taken court action to 'divorce' her parents pleaded last night for her to come home.

viii *PRIVATE HEALTH PRICE FIXERS FACING _____* . Fees charged for private medical treatment are to be investigated by monopoly watchdogs.

ix **SRI LANKA PEACE _____** . A Sri Lankan government negotiator is expected to try to reopen talks with the Tamil Tigers today in an attempt to end the outbreak of fighting between Tigers and the Army.

x **TEENAGE PAIR KILLED IN _____ ACROSS M-WAY**. A teenage judo champion and a girl pal were killed in front of friends as they took a short cut across a motorway.

Ladies and gentlemen of the press

editor	The people in charge of newspaper content are **editors**. The people who write for them are **journalists**, sometimes referred to informally as **journos** or insultingly as **hacks**. Someone who writes articles that appear regularly, usually in the same place in the paper, and often with powerfully expressed opinions, is a **columnist**.
journalist journo hack	
columnist	
Fleet Street	The British national press is referred to as **Fleet Street**, although no national paper is now produced in this London street.

editor *206* ⇓

columnist *36, 214* ⇓

With rapidly falling circulation figures, journalists have demanded the editor's dismissal.

He's also spending time keeping hacks out of the way because they keep asking Dennis about girlfriends.

Courier is like the hard-news journo of cliché, who thinks only about the glory of the story.

Most journos know of a colleague who abandoned journalism for advertising. We curl our lips at such a fellow. He's a sell-out, a loser, somebody who couldn't stand the pace in the real game.

A respect for the role of the king prevents the Spanish media from taking the aggressive Fleet Street approach to monarch's private lives.

At the bar, we found vituperative columnist Julie Burchill and thought, at last, here is someone who is bound to be rude and abrasive. But Burchill was a babe.

story
piece
article
run an article
carry an article
editorial
leading article
leader
leader writer

Newspapers **run** or **carry articles** or **stories**. Articles other than the most important ones can also be referred to as **pieces**.

Editorials give the paper's opinion about the news of the day. In a quality paper, the most important editorial is the **leading article** or **leader**. These, and the other editorials, are written by **leader writers**.

'The Financial Times' carries an article on the situation in Albania.

'The Wall Street Journal' ran an article about people in Belgium who have seen flying triangular-shaped craft.

'The National' ran a piece about a boxer who'd had to have his legs amputated because of the damage steroid use had done.

The resignation was the top story for the 'New York Times'. In a leader, the paper said that on the issues affecting America most, substantial continuity would be assured under any of the contenders for the leadership.

Following his criticism of social workers, may I suggest that your leader writer should spend a month as a social worker to see just how stressful and demanding the job is – and be paid the same salary as the social worker.

Some of the editorial leader writers put their fingers on the pulse of several points worth discussing.

12 Naming of parts. Match these newspaper expressions
to their descriptions, and then use the expressions to
complete the extracts below.

1	**obituary**	a	small advertisements about films, plays, concerts, things for sale, and so on
2	**gossip column**	b	news about the country the paper is published in
3	**classified**		
4	**home**	c	exclusive story, especially an exciting one
5	**masthead**	d	(often critical) stories about the social activities and private lives of famous people
6	**banner headline**		
7	**scoop**	e	headline in extremely large print
		f	top of front page carrying the name of the paper
		g	article about the life of someone who has recently died

gossip column *195* ⇓

i   *The Sun's* _____ is 'Come Home Dad'.

ii   The discovery of the Goebbels diaries was yet another *Sunday Times*
_____ that left our rivals gasping.

iii   …*The Observer's* front page headline – under its new royal blue _____ .

iv   Among the _____ stories covered in British papers is the continuing legal
row over the finances of the country's National Union of Mineworkers.

v   May I add a personal note to your excellent _____ of Charles Abell?
Throughout his career, he was faced with difficult problems but never hesitated to
take firm decisions and to stand by the consequences.

vi   MGN's move has been seen as part of an attempt to get its share of the regional
newspapers' advertising cake – particularly _____ – and other tabloid
national papers are expected to follow.

vii   Having failed at show business he ended up in journalism writing about it. By the
mid-thirties he had his _____ . Broadway was his beat. Table 50 at New
York's Stork Club was his office.

Gossip and the glitterati

| celebrity |
| celeb |
| |
| glitterati |
| beautiful people |
| jet set |

Newspapers, especially tabloid newspapers, are often
accused of taking an excessive interest in the private
lives of famous people such as film stars: **celebrities**,
or, very informally, **celebs**.
   Celebrities are sometimes referred to slightly
humorously, and perhaps critically, as **glitterati**. This
expression has replaced **beautiful people** and **jet set**,
reminiscent now of the 1960's.

glitterati *208* ⇓

◆ **LANGUAGE NOTE**
   Glitterati has no singular form.

Are there enough <u>celebrities</u> in the world to sustain yet another chat show?

Most of the <u>celebs</u> are very down to earth with backgrounds like mine.

Zermatt was fashionable with 'le <u>jet-set</u>' (Johnny Halliday, Sacha Distel, etc) in the Sixties which means that its idea of chic is nowadays very unobtrusive.

It started in New York with Studio 54, and what they do is get this elitist door policy where they pick and choose, you know, whoever they figure is (sic) a <u>beautiful people</u>.

Hong Kong's <u>glitterati</u> were downing buckets of champagne, puffing Cuban cigars and dancing their way through a night of opulence.

privacy
  invasion of
  privacy
  breach of privacy
 	
intrusive
  reporting
 	
paparazzi
 	
doorstepping
 	
bug
bugging
	Celebrities, as well as more ordinary people, complain about **invasion of privacy** or a **breach of privacy** when they feel their private lives are being examined too closely.
	
	They complain about **intrusive reporting** techniques like the use of **paparazzi**, photographers with long-lens cameras who take pictures without the subject's knowledge or permission. Other intrusive methods include **doorstepping**, waiting outside someone's house or office with microphone and camera in order to question them, and secretly recording conversations by **bugging** rooms with hidden microphones, or **bugs**.

bugging *43* ⇓
bug *42* ⇓

◆ **LANGUAGE NOTE**

The singular of **paparazzi** is **paparazzo**.
Doorstepping can also be spelt with a hyphen.

To hope that pictures like these would not appear is like trying to put a cap on an active volcano. The behaviour of the royal family is not just a matter of intense public curiosity, not in itself a justification for a <u>breach of privacy</u>, but is also of some public importance and concern.

It is bad enough to spy on her during a private early morning swim, but then to criticise her choice of swimwear for the occasion is the worst <u>invasion of privacy</u> imaginable.

They call on the government to consider the introduction of a privacy law to protect people from unjustly <u>intrusive</u> newspaper reporting.

Picture editors must also maintain relationships with the scores of British and foreign <u>paparazzi</u> who haunt showbusiness personalities and royalty, while courting the more respectable agencies or photographers who specialise in winning authorised access to film, television and pop stars.

Reporters and photographers crowded every exit from the Mirror building to cross-question Maxwell as he left. 'We are <u>doorstepping</u> our own chairman,' said a newsroom executive. 'Can you believe this?'

She was so frightened that she had her private rooms searched in case they were <u>bugged</u>.

13 **Privacy and the paparazzi** 1. Read this extract of a letter from a member of parliament to the editor of *The Times* and answer the questions.

MELLOR: THE RIGHT TO KNOW AND THE RIGHT TO STAY IN OFFICE

Sir,

As might be expected from a Press Complaints Commission which includes tabloid editors, it has now stated that the public have the right to be informed about the private behaviour of politicians if it affects the conduct of public business.

Was it therefore in the public interest for the tabloid editors to pay an 'electronics expert' who had bugged a bedroom then sold the tapes and photographs of it? Have we now reached the stage where it is easier for those who acquire other people's damaging personal secrets to sell them to the tabloids rather than risk jail over blackmail?

The statement amounts to a simple approval of the tabloids' use of paid informers, as, for example, did the KGB in Moscow or the Stasi in East Germany. Like them, the tabloids use such information to destroy lives without trial, defence or jury.

It endorses the practice of allowing a picket line of doorstepping journalists outside a house, to barricade relatives and children and cause them enormous distress, all in the interests of 'a good story'.

1 Why is 'electronics expert' in inverted commas?
   a) the person doing the bugging didn't know much about electronics,
   b) the person was less interested in electronics than in earning money by selling the secret recordings to newspapers,   extortion *141* ⇓
   c) you don't really know, but it might be a combination of a and b.

2 What sort of state employs large numbers of informers?
   A p _ _ _ _ _ state.

3 If you endorse an activity, do you support it and approve of it?   trial *143* ⇓
          jury *146* ⇓

4 Is this a picket line in a literal sense?   picket line *121* ⇓

5 If someone barricades people into a house, do they let them leave?

6 If someone causes someone distress, do they upset them?

Suing for libel

<table>
<tr><td>

libel
  sue for libel
  libel damages

libel action

actionable

writ
  issue a writ

lawsuit

</td><td>

In some countries, you can take legal action and **sue** newspaper editors for invasion of privacy: different countries have different laws about what breaches of privacy are **actionable**.

You may also **sue for libel** in a **libel action**, if you think that you have been libelled: in other words, that something untrue, and that damages your reputation, has been written about you. When someone starts legal action for libel, they **issue a** libel **writ**.

In both cases, the objective of the **lawsuit** is financial compensation in the form of **damages**.

</td></tr>
</table>

sue *110, 192* ⇓

◆ **LANGUAGE NOTE**

> **Libelled** and **libelling** can be spelt **libeled** and **libeling** in American English.
> **Lawsuit** can be spelt with a hyphen or as two words.

Rod Stewart has won the first round in a £15 million <u>libel action</u> against a newspaper which claimed he cheated on wife Rachel Hunter with her agreement. A judge in Los Angeles refused to drop the invasion of privacy part of the 47-year-old singer's <u>lawsuit</u> which claims the story is filled with 'baseless lies'. Attorneys for the Canadian tabloid 'News Extra' had argued the claim was without justification, because the lawsuit also alleges <u>libel</u>.

allege *138* ⇓

Germany: grosser invasions of privacy are widely <u>actionable</u> in the civil courts and there is a civil remedy for a newspaper publishing inaccurate personal information and refusing to correct it.

Each airline chief is <u>suing</u> the other <u>for libel</u> arising from accusations of alleged dirty tricks and smear tactics.

dirty tricks *42* ⇓
smear campaign *39* ⇓

TV wine expert Jill Goolden won substantial <u>libel damages</u> in the High Court yesterday over allegations that her kitchen was <u>filthy</u>.

The Aga Khan has <u>issued a writ</u> for libel damages against Express newspapers and the Daily Express columnist Ross Benson over a gossip column story on the BCCI [Bank of Credit and Commerce International] collapse.

14 Privacy and the paparazzi 2. Read this article from *Newsweek* and use these words to complete the gaps. One of the words is used three times, two are used twice and the rest once each.

a lawsuits	c paparazzi	e photographers	g scoop
b privacy	d paparazzo	f photography	h celebrity

Stalking the Stars

...You can't see them. But they're there, lurking outside the hotels of Majorca, reconnoitering the beach clubs of the French Riviera, eavesdropping in ritzy restaurants from Madrid to Monte Carlo, hiding behind evergreens in St Moritz and palm trees in St Tropez.

Taking pictures is the least of their work, and many aren't even very good _____ (1). 'I have no talent for _____ (2),' admits Rostain, who together with Mouron nevertheless earns 1.5 million francs a year peddling snapshots of all the right people doing all the wrong things. '_____ (3) aren't supposed to do quality _____ (4), but to get exclusive documents.'

Real _____ (5), that is – not celebrity _____ (6), who work with the consent of their subjects, whether implicit or explicit. Real paparazzi are a rare breed: about a dozen each in France, Italy and Spain, fewer in Britain. Even so, the competition is cutthroat. To survive a _____ (7) must be intrepid, diligent, well-connected – and patient. A true _____ (8), such as the one that linked the Duchess of York to her financial adviser, takes weeks, sometimes months, of preparation. ...

If Rostain and Mouron manage to get the pictures they want, and if a celebrity chooses to sue, chances are that they will win. In France, a legal principle known as the *droit à l'image* (right of image) prohibits the publication of photographs without the explicit consent of the people in them, except in news situations where the photos have clear news content.

'I can't complain,' says Paris _____ (9) lawyer Gilles Dreyfus, who is representing Brigitte Bardot in a suit against *Voici*, which in August ran clandestine photos of the reclusive star frolicking on a yacht in the company of a 51-year-old high-up in the far-right National Front party. 'To my knowledge, French law is the strictest in the world.' As a result, *Voici* faces 10 to 15 _____ (10) a year. In most cases, courts order publishers to pay damages ranging between 25,000 to 50,000 francs – a burden that *Voici*, with sales of 200 million francs a year, can easily afford. 'It's a budget item,' says its editor in chief, Patrick Marescaux. ...

Some _____ (11) hope to penetrate the few remaining pockets of _____ (12). In France, for example, the personal lives of politicians are off-limits. 'It's a taboo,' says Paris-Match news editor Chris Lafaille. Rostain and Mouron hope to change that. They're trying to catch one prominent French politician with his mistress, they say. Getting the photos isn't easy, but the hard part is finding a periodical willing to run them. 'If we succeed,' says Rostain, 'maybe we'll open up a whole new market.'

Gagging the press

gag
watchdog
  toothless
   watchdog

censorship
statutory
  controls

crackdown
clampdown

press freedom
freedom of the
  press

Governments that limit press freedom are accused of **gagging the press**. This may take the form a voluntary code of practice overseen by a body referred to informally as a **watchdog**. If the watchdog is ineffective, it is described as **toothless**.

If this is not enough for the government, it may impose **statutory** (legally enforceable) **controls**. The authorities are then described as **cracking down** or **clamping down** on the press. They may also be accused of press **censorship** and of limiting **press freedom** or the **freedom of the press**.

crackdown *71, 126* ⇩
clampdown *71, 126* ⇩
censorship *71* ⇩

◆ **LANGUAGE NOTE**

The nouns corresponding to the verbs **crack down** and **clamp down** are **crackdown** and **clampdown**.
Watchdog, crackdown and **clampdown** are also spelt with a hyphen.

The chances of a privacy law to gag the Press are now 'a lot less than they were a few days ago'.

'The state of the marriage has been put into the public domain in part at least by the outward behaviour of the partners. It is therefore a legitimate subject within the public interest for report and comment by the press.' But the press watchdog criticised broadcasters for 'intrusive and speculative reports'.

The proposed watchdog will not be as toothless as doubters suggest.

Commons all-party media committee chairman Nicholas Winterton said the pictures appeared to be a 'flagrant breach of privacy' but should not prompt calls for a legal clampdown. But Lord St John of Fawsley said: 'It seems to me that it marks a further milestone on the way to introducing a general right of privacy which would benefit all citizens.'

...a whole succession of reactionary initiatives in relation to the freedom of the media, television and news agencies that have been cracked down on.

On privacy, he is as opposed to press censorship as the newspapers.

The Times says that the proposals give the newspaper industry a 12-month deadline to put its house in order of face tough statutory controls. Many papers comment editorially that the proposals could damage press freedom.

Nobody ever said the freedom of the press was a freedom that would never be troublesome.

15 **The Last Chance Saloon.** This extract from *The Times* is about limiting press freedom to report on people's private lives. Read it and answer the questions.

Was it a hollow press victory?

As editor of Britain's biggest selling Sunday tabloid, Patsy Chapman is used to juicy tips about scandals involving politicians. But Chapman is also a member of the Press Complaints Commission (PCC), set up to ensure that editors observe the code of conduct drawn up last year after Fleet Street narrowly repelled legislation to curb the press over intrusion into private lives.

That was why she agonised when she was tipped off that David Mellor was having an affair with an actress. Although the *News of the World* lives by scandal, Chapman has to be satisfied that its stories pass muster by the PCC code. And Mellor, after all, was the minister responsible for initiating any new press legislation.

When the story broke in *The People* last Sunday, there was already a widespread conviction in Fleet Street that John Major was in favour of new press laws, angered by reporting of the rift in the marriage of the Prince and Princess of Wales.

Alarmed, Sir Nicholas Lloyd, the Fleet Street editor closest to Mr Major, published a leading article last Monday accusing *The People* of committing suicide. 'Its behaviour threatens all sections of the press, however responsible, by giving the most powerful ammunition to those demanding a crackdown on media freedom,' the *Daily Express* declared.

1 Look through the whole article and identify all the papers and editors mentioned. Who edits which paper?

2 Which is the biggest Sunday tabloid?
a) *The People,* b) *The News of the World?*

3 British national papers narrowly repelled, or only just succeeded in resisting, legislation to curb the press. If you curb something, do you give it a) less freedom or b) more freedom?

4 What noun already used in the article is 'tip off' related to?

5 If something passes muster is it acceptable?

6 If there is a widespread conviction about something, do a lot of people believe it?

7 Was the Mellor story first published in the *News of the World?*

8 Who normally gets ammunition given to them?

But other tabloid editors sniffed the reek of hypocrisy. The minister who had once warned editors that they were drinking in the Last Chance Saloon had, as *The Sun* cruelly put it, been playing the piano in the bordello next door.

So here was a minister for press intrusion who had something to hide and had desperately tried to hide it. If the government was seriously considering a new press bill, it was open to the accusation of trying to conceal the sins of its own ministers. It was Mr Major's most avid supporter, Kelvin Mackenzie, editor of *The Sun*, who delivered the killer blow.

On Tuesday he revealed that a prominent member of the cabinet had phoned his newspaper during the general election campaign with the names and addresses of three women whom he claimed were having affairs with Paddy Ashdown.

The allegations had been checked and found untrue. Mackenzie, by demonstrating that a minister had peddled a sexual scandal to *The Sun*, encouraging it to intrude into a rival politician's private life, a claim bolstered the next day by *The Independent*, effectively scuppered Major.

9 If you sniff the reek of hypocrisy, you sense it: hypocritical people tell people to do one thing and do another thing themselves. What is the hypocrisy involved here?

10 What word is used here to mean the same as 'hide' earlier in the article?

11 If you are someone's avid supporter, do you support them strongly?

12 If you peddle information, are you keen for people to believe it?   allegation *39, 138* ⇓

13 If you bolster a claim, do you back it up?

14 If you scupper someone's plans you destroy them. Who scuppered Major's plans in this situation? What plans were scuppered?   scupper *163* ⇓

Political correctness

political correctness politically correct politically incorrect PC speech code	Journalists and others such as university teachers are increasingly asked not to use certain words and expressions because they are **politically incorrect** and might cause offence, and to use other, **politically correct**, or **PC**, words. Where organisations such as universities have rules about words to be avoided in conversation and elsewhere, these rules constitute a **speech code**. Politically correct language is part of a wider phenomenon: politically correct thinking, or **political correctness**.

A set of attitudes has come to dominate the university campus which 'Newsweek' and other publications would call <u>politically correct</u> attitudes – that is to say one has to have a single attitude toward the Third World, the situation of women, etc. The Dartmouth Review feels that it's almost a duty to violate these very dubious assumptions that are being imposed as politically correct.

"Welcome to the University. I'm your faculty adviser. This is your dorm room. That's your study desk. And Boris here will be your thought policeman."

Henry Payne, USA – United Features Syndicate

<u>PC-things</u> include ethnic pride (especially Afrocentrism), recyclable products, Malcolm X, being 'gay' or even 'queer' (not homosexual), saying 'people of colour' (never coloured people), 'women' (not girls) and 'Ms' (not Mrs or Miss), sensitivity to unconscious racism, and 'diversity' in all things. Non-PC things include polystyrene cups, buying petrol from Exxon, saying 'businessmen' or 'congressmen' (as opposed to 'persons'), talking about dead white European male (DWEM) thinkers and writers (Plato to Proust).

<u>Political correctness</u> and the banning of words does not drive out prejudice: it merely hides it.

It reminds me of Kipling saying the loveliest sound in the world was 'deep-voiced men laughing together over dinner'. Nowadays remarks like that are deemed sexist, chauvinist, <u>politically incorrect</u>, and, for all I know, actionable.

16 **Lexicographically correct or verbally challenged?** Read this article about politically correct language from *The Economist* and answer the questions.

AN ALL-AMERICAN INDUSTRY

Something odd is happening to political correctness. On the one hand, it is thriving, right up to the highest levels of government (witness the equally-sized Christmas tree and Chanukah memorial outside the White House). On the other hand its opponents are thriving too (look at the best seller lists, headed by Rush Limbaugh and Howard Stern).

Seemingly irreconcilable arguments surround it. Some dismiss political correctness (PC) as an irrelevance hyped up by the right; others see it as a leftist danger to the very fabric of American life; still others argue that it is plain passé. Is America in the throes of neo-PC, anti-PC or post-PC? It is hard to tell.

So much the better for the PC industry. For that is what political correctness has become. It is no longer a matter of who wins or loses the

1 Both PC and its opponents are thriving. Does this mean they are both doing
a) well, or b) badly?

2 If something is a danger to the very fabric of something else, is it
a) very dangerous, or b) not dangerous?

3 If you are in the throes of something, is it finished?

arguments. The arguments themselves are what sustain the industry. Competition in the PC industry is not only healthy, it is essential.

Few industries can boast such rapid growth as this one. A computer search by the *New York Times* found 103 newspaper references to 'political correctness' in 1988. In 1993 the number was roughly 10,000.

Such extraordinary growth would quickly slacken if the driving force behind it – the language of political correctness – were to go out of fashion. But there seems little prospect of that happening. The current controversy over style at the Los Angeles Times shows that there is still plenty of fuel for the PC industry.

The *Los Angeles Times's* 19-page 'Guide on Ethnic and Racial Identification', drafted by a committee, was sent to the paper's staff on November 10th. Journalists are told never to use the word 'Jewess', but to remember to call a Latino woman a 'Latina'.

They are urged to avoid referring to African 'tribes', because this offends many blacks (who are more often 'African American'). 'Eskimos' disappear (they are 'not a homogenous group and may view the term Eskimo negatively'). 'Dutch treat' and 'Dutch courage' are offensive (to the Dutch?), as are French letters (to condom-makers?)

There is more. The term 'deaf and dumb', is, apparently, pejorative, much as 'birth defects' are best replaced by 'congenital disabilities'. Because many women do the job, 'letter carrier' is preferable to 'mailman'. 'Mankind' is frowned upon. 'Gringo', 'savages' and 'redskin' are among the words to be used only in quotes with the approval of the editor, associate editor and senior editor.

Not surprisingly, the guidelines provoked a reaction, and the controversy has become public. A memo signed by journalists at the *Los Angeles Times's* Washington bureau gives warning that it is a short step from 'shunning offensive words to shying away from painful facts and subjects'. All this is splendid for the PC industry (language fuss, for example, does wonders for the dictionary business).

4 If X sustains Y, does X keep Y going?

5 If something boasts a characteristic, it possesses it. Is it possible for something to boast an unimpressive characteristic?

6 If the rate of something such as growth slackens does it a) speed up, or b) slow down?

7 An example of a Dutch treat is going to a restaurant with someone and splitting the bill equally. Dutch courage is the courage people get from drinking alcohol. If you were Dutch, would you be offended by these expressions?

8 Pejorative expressions are not approved of, or frowned upon, because they are critical or insulting. Why is 'mankind' frowned upon?

9 If you shun something or shy away from something, do you like discussing it?

10 If there is fuss about something, are people nervous and anxious about it?

Crossword

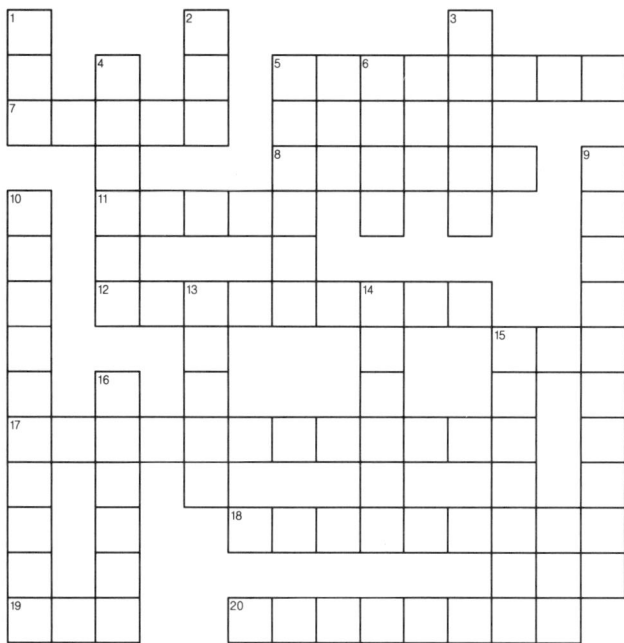

Across

5   See 8

7   Exclusive and often sensational (5)

8   and 5   Take legal _____ if you think you've been _____ (and if you can afford it) (6, 8)

11 and 6 down   This political message is a mouthful (5, 4)

12 The lads with the long lenses (9)

15 Attempt at a headline (3)

17 Breach of privacy outside someone's house (12)

18 This type of reporting is invasive (9)

19 Typical British tabloid (3)

20 Media attention of an intense kind: blanket _____ (8)

Down

1   Politically correct computers? (3)

2   Change channels (3)

3   Gore (5)

4   and 16 Celeb-packed article (6, 6)

5   Editorial (6)

6   See 11 across

9   Bigger and better quality than a tabloid (10)

10 Very similar to crackdowns (10)

13 This could be gutter or quality, national or local (5)

14 Channel changer (6)

15 This is done with secret microphones (7)

16 See 4 down

The campaign trail

candidate
election
run for election
stand for election
campaign
campaign trail
campaigning
run-up to the
election

In a democracy, the country's rulers and law-makers are chosen in **elections**. In American English, **candidates run for election** and in British English they **stand for election**.

The **campaign** is the series of advertisements, television appearances, meetings and speeches designed to get support for a candidate. The expression **campaign trail** emphasises the number of places candidates have to go to and things they have to go through while **campaigning**.

campaign 8 ⇑

Campaign also refers collectively to all the parties' campaigns.

The **run-up** to an election is the period leading up to an election, perhaps a longer time than the campaign itself.

If Mahatma Gandhi came back to life and <u>stood for election</u> in the eastern Indian state of Bihar, he would probably lose.

Mrs Thatcher hoped most of them were against a federal Europe. 'Otherwise what's the point of standing as <u>candidates</u> in the next general election?'

Vargas Llosa, who constantly glances backwards into his own life or into the dark recesses of his continent for his fiction, is preoccupied by 'something larger than politics'. Coming from a man who, in 1990, <u>ran</u> for president in Peru, and lost, this seems hard to take.

He is hurt by the perception that he is afraid to face his opponent. He is followed on the <u>campaign trail</u> by people dressed in chicken costumes.

There are ten weeks to go to the election, yet we are already mind-numbingly bored with the <u>campaigning</u>.

Shots were fired and explosives thrown into the offices of two political parties in Tiblisi in what the BBC Moscow correspondent describes as the increasingly violent <u>run-up</u> to elections next month.

1 **On the campaign trail.** Match the two parts of these extracts.

1 The Colombian election campaign,

2 Whatever the political and economic situation,

3 It's been so long since the last election that we've forgotten how difficult it is

4 The tribunals would disqualify those found guilty

5 Senator Garn told a press conference at the Utah state capital that

6 Elected for six years, Mexican presidents

7 When Lincoln ran for his second election,

a from standing for election for a period of up to seven years.

b are barred from standing for re-election.

c due to culminate in a presidential poll on 27 May, has become more a matter of physical survival than political persuasion.

d he will not run for re-election next year.

e it was not as the Republican candidate.

f the party in office has always gained support in the run-up to the election.

g to avoid media coverage of the campaign trail.

coverage 2 ⇑

The campaign platform

party

platform
  plank in the
  platform
manifesto

soapbox
stump
  on the stump

heckle
heckler

hustings
  at the hustings
  on the hustings

electioneering
cynical
  electioneering
blatant
  electioneering

A political **party** is a group of politicians and their supporters who have similar views on how the country should be run.

A party's **platform** is the policies that it says it will put into effect if elected. Individual policies are **planks** in the platform. Proposed policies may be outlined in a document known as a **manifesto**.

manifesto 186 ⇓

Speeches were traditionally made in Britain standing on a **soapbox** and in the United States **on the stump**, and these things are often referred to in connection with campaigning even if they are not now often actually used. People who shout out their disagreement when a politician makes a speech are **hecklers**, and what they do is **heckle**.

heckle 191 ⇓
heckler 191 ⇓

Politicians on the stump or **at** or **on the hustings** are **electioneering**. Electioneering can be used neutrally to talk about what candidates do during a campaign, but it can also be used to show disapproval of 'unfair' methods. In this case, electioneering may be described as **cynical** or **blatant**.

The King announced that he is ready to talk with the country's political parties about political change.

The Democrats plan to capitalise on public frustration by making health one of the main planks in their platform.

The party's manifesto was so full of generalisations that most South Africans have been amazed by the reforms the government has passed.

The rousing speech, the last of six soapbox addresses, came at the end of 10,000 miles on the battlebus and tours to more than 60 constituencies.

Dos Santos, Angola's dour leader, is an unconvincing convert to democracy. <u>On the stump</u> in Huambo, he looked uncomfortable with the razzmatazz of electioneering.

With only days to go before elections in Pakistan, candidates are battling it out at the <u>hustings</u>.

Government ministers had a rough ride during their nationwide tour, <u>heckled</u> in some places, greeted with stony silence in others.

Belgrade television were even accused of using crude techniques to superimpose enthusiastic cheers over the sound of <u>hecklers</u> at one of Milosevic's campaign rallies.

<u>Electioneering</u> in Mandalay has been more enthusiastic, with members of the opposition parties encouraging supporters to vote.

Labour accused Mr King of <u>blatant electioneering</u> as he placed the crucial order for short range air-to-air missiles. Labour defence spokesman Martin O'Neill said, 'It will come as a relief to the workforce of those companies. Whether it will come as a relief to the Conservative candidates in those seats, it will remain to election day to find out.'

2 **Electioneering clichés.** Find combinations in the table that correspond to the definitions 1–8. Then use the combinations to complete the extracts a–h.

1   Trips that candidates go on

2   Things that candidates say to get elected but that they don't really mean

3   Something that a candidate says they will do if elected

4   Unoriginal things that candidates say and do

5   An attack made by a candidate on others

6   Methods, honest and dishonest, that are used by candidates to gain electoral advantage

7   A government's financial plan that is designed to win votes

8   Violence that is encouraged by candidates

		clichés	
	promise		thuggery
tours		**electioneering**	assault
	tactics		budget
		rhetoric	

a   ...shaven-headed youths who combine football violence with electioneering
_____ .

b   He did everything in the book of electioneering _____ short of kissing babies.

c He followed this up with an electioneering _____ on Labour, claiming businessmen had no enthusiasm for a Labour government.

d He has already been round the country three times on thinly veiled electioneering _____ .

e Mr Reagan's great achievement of his second term – tax reform – was first aired as an electioneering _____ in his State of the Union speech in 1984.

f The prospect of an electioneering _____ and a cut in interest rates as an additional sweetener gave shares a welcome boost yesterday.

g Voters complain about electioneering _____ that verge on the dishonest.

h What the Soviets at first took to be electioneering _____ they discovered to be theological conviction. 'Evil empire' meant what it said.

Whistlestop tours and spin doctors

whistle-stop tour rally walkabout	A very fast campaigning trip, with a candidate making a lot of speeches and appearances in a lot of places in a short time, is a **whistlestop tour**.
glad-hand	A tour such as this might consist, among other things, of: **rallies**: large, often open-air, political events with speeches and entertainment, and rally *8* ⇑
gaffe	**walkabouts**: the candidate walks about in a crowd and shakes hands, or in this political context, **glad-hands** people. glad-hand *8* ⇑
image	Candidates must be careful not to make **gaffes**. Gaffes are slips of the tongue or offensive remarks that damage their **image**: the perception that people have of them. gaffe *216* ⇓
spin doctor spin controller	**Spin doctors** or **spin controllers** are consultants who try to minimise the effects of gaffes, and otherwise improve the way candidates are presented in the media generally.

◆ **LANGUAGE NOTE**

Whistlestop is also spelt with a hyphen and as two words.

And in the film 'Abe Lincoln in Illinois', where the part was played by Raymond Massey – in one of the scenes when Abe Lincoln is leaving on a <u>whistle-stop tour</u> – you'll hear the crowd saying: 'Goodbye, Mr Lincoln. Goodbye, Mr Lincoln.' And you'll hear one lone voice saying: 'Goodbye, Mr Massey. Goodbye, Mr Massey.'

At political <u>rallies</u> across the state, opinions on Helms are anything but ambivalent. Unidentified group: 'Two, four, six, eight, Jesse Helms is full of hate.'

Mrs Robinson admits she is not a natural politician in the Irish sense; she lacks the <u>glad-handing</u> skills so valued in the small world of Irish politics.

Mr Major and his wife Norma were jostled by a crowd of demonstrators during a <u>walkabout</u> in Bolton. Police tried to hold them at bay as they shouted 'Tories Out' and 'Go back to London', but the Premier stayed calm and kept smiling.

Livkov is keeping a very low profile during the campaign. Probably this is because his <u>image</u> has been badly dented by attacks in opposition newspapers, which have dwelt on his communist past.

<u>Gaffe</u> of the campaign: 'I don't want to run the risk of ruining what is a lovely recession.' He meant to say reception. (George Bush)

The disarray in the cases of Cavazos and Bennett was the abrupt way the news broke – that is to say before the <u>spin-controllers</u> could set the stage, if I'm not mixing metaphors here.

A recent question to Mr Clinton and Al Gore on a CBS television phone-in programme was prefaced with: 'Good morning Governor Clinton, Senator Gore, our future president and vice-president', the sort of sound-bite that is a <u>spin doctor's</u> dream come true.

sound-bite 7 ⇑

3 **Controlling the spin.** Read this extract from *The Times* and answer the questions.

Bite-sized campaigners

'Negative advertising and negative campaigning works,' Peter Jennings, chief ABC anchorman in New York. 'We all like to say it doesn't work and it's really beneath contempt, as it is in many cases. But until American people either individually or as a whole reject negative advertising, I think that's the way it's going to go.'

The image of the candidate is so much more important in America than in Britain, because the combination of the greater size of the country and the much less cohesive party system means that in the early stages of the campaign, many candidates are relatively unknown.

I pressed the respected American columnist George Will on whether that meant that television impact now determined the choice of candidates. Was it a case of the more telegenic they were, the more chance they had of success?

1 If something is beneath contempt, do you have a high opinion of it?

anchorman 7 ⇑
advertising 10 ⇑

2 Is the party system stronger in the United States than in Britain?

3 If you press someone on a question, do you care if they don't give you a clear answer?

columnist 19 ⇑

4 Do telegenic people look good on television?

telegenic 7 ⇑

'No,' he said, 'whatever we're getting from television it's not glamour. Television is at best a terrible temptation, because you can get away with murder on it, by condensing your campaign into slogans. But television needn't be quite as lazy or ignorant in doing it.'

Still, the absence of a national daily press cannot do other than enhance the importance of television in a presidential campaign.

Politicians themselves are critical of the way in which they feel the political agenda has shifted out of their control into the hands of the media manipulators and spin doctors.

Henry Kissinger, former Secretary of State was particularly unhappy: 'The risk we're running in our campaigns is that they've reached a stage where the media become part of the electoral process; they no longer report it, they become a part of the electoral process.'

5 If you can get away with murder in doing something, do people care what you do?

6 If you condense something, do you make it   a) bigger, or   b) smaller?

7 Are lazy people energetic?

8 If X enhances the importance of Y, does it increase Y's importance?

9 The political agenda consists of the issues and problems that politicians deal with. Do politicians feel they are getting more control over it?

10 If you run a risk, is the risk a danger for you?

11 The media have reached a p _ _ _ t where they are part of the electoral process.

Seeking nomination

primary elections
  primaries

nomination
  seek nomination

delegate

convention

smoke-filled
  room

In the United States, a party's presidential candidate may be selected in a series of **primary elections** or **primaries**. Primary elections are held in some, but not all, states as a way of finding which candidate has most support. The final choice of presidential candidate is made by **delegates** representing each state at the party **conventions**, famous for late-night bargaining, supposedly in **smoke-filled rooms**, between supporters of each candidate. The expression smoke-filled room is used to refer to meetings where intense, secret negotiations take place, usually between members of the same group or party, to the exclusion of outsiders.

convention *178* ⇓

Candidates looking for selection **seek nomination** as the party's presidential candidate.

It is that time again, and that place too. On the first weekend of November, five of the six declared candidates for the Democratic nomination *made their way, as so many of their kind have done before, to New Hampshire. Its* primary *will be held on February 10th; and it is, as always, the first in the nation.*

The reform changed the <u>delegates</u> to the national party convention were selected. By forcing delegates to declare their allegiance and run for election, that reform was intended to replace the <u>smoke-filled rooms</u> and deal-making with the intra-party primaries that had until then been mainly 'beauty contests' of little consequence.

presidential bid	An attempt to become president is sometimes referred to as a **bid for the presidency** or a **presidential bid**.
bid for the presidency	The candidate running for the vice-presidency is the presidential candidate's **running mate**. An ideal combination of candidates for these two posts is known as the **dream ticket**. The expression is also applied to other attractive political partnerships in the US and elsewhere. It is even sometimes used to describe a single candidate with attractive qualities.
running mate	
dream ticket	

His <u>presidential bid</u> has attracted to this small city roughly 350 highly paid consultants, strategists, and idealistic young volunteers, not to mention scores of expense-account journalists and thousands of tourists.

Gary Hart's <u>bid for the presidency</u> failed after the evidence of his romantic link with Donna Rice.

If Hillary is the perfect partner, then in Al Gore he had the perfect <u>running mate</u>. It really was the <u>dream ticket</u> for women. Where Clinton is rugged and earthy, Gore is clean cut and preppy.

This new dawn is not to be confused with the last new dawn, when Neil Kinnock and Roy Hattersley were described as a <u>dream ticket</u>.

Peterson, Canada – Cartoonists & Writers Syndicate

4 **The right candidate.** The same word or expression from this section is missing from all these extracts. What is it? In which extracts is the singular form of the missing item used and in which the plural?

1	Labour party policy was determined by a few trade union bosses in	. . .	. That is now beginning to change.
2	The Conservative leadership was once decided in	. . .	of London clubs by the party's grandees.
3	It took 15 hours in a	. . .	but the outcome was never in doubt.
4	Those attending the Maastricht summit will be sweating it out in the	. . .	of Euro uniformity.
5	Despite all the talk of democratic reforms, Japan is still run by what Americans used to call the politics of the	. . .	. The godfather of Japanese politics, Shin Kanemaru, has begged the public to show 'understanding' of the way the ruling LDP is picking its new president.
6	The danger is that professionals in	. . .	will impose an over-centralised European Union which many Europeans may not want.
7	On one side is the	. . .	approach to political change, negotiated by 'professionals'. On the other is reform brought about by popular pressure.

The sleaze factor

**digging for dirt
muckraking
mudslinging**

sleaze

Sometimes candidates or the media search for damaging information about a politician's personal life, or business or secret political activities. When they do this they are said to be **digging for dirt** or **muckraking**. Damaging information of this kind is **sleaze**. If they then use this information to attack their opponents, they are accused of **mudslinging**.

smear campaign

vilification

Victims of muckraking say that their opponents are guilty of conducting a **smear campaign**, or more formally, a campaign of **vilification** against them.

smear campaign *24* ⇑

Teflon coating

If allegations or charges against someone cannot be proved, or made to stick, that person is said to have a Teflon coating. (Some saucepans have **Teflon coatings** to prevent food sticking to them.)

allegation *28* ⇑, *138* ⇓

charge *140* ⇓

◆ **LANGUAGE NOTE**
Muckraking and **mudslinging** are also spelt with a hyphen and as two words.

In preparation for potentially the nastiest campaign yet, the Democrats have been digging for dirt with which to undermine Mr Bush's image. During his presidency, one brother and one son have been fined for financial irregularities. Another brother and two other sons have been involved in questionable business deals.

fine *149* ⇓

ASHDOWN CASE JURY WARNED ON MORALITY. Jurors were warned yesterday not to let their views on the morality of politicians' private lives or the muckraking of newspapers influence them in the case of the man accused of stealing the document that disclosed details of Paddy Ashdown's sexual relationship with his former secretary.

juror *146* ⇓

The campaign has taken on a mud-slinging violence that makes Mrs Ferraro's 1984 experience seem clean by comparison. Her opponents have seized on her family's alleged links with the Mafia to undermine her.

A parliamentary commission was set up to investigate charges that Garcia personally embezzled $50 million. He has denied any wrongdoing. He puts all accusations down to a smear campaign by his political opponents, who he claims are worried he may choose to stand again for president in the next elections in 1995.

wrongdoing *95* ⇓
embezzlement *96* ⇓

Mr Markovic said he and his government were being subjected to an intense media campaign of lies and vilification.

'We will continue to run a good, clean, hard-hitting campaign. The president is determined to keep this campaign out of the <u>sleaze</u> business,' said a spokesman with Mr Bush in Florida.

Reagan was the so-called <u>Teflon</u> President, whose impeccable image protected him from scandal and charges of incompetence.

bimbo	Politicians sometimes fail electorally because of allegations of extra-marital affairs. Women involved in affairs such as these are often referred to as **bimbos**, implying that they are sexually attractive but intellectually limited, even if evidence of their intellectual qualities, or lack of them, is rarely discussed.

The only top Republican aide with the common touch is Mary Matalin, the political director. But when Ms Matalin raised Bill Clinton's problems with '<u>bimbos</u>' last week, she was, to her disgust, rebuked and made to retract by Mr Bush.

5 **Digging for gold and digging for dirt.** Read this article from *The Times,* written during Bill Clinton's bid for the presidency, and answer the questions.

Clinton hires tough Texan to ride shotgun

The Democrats know that Mr Clinton, of all men, enjoys no Teflon coating. They all know he will be assailed as the 'failed governor of a small state' and as a man who cannot be trusted.

Could the Republicans be sitting on another explosive revelation about his private life? 'Not a true one,' said Miss Wright in an interview. 'I am not at all sure there are not lies in the making out there, but my job is to dispel and discredit them as fast as possible. I have gotten to where I expect anything.'

Last September, loathing the strain of campaigns, she accepted a fellowship at Harvard. By March, Mr Clinton faced multiple charges of infidelity, draft-dodging and financial skulduggery in Arkansas and was being savaged like 'a piece of meat'. Miss Wright alone knew his record well enough to refute the allegations. He begged her to return, and when she did, she found Little Rock overrun by reporters digging for dirt.

1 Do Democrats think allegations might be made to stick to Clinton?

2 The Republicans may be about to r _ v _ _ _ more about Clinton's private life.

3 If you dispel and discredit lies, do most people go on believing them?

4 Are people who indulge in skulduggery honest?

5 If someone is viciously attacked, they are s _ _ _ a _ _ d.

6 If you refute an allegation, do you prove that it is false?

To counter endless spurious claims of adultery by Mr Clinton, she employed a leading private investigator, San Francisco's Jack Palladino, who by May alone had received $28,000 from the campaign.

Miss Wright and Mr Palladino learnt that Sally Perdue, a former Miss Arkansas, was about to profess a past affair with Mr Clinton. They found four friends and relatives to dispute Ms Perdue's veracity and managed to kill the story.

Miss Wright calls such episodes 'bimbo eruptions'. She has counted at least 26, but only Gennifer Flowers has made the headlines. She admits Mr Clinton has on occasion been 'naively careless about appearances', but blames 'gold-diggers', tabloids who offer them six-figure sums to lie, and the Republicans, who, she insists, are generating the stories.

7 If you offer evidence that a claim or allegation is false, you c _ _ _ _ _ _ it.

8 If an allegation is not backed up by evidence is it spurious?

9 If you dispute someone's veracity, you accuse them of _ _ _ i n g.

10 If someone digs for gold, they look for an easy way of getting rich. Which of the following are six-figure sums?
   a) $150,000
   b) $44,532
   c) $35,789.50.

tabloid *18* ⇑

Dirty tricks

dirty tricks
disinformation

Watergate
-gate

cover-up
cover up

Politicians may accuse their opponents of using unfair or even criminal methods against them, such as paying people to make false accusations, stealing documents, bugging phone conversations, and so on. These methods are known as **dirty tricks** and are usually part of a campaign to spread **disinformation**: half-truths and lies.

bug *22* ⇑

The most famous dirty tricks campaign of all was in 1972, when President Nixon ordered the Democratic party's offices in the **Watergate** building in Washington to be burgled. Watergate may now be mentioned and the suffix **-gate** used when referring not only to dirty tricks campaigns, but to any case of political or business corruption and its associated **cover-up**: the associated attempts to **cover up**, or hide, the truth.

dirty tricks *24* ⇑

burglary *129* ⇓

◆ **LANGUAGE NOTE**

The noun **cover-up** is also spelt as two words.

Friends of Mandela, while not disputing the letter's authenticity, accused enemies within the ANC of waging a <u>dirty tricks</u> 'smear campaign' against her. 'They are trying everything they can to destroy her,' one said.

So, in some sense there is truth in <u>disinformation</u>. That's always what disinformation's about.

A Puerto Rican Senate committee is investigating the killings and subsequent <u>cover-up</u> of two independence activists 13 years ago. NPR's Maria Martin reports on the case, which is being called the <u>Watergate</u> of Puerto Rico.

The controversy now being dubbed Inkatha-<u>gate</u> took a new turn with the resignation of Chief Buthelezi's personal assistant, M. Z. Khumalo, who said he alone knew about the security police payments.

Now and then a conspiracy in high places is uncovered, like <u>Watergate</u>, Irangate, or any other <u>-gate</u> you care to mention.

The 'Observer' says there is evidence of large-scale British involvement in the <u>Iran-Gate</u> affair now emerging following the collapse of the Bank of Commerce and Credit International. And it goes on to list a series of complicated manoeuvres in which the Colonel is said to have used accounts at the Bank to transfer money from arms sales to Iran to Nicaragua's contra guerillas.

6 **Presidential paranoia.** Read this extract from an American National Public® Radio broadcast made on the 20th anniversary of the Watergate break-in, and answer the questions.

WHAT WATERGATE WAS ALL ABOUT

The botched break-in at Watergate, which gave the era its name, was only a minute part of what it was all about. Bugging the Democrats and rifling their files, apparently to learn what they might have on Nixon, was only one manifestation of presidential paranoia fanned by anti-war protests.

Once critics and opponents were perceived as 'enemies', a word until then unfamiliar to American politics, then the law and the Constitution could be flouted in the name of national security, and so taps could be put on the phones of White House aides and the journalists to whom they might be leaking, and so explicitly illegal plans could be drawn up for widespread FBI and CIA surveillance on American dissenters.

1 If a plan is botched, is it carried out successfully?

break-in *129* ⇓
bugging *22* ⇑

2 The files were rifled, or stolen, to see what d _ _ _ _ , or damaging information, the Democrats had on Nixon.

3 Paranoia is abnormally intense suspicion and distrust. Nixon's was 'fanned' by anti-Vietnam war protests. Did it get a) more intense, or b) less intense?

4 If you flout the law, do you obey it?

5 If you put a tap on someone's phone, you _ _ g it.

6 If an official leaks information to the press, do they wish their identity to be known?

7 In a surveillance operation, do organisations such as the police spy on people?

All this was only the first installment of the conspiracy. Re-elected by a landslide, Nixon had more ominous plans for his second term which were aborted by the unraveling of Watergate. He planned a clean sweep of officials unresponsive to his designs and the stationing of White House commissars and departments and agencies to bring them under tighter control.

He had told counsel John Dean to 'keep notes on all of those who try to do us in,' and said he would use against them the full powers of government that he had not used in the first four years. He planned to expand the plumbers, the White House intelligence unit, into a large-scale intelligence and surveillance operation.

So when you are asked, 'Grandpa, what was Watergate all about? Was it about dirty tricks and politics as usual?' Then you should answer, 'No, it was about a paranoid politician who saw enemies all around him and who tried to hijack the whole government in order to punish them.'

8 Someone in a conspiracy conspires or p _ _ _ _ with other people to do something illegal.

9 Nixon had more ominous, or threatening, plans for his second term, but they weren't carried out because of the 'unraveling' of Watergate, which was investigated and explained. For example, Nixon had planned a 'clean sweep' of 'unresponsive' officials. Did he intend to neglect any of these people?

10 If you do someone in, do you
a) help them,   b) attack them?

11 What do plumbers normally work on? a) pipes, taps and leaks
b) electricity, or c) woodwork

12 A paranoid person suffers from p _ _ _ _ _ _ a .

13 If someone hijacks something, do they bring it under their control using illegal methods?

Polls and pollsters

opinion poll
opinion survey

poll
polling
  organisation
pollster

sample

results
findings
  reliable results
  reliable findings
  accurate results
  accurate findings

Between elections, especially during election campaigns, **opinion polls** or **surveys** are conducted to **measure public opinion** and to **predict** or **forecast** election results.

Polling organisations and the people working for them are **pollsters**. They interview or **poll** a number of people, a **sample** typical in its mix of ages, social classes and professions of the population as a whole.

An **exit poll** is carried out just after people have voted as they are leaving the polling station.

Results or **findings** of opinion polls are more or less **reliable** or **accurate**.

◆ **LANGUAGE NOTE**

The nouns corresponding to the verbs **forecast** and **predict** are **forecast** and **prediction**.

The opinion poll was conducted among a sample of 15,000 adults randomly and scientifically selected from all 450 local government areas in Nigeria.

It puts Labour support at 53 per cent of the electorate, the highest figure recorded in the poll of polls. The results were taken from surveys by six polling organisations: Gallup, Harris, Mori, ICM, NOP and Audience Selection.

Pollsters are to change the way they measure public opinion after getting the result of the last general election badly wrong.

Opinion polls predict that the M-19 party may either win the polling or emerge with sufficient votes to threaten the hold of the country's principal parties.

Opinion polls are forecasting that a non-Communist coalition of parties, Demos, will win at least 40 per cent of the vote.

It also concluded that most of the voters who had chosen to remain silent would probably back the opposition. Because of this, it is essential to view the poll's findings with some scepticism.

NOP's unadjusted forecast was one of the most accurate of any by-election exit poll, in which people leaving the polling booths are asked how they voted.

7 **Last-minute polls.** This column, by Bernard Levin, published in *The Times* (29.7.91) looks at the question of whether polls should be banned in the last week before elections. Complete the gaps with the words listed. (a is used four times, b and c twice each, and the other words once each.)

a polls	c pollsters	e accuracy	g campaign
b polling	d poll	f inaccuracy	h election

Poll late and poll often

Opinion _____ (1) have been with us, in their present form, since the 1930s; originally crude and liable to substantial error, they have been repeatedly refined (I am speaking of the recognised _____ (2) organisations) and now regularly demonstrate very remarkable _____ (3) . At first, some voters found them irritating, but that feeling has long disappeared, and it is clear that the electorate as a whole enjoy the political swings and roundabouts.

But one thing must be emphasised: there is no evidence that voters' intentions are changed by the _____ (4) results, though I must add that if they were it would be perfectly acceptable, for the voters are entitled to be swayed by anything they wish, even, for instance, the promises of the politicians.

France, for no discernibly logical reason, bans the publication, though not of course the taking, of _____ (5) figures, during the final week of the _____ (6) _____ (7) ; in all other democratic lands the _____ (8) can take their soundings up to the last minute, and so it should be.

Of course, the parties which are trailing in the _____ (9) regularly denounce them as instruments of Satan, or at least instruments of shocking _____ (10), but as soon as the _____ (11) reveal that the party order has been reversed they hasten to proclaim that the _____ (12) are the finest fellows alive; neither attitude has any sense in it, for the reason I have given: there is no evidence that the _____ (13) themselves do, or can, affect the outcome, though of course the voters may use the findings for their own electoral purposes.

trailing 219 ⇓

Trailing or riding high?

rating
  approval rating
  popularity rating
	Between elections, pollsters ask people if they approve of the performance of politicians and parties, and the results are given as **approval ratings** or **popularity ratings**.

lead	In the run-up to an election, pollsters and journalists may talk about a **race** in which the party or candidate most likely to win is the **favourite** or the **front runner**.
ride high	
trail trail behind	Candidates or parties with the best results in opinion polls are said to be **ahead** or **riding high**. Their **lead** is often given in percentage **points** over the others.
points	
race favourite front-runner	When two parties or candidates have about the same amount of support, they are said to be **level pegging** or **running neck and neck**.
running neck and neck level pegging	Candidates or parties not doing so well are said to be **behind** or **trailing** or **trailing behind**. If their results improve, they **gain ground**.
gain ground	

ratings 10 ⇑

race 218 ⇓
favourite 218 ⇓
front-runner 219 ⇓

neck and neck 219 ⇓

◆ **LANGUAGE NOTE**

Favourite is spelt **favorite** in American English.
Front runner and **level pegging** are also spelt with hyphens.
Neck and neck is also spelt with hyphens, especially in the expression **running neck-and-neck**.

8 **Ahead in the race, level pegging or trailing behind.** Match the two parts of these extracts.

1 A poll published on December 7th shows that President Mitterrand's popularity rating has slipped to a new low of 31 per cent,

2 During the last 12 years this government has involved us in two wars, two recessions, record unemployment, crime and hospital waiting lists,

3 Prime Minister Kaifu was riding high in the popularity polls.

4 The Socialists are trailing in the opinion polls but are gaining ground and are currently in

5 There's been a lot of pressure on him, saying that he's at 91 per cent approval rating in the polls, and he could use that tremendous approval to do something, not just sit on it.

6 Two months ago, Father Jean-Bertrand Aristide, a priest who advocates power for the impoverished Haitian masses made a late entry into the race

7 Unpublished polls by Gallup confirmed that

8 Weekend polls showed he had halved his opponent's pre-convention lead of 15 to 25 points. He was shown to be trailing by 14 points (*Newsweek*), 11 points (*Time*), nine points (*Washington Post*) and eight (*Los Angeles Times*).

a 'This is the most open, fickle, volatile electorate we have ever seen,' said Peter Hart, a Democratic pollster.

b a fall of 21 points in just three months. Another poll shows that the level of satisfaction with his performance is the lowest for any president under the Fifth Republic.

c and instantly became the front-runner for president.

d And of course, if he succeeded in getting a peace in the Middle East, he would go down in history. He could win the Nobel Peace Prize. He would be remembered forever.

e far better shape to fight an election than the bitterly split Union of Democratic Forces.

f So high, in fact, that faction leaders in the Liberal Democratic Party were starting to worry.

g the two main parties are now virtually level-pegging.

h yet the polls still show them running neck and neck with the opposition. It seems crazy to me.

Casting your ballot

elect
election
  election day

poll
  go to the polls

vote
  cast votes
ballot
  cast ballots

electorate
turnout
abstain
abstention

On **election day**, voters **go to the polls**. They **vote**, or **cast their votes** or **ballots**, to **elect** candidates.

People with the right to vote are **voters**, and together make up the **electorate**. The proportion of people actually voting is the **turnout** and the total number of votes cast is the total **vote**. People not voting **abstain** from voting and are counted as **abstentions**.

◆ **LANGUAGE NOTE**

The noun **turnout** is also spelt with a hyphen.

Mitchell, Australia – Cartoonists & Writers Syndicate

It's election day in Chad – people throughout the country have been casting their votes at the first contested election since independence from France in 1960.

On September 15th the voters of Hong Kong, casting ballots in the British colony's first truly democratic legislative election, delivered China a slap in the face.

This Sunday, Peruvians vote to elect their 23rd president.

It is the second time in a fortnight that the people of Hungary have been asked to go to the polls and today the atmosphere is matter of fact, with none of the sense of occasion which prevailed two weeks ago when voters were voting freely for the first time in 40 years.

'The sunshine has brought out the voters in droves, and we expect a very high turnout,' a Tory official said last night.

But many liberals and conservatives may abstain from voting because in recent months they have been hit by inflation and unemployment and the colourless platforms of the establishment parties have but limited appeal for them.

A growing proportion of Europeans are not bothering to vote. In Portugal abstentions leapt from 22 per cent in the 1987 general election to 32 per cent in 1991.

9 **The ballot or the bullet?** Look at the extracts and complete the definitions below using the key words.

In the separate women's <u>polling booths</u> it is specially difficult to detect false voters since many of the women are in purdah.

Current estimates are that fewer than half of eligible Americans are expected to cast their <u>ballot</u> on November 3.

Voting will not be by <u>secret ballot</u> but by the controversial method of queuing behind your favourite candidate. Many people fear that the queuing system will create conditions for chaos at the <u>polling stations</u>, but the government says it is an open system which will stop the practice of filling <u>ballot boxes</u> with fictitious <u>ballot papers</u>.

Mr Rao was certain of victory, yet there were reports that his supporters had captured booths and stuffed ballot boxes. In Bihar many people died and new <u>balloting</u> was ordered in hundreds of polling stations.

Israel is a democratic society where governments are changed by the <u>ballot box</u>, not the bullet.

ballot cast ballots ballot box ballot papers secret ballot balloting **polling** polling booth

Voting, p _ _ _ _ _ _ or _ _ _ _ _ _ _ _ takes place at p _ _ _ _ _ _ t _ _ _ _ _ _ _. In a c _ _ _ _ _ _ l _ _ _ , voters mark their b _ _ _ _ _ p _ _ _ _ _ in a _ _ _ _ _ _ g b _ _ _ _ and place them in a _ _ _ _ _ o _ _ o _ . The ballot box is often mentioned when contrasting democratic methods with terrorist ones.

Getting elected

legislature **seat** gain a seat win a seat lose a seat **electoral system** **first-past-the-post** **proportional representation** **PR** **list** **constituency**

A body that passes laws is a **legislature**. Candidates **win** or **gain seats** in legislatures under different systems in different countries. Existing members of a legislature who are not re-elected **lose their seats**.

The two main methods of electing candidates are:

proportional representation, or **PR**, where winning candidates are elected from a **list** in proportion to the number of votes cast for each candidate, and

first-past-the-post, where the candidate with the most votes in the **constituency** wins, even if he or she has fewer votes than the other candidates combined.

Some countries use a combination of both **electoral systems**.

His promise to make the Senate an <u>elected body</u> with effective power, the main demand of western Canadians, is vaguer.

Mongolia has promised free multi-party elections to the <u>legislature</u>, the Great Hural and has become the first Asian nation to bow to the winds of change sweeping in from Eastern Europe.

In the Bulgarian elections, computer predictions give the Socialists – formerly the Communists – nearly half the <u>vote</u> and therefore about 100 <u>seats</u> of the 200 decided under the <u>PR</u> system. The figures obtained by the BBC show that of the 200 seats decided under the <u>first-past-the-post</u> system, the Socialists have won 76 seats.

Israel's electoral system is one of <u>proportional representation</u> by list. Each party lists its candidates for the Knesset in order of seniority, and as the votes accumulate, another name on the list enters the Knesset.

In 1989 the Green Party received 2 million votes, 15 per cent of the vote, in the European elections. However, because of Britain's first-past-the-post <u>electoral system</u> (whereby only the candidate who receives the most votes is elected) the Greens did not <u>gain</u> a single <u>seat</u>.

About 1.3 million people voted Labour in Scotland. There, it <u>won</u> 50 seats. In the English heartland, between the Wash and the Avon (excluding London), some 1.7 million people voted Labour. There, it won 3 seats.

The supporters of <u>PR</u> point to the unfairness of the present system where one member of parliament represents one diverse <u>constituency</u> where the majority of people may have voted for a number of other candidates.

10 **Legislature quiz.** Legislatures are often divided into upper and lower houses or chambers. Match these legislative chambers to their countries.

1	House of Commons	a	Germany
2	Sejm	b	United Kingdom
3	Bundestag	c	Ireland
4	Riksdag	d	Mongolia
5	Great Hural	e	Poland
6	Cortes	f	Sweden
7	Dáil	g	Spain
8	Lok Sabha	h	India
9	Knesset	i	Denmark
10	Folketing	j	Israel

Knocked out in the first round

rounds of voting
first round
second round

run-off

In some countries – France is one – there are two **rounds of voting**, usually a week apart. If no one candidate in the **first round** of voting gets more than 50 per cent of the vote, the top two candidates go on to a **second round** in a **run-off**, with each trying to attract the first round supporters of the other candidates.

◆ **LANGUAGE NOTE**

Run-off is also spelt as one word.
Run off, **first round** and **second round** can be spelt with a hyphen.

About half the 120 seats in the National Assembly remain to be decided. These include constituencies in and around the country's most important cities, Libreville and Port Gentil, where because of irregularities the ballots cast in last month's <u>first round of voting</u> were annulled.

Among the NDP victors were at least eight government ministers, including Dr Amal Osman, one of only five women who have so far secured parliamentary seats. The <u>second round run off</u> will be on December 6th and only then will a full list of members be available.

11 **A political killing?** Put this BBC report into a
logical order. (The first section is a.)

BRAZIL'S WILD WEST

a A 42-year-old Brazilian senator, Mr Olavio Gomez Pires, who is also a candidate for the governorship of the western state of Rondonia, has been shot dead. Reports say two men drew up in a car as the candidate was leaving his office in the state capital Porto Velho. They opened fire with machine guns.

b Senator Olavio Gomez who was standing in a coalition led by the Socialist Party, the PTB, had a narrow victory in the first round of voting on October 3rd but he faced a run-off second round on November 25th.

c The attackers got away. A commission of senators is going to Rondonia to investigate the assassination.

d The election campaigning in that state was marked by accusations of corruption. It's on the fringes of the Amazon region and has been extensively colonised only in the last 20 years. Rondonia is afflicted by crime typical of a frontier region – the smuggling of gold and tin and more recently by drugs trafficking. Rondonia borders the state of Acre where the conservationist and political campaigner Chico Mendes was murdered two years ago.

e The motive for the assassination is not clear. If it was a political killing the elections in that state may have to be staged again.

Electoral fraud

election returns	Results in an election are also known as **election returns**. An opposition party or outside observers may accuse the organisers of the election of **electoral fraud**, saying that the elections have not been **free and fair**.
free and fair elections	
electoral fraud electoral irregularities	**Vote-rigging** occurs, for example, when ballot boxes are filled with fictitious ballot papers or when votes are not counted properly. Where a lot of vote rigging is alleged to have taken place, it may be characterised as **massive** or **widespread**.
vote-rigging massive vote-rigging widespread vote-rigging	Another form of **irregularity** may take place before the election, when boundaries between constituencies are drawn. If the governing party draws the boundaries to their own advantage they are guilty of **gerrymandering**.
gerrymandering	

fraud 96 ⇓

Elections were held, but when returns showed that Doe was losing heavily, he confiscated all the ballot boxes, announced he had won over 50 per cent of the vote and declared himself President.

The State Department said on Monday that the Romanian elections on Sunday were peaceful with a heavy voter turnout, but Spokesman Richard Boucher said it was too early to determine if the elections were free and fair. Election day irregularities seem to have been minimal, Mr Boucher said, although opposition political party leaders have complained of breaches of election law procedures.

She has accused her opponents of massive vote-rigging. She said ballot boxes were stolen and switched, and agents of her party had disappeared.

In 1986, the Supreme Court conceded that gerrymandering – the practice of drawing boundaries to help one political party – can be subject to judicial review.

12 **Witch way to vote?** Read this report from *The Times* about the use of witch doctors to prevent, or check, electoral fraud. A witch doctor is someone thought to have magic powers. These powers are often invoked through the casting of spells: actions and utterances thought to have magical effects. Fill the gaps using six of the words listed. Two words are not used.

a booths	c voting	e gerrymandering	g constituency
b electoral	d poll	f vote-rigging	h irregularities

Thais cast spells to check poll fraud

As the election campaign that has seen the most strenuous efforts ever in Thailand to stop vote-buying and other _____ (1) came to an end, the government-appointed _____ (2)-watch committee hired witch doctors to invoke benign spirits to stop _____ (3) fraud.

The committee said: 'Superstition is needed to fight satanic influences.' The witch-doctors had their biggest ceremony in the _____ (4) of General Chatichai Choonavan, a former prime minister, who with other ministers was accused of corruption while in office. The army cited their corruption as justification for the coup last year.

Reciting magic words, the witch doctors cast spells on pieces of animal hide and iron nails that were later scattered around the houses of suspects. The committee said the items would creep into the bodies of corrupt politicians. More than 60,000 volunteers have been on the lookout for attempts to manipulate the election. Tomorrow they will man polling _____ (5) to stop fraudulent _____ (6) .

suspect *138* ⇓

Election results

victory
  claim victory

defeat
  admit defeat
  concede defeat

margin

landslide

When it becomes apparent which parties or politicians have won an election, the winners **claim victory** and the losers **concede** or **admit defeat**.

If a party or a candidate wins an election by a large amount or **margin**, commentators talk about a **landslide**.

The conservative New Democracy Party are <u>claiming victory</u> in the Greek elections after winning half the 300 seats.

Benazir Bhutto has <u>admitted defeat</u> in Wednesday's general elections, even before official results have confirmed what seems to have been a major electoral upset.

Opposition leaders in Zambia say that President Kenneth Kaunda has <u>conceded defeat</u>. Presidential challenger Frederick Chiluba told reporters that he'd spoken with Kaunda on the telephone.

They received 55 per cent of the vote, a comfortable <u>margin</u> in the first parliamentary elections in the unified Germany.

Now with Communism in all its forms discredited, he has come down in favour of social democracy within a pluralist framework. But his party's apparent <u>landslide victory</u> in the elections appears to make a multi-party system something of an irrelevance for the time being.

13 **Surprising victory or massive defeat?** These words are used to describe victory and defeat. Complete them.

a) c _ t _ g _ r _ c _ l

b) c _ m f _ r t _ b l _

c) c _ n v _ n c _ n g

d) c r _ s h _ n g

e) d _ c _ s _ v _

f) d _ v _ s t _ t _ n g

g) h _ _ v y

h) _ v _ r w h _ l m _ n g

i) _ _ _ _ _ _ n d _ n g

j) s p _ c t _ c _ l _ r

Throwing the incumbents out

swing

incumbent
re-elect

mandate
  fresh mandate

office
  in office
  term of office
  thrown out of
    office

The **swing** from Party X to Party Y is the percentage of voters who previously supported X who now support Y.

If **incumbent** parties or politicians (that is, parties or politicians in power or **in office**) get **re-elected**, they receive a **fresh mandate** from the electorate for a new **term of office**. If they don't, they are **thrown out of office**.

The Labour council's decision to move the Northern Ballet from Manchester to Halifax at a cost of £200,000 so angered the locals that there was a huge 10 per cent <u>swing</u> against Labour in the district election in May.

The possibility of a new left-of-centre party emerging will be frustrated by a combination of Labour's declining presence and our first-past-the-post electoral system. The Tories will remain <u>in office</u> for many years to come.

The opposition parties in the tiny island nation are to contest only 40 of the 81 seats in parliament. The People's Action Party is therefore guaranteed to be returned for a seventh consecutive term of office.

Of course politicians will sometimes make bad decisions. At least they can be thrown out of office unlike unaccountable central bankers.

The general anti-incumbent feeling could well give her victory despite the campaign gaffes she is making.

Señor Solchaga optimistically wants a fresh mandate to raise value-added tax.

14 **Throw the rascals out.** Read this extract from National Public Radio® about limiting the time members of Congress can stay in office. Say where a) the radio reporter and b) the politician who is an opponent of term limitation each start speaking. They each speak twice: not all the numbers indicate a change of speaker.

LIMITING TERMS OF OFFICE

(1) But just as Republicans who support term limits are suspect as losers who can't win by the rules the way they are, Democrats who oppose the limits are suspect as incumbents who want to hold on to their jobs, says Washington Democrat Al Swift, who's in his seventh term.

(2) Any incumbent who is affected by term limitations is not taken seriously when they speak out about term limitations.

(3) People – and I think naturally so – say, 'Well, you're just trying to protect your job.'

(4) In order to make his case against term limits more credible, Swift announced he's retiring in 1994, the year the Washington ballot initiative would force him out if it passes.

(5) By then any incumbent who's already served the newly imposed 12-year maximum would be ineligible to run again. Congressman Swift claims that people are now much more ready to listen as he makes his case.

(6) Term limitations at heart is a limitation on the citizen who goes into the voting booth.

(7) It is being sold on a 'throw-the-rascals-out' kind of theme, which is always somewhat popular and today is enormously popular. But you've got to be careful of these things as they often bite back.

Absolute majorities and hung parliaments

majority
  absolute majority
  overall majority

government
  form a
    government

coalition
  coalition
    government

minority
  minority
    government

If one party obtains more seats than all the others combined, it has an **overall** or **absolute majority** and is able to **form a government** on its own.

If no one party has an overall majority, a **coalition government** is formed, often after much inter-party bargaining and negotiation. If the governing parties do not between them hold a majority of seats, they form a **minority government**.

India's lower house of parliament, the Lok Sabha, convenes tomorrow. The Congress party and its allies are about 12 short of an overall majority. Sam Miller in Delhi considers how Congress can find enough support to remain in power.

The Free Democrats are the kingmakers of German coalition governments and their high showing in the polls could give them a strong bargaining chip with which to put pressure on Chancellor Kohl's CDU. Since he's unlikely to get an absolute majority, he'll have to rely on the Free Democrats to form another government.

Indira Gandhi, installed as prime minister in 1966, was supposed to be a pussycat. She proved to be a tiger instead, running a bold minority government for two years.

15 Hung parliaments and splinter parties. Read the examples and complete the commentary with the key words.

The Liberal Democrats are hoping that these policies will be implemented after the next election as a price they would demand for forming a coalition government in a hung parliament.

The union will have to make an alliance with a minority party representing the Turkish population in Bulgaria.

…the Bharatiya Janata Party: a fringe party of Hindu extremists only a few years ago, it looks as though it could be part of the government after the election.

The opposition Social Democratic and Green parties, meanwhile, lost strength and split their votes among small splinter parties.

Bulgaria's ruling Socialist party yesterday lost its majority in parliament when a splinter faction declared independence from the party.

Dr Mahatir's United Malays' National Organisation, the dominant party of the ruling coalition, accused Tonku Razaleigh, who leads a breakaway party from UMNO known as Semangat 46, of splitting and therefore weakening the Malays.

hung parliament
 	
party
  fringe party
  minority party
  breakaway party
  splinter party
 	
faction
  splinter faction
	If, in a system usually dominated by two parties (usually the British one), neither party gets an overall majority, commentators talk about a _____ _____ .
	
	A _____ party is a party holding a relatively small number of seats, and a _____ party is one with extreme views and very little support.
	
	A party may be made up of rival groups or _____ . A _____ faction may break away to form a separate party, known as a _____ party or a _____ party.

Rainbow coalitions and political horse-trading

opposition
 	
coalition
  opposition
  coalition
  rainbow coalition
 	
horse-trading
	Parties opposed to the government form the **opposition** and may work together in an **opposition coalition**.
	
	A **rainbow coalition** is one containing many different interests; the expression is sometimes used to indicate approval of unity between different groupings, and sometimes to indicate disapproval of the fact that the groups have so little in common that they should not get together.
	
	Critics of proportional representation say that one of its defects is that it does not often produce absolute majorities, and they refer to the bargaining between the coalition parties, disapprovingly, as **horse-trading**.

The opposition coalition, led by the Mongolian Democratic Party, has accused the ruling party of being insincere about reform.

Jackson said his Rainbow Coalition will be working to build what he called 'a new independent Democratic majority'.

Mr Lenihan said he was beaten by a rainbow coalition that did not reflect the normal divisions in Irish politics.

After a short honeymoon, the ruling coalition will begin its horse-trading, haggling over ministerial posts.

16 **Creaking coalitions.** Read this article from *The Independent,* written by a politician who believes in the first-past-the-post electoral system, and answer the questions.

OUT OF ALL PROPORTION

The general theory of proportional representation is simple and appealing: each political party receives a number of seats in the legislature in proportion to the number of votes cast in its favour. In that way, so the argument runs, Parliament would accurately reflect public opinion. That is the theory, but what about the practice?

Let us take the result of the 1987 General Election. The Conservatives took 42 per cent of the vote, Labour 31 per cent and the now-defunct 'Alliance' 23 per cent. If seats had been distributed under a PR system, neither the Conservatives nor Labour would have been able to form a government on their own. Whoever did would be reliant on – and therefore beholden to – the votes of the 'Alliance'.

So who then would be calling the tune in Parliament? Which party above all could be sure that its policies were the ones that would be put into action? Answer: the one with just 23 per cent of the popular vote. The alternative would be a creaking coalition, paralysed by fear of losing control. And it needn't be a percentage as high as 23. Look at Israel where tiny parties, with only one or two members in the Knesset, regularly threaten to bring down the government unless their policies – often extreme ones – are accepted.

1 If something is appealing, is it attractive?

2 Instead of 'runs', the word g _ _ _ could be used here.

3 If something is defunct, it is no longer in e x _ _ _ _ _ _ _ _ .

4 'Whoever did'. Whoever did what?

5 If you are reliant on someone, are you independent of them?

6 It you are beholden to someone, do you owe them a favour?

7 If you call the tune, you are in c o n _ _ _ _ _ of events.

8 Is a creaking coalition a workable one?

9 If you are paralysed with fear, are you able to act?

10 Is an extreme policy a reasonable one, in most people's opinion?

People who support PR think that it would be fairer, but in practice it gives totally disproportionate power to minority groups – to the fascist right in France, and the communist left in Italy.

Closer to home, take the Irish Republic, which under PR held elections in 1981, 1982 (twice), 1987 and 1989. Mr Haughey's Fianna Fáil party, with 77 seats, failed to secure an overall majority. The result, after weeks of horse-trading, was a coalition with the Progressive Democrats, who held just six seats in the Dáil, yet managed to extract two cabinet posts in return for their co-operation – a degree of influence out of all proportion to their popularity, especially considering they held 14 seats prior to the election.

But 'fairness' is only one aspect of the electoral system that those who advocate reform must consider; the link between a constituent and his or her representative is equally important. One of the strongest, most enduring and attractive aspects of our democratic system is the relationship between MPs and their own constituency. MPs at weekends go back to their roots, to those people who gave them authority to be MPs.

Under some versions of PR, MPs would not represent any area in particular. The nearest thing that PR could come to fulfilling this requirement would be by having huge multi-member constituencies – of a whole county or more. The link of mutual dependence and responsibility that currently exists between MPs and their constituents is central.

11 Did the Progressive Democrats have disproportionate influence in relation to their electoral support?

12 If you have a link with something, are you connected with it?

13 A constituent is someone who votes in a given c _ _ _ _ _ _ _ _ _ _ _ .

14 If something endures, is it temporary?

15 If something fulfils a requirement, does it satisfy that requirement?

16 If something is central to something, it is very i m p _ _ _ _ _ _ .

Honeymoons, lame ducks and the political wilderness

honeymoon

cabinet reshuffle

crisis

resign
stand down
quit

collapse

lame duck

political
  wilderness

When a government is elected, there is often a **honeymoon** period when people are not too critical of it mainly because they are waiting to see what it will do in the longer term.

After a while, normality sets in:

ministers may be given new posts, or lose their posts, in a **cabinet reshuffle**;

they may leave the cabinet, or **resign**, **stand down** or **quit** because of incompetence or wrongdoing;

there may be **crises**, when confidence in the government is so low that people wonder if it can continue and think it may **collapse**. Governments or politicians that have lost all credibility and authority are described as **lame ducks**.

collapse *100, 163* ⇓

lame duck *99* ⇓

Politicians or parties who leave office and no longer have power or influence are said to be in the **political wilderness**.

◆ **LANGUAGE NOTE**

The singular of **crises** is **crisis**.

In any new presidency – in any new anything – everybody is hopeful, there's a <u>honeymoon</u> *period and there are stars in everyone's eyes.*

On Sunday, nine ministers who favoured opening talks with the opposition lost their jobs in a <u>cabinet reshuffle.</u>

Among the casualties in this ruthless <u>cabinet reshuffle</u> *were some of the prime minister Harold Macmillan's oldest and closest colleagues, prompting Jeremy Thorpe to remark, 'Greater love hath no man than this, that he lay down his friends for his life.'*

The Daily Telegraph reports that Mrs Thatcher only changed her mind about not fighting on after the majority of her cabinet urged her to <u>resign</u>. *It says that three cabinet ministers had threatened to resign if she did not* <u>stand down</u>.

A minister <u>quit</u> *two weeks ago saying, 'I'm tired of signing decrees no one pays attention to.'*

The anniversary finds the Socialists in <u>crisis</u>, *facing the danger of* <u>collapse</u>. *Yesterday, the party lost its parliamentary majority when 16 of its deputies formed a breakaway group.*

Riddell, UK – The Economist

Whoever wins faces the prospect of leading a <u>lame duck</u> administration. Too many hostile things have been said on both sides to give either man any real hope of turning the Tories' nominal 21-seat majority into a viable long-term government.

His car headed for the House of Commons, its occupant for the <u>political wilderness</u>. Today Mr Mellor will make a statement to the Commons at 11 am. He is expected to blame everyone, apart from himself, for his resignation and destruction of political career.

17 Political lame ducks. Not only governments can be lame ducks. Put an appropriate noun from the list into each extract below.

a prime minister	c administration	e congressman
b government	d leader	f governorship

1 He could have lost so much political impetus that he would have found himself leading a lame duck _____ .

2 Lukens is appealing that conviction. Lukens is a lame duck _____ . He was defeated in the Republican primary and he has only a few more weeks to serve in congress.

3 ...his claims to have been sole architect of the state's prosperity for most of the 1980s. But Governor Dukakis identified himself with the success and is therefore identified with the failure. He is rarely seen about now as he lives out the last days of his lame duck _____ .

4 What Britain doesn't need after a year of lame duck government is another lame duck _____ .

5 Mr Olszewski may have felt that he would end up becoming a lame-duck _____ . Mr Walesa's spokesman has dismissed the significance of Mr Olszewski's decision to abandon his mission, saying the President has at least three other candidates for the post of prime minister.

6 If he succeeds, he could only become a lame duck _____ , his tenure of office would be decided by Congress, whose long-term ambition is to win an election and govern India again.

Grassroots support and votes of confidence

grassroots
by-election
marginal
constituency
marginal
vote of
confidence
vote of no
confidence
call elections
call fresh
elections
go to the country
interim
government
caretaker
government

A government's **grassroots** support during its term of office may become apparent during a **by-election**. Grassroots support is the support of ordinary voters. A by-election is held in a constituency when the person representing it resigns or dies.

In a first-past-the-post system a **marginal constituency**, or **marginal**, is one where the incumbent member's majority was so low in the previous election that it may easily by won by another party in the next election. A governing party may lose its majority by losing by-elections in marginals.

If a government wants to establish that it has a majority, or if it loses its majority, or if confidence in the government is low for other reasons, it may ask for a **vote of confidence** in parliament. If it loses this vote, the government may **call (fresh) elections**, or, in British English only, **go to the country**.

An opposition party may call for a **vote of no confidence** in the government, perhaps with the intention of bringing about new elections.

There may be a period before elections when an **interim** or **caretaker government** takes care of the everyday running of the country, but makes no important decisions.

◆ **LANGUAGE NOTE**

Grassroots can also be spelt with a hyphen or as two words.

The results are also a major blow to the prime minister's hopes of using these elections to demonstrate the grass-roots popularity of his economic reforms.

Gladstone emerged from retirement to fight a by-election in the marginal Conservative seat of Midlothian in 1878, winning it and retaining the seat at the general election.

Charan Singh was eventually asked to form a government, but had to ask for Congress party support to do so. This support was withdrawn even before that government could face a vote of confidence, and the president then decided to call fresh elections in which Mrs Gandhi was able to gain a majority.

The government overwhelmingly rejected a call by radical deputies to hold a vote of no confidence on the proposals.

If you were the Chancellor knowing that in the next year or 18 months you have to go to the country on your economic record this news would scare the life out of you.

They have repeatedly called on him to resign and say a caretaker government should take over to supervise elections with the help of international observers.

No date has been set for multi-party elections in Nepal, but the interim government has said it will hold them within a year of taking power, this is before next April. Politically, the coalition interim government is holding together.

18 **Grassroots partners.** Make combinations from the table
and use them to fill the gaps in the extracts below.

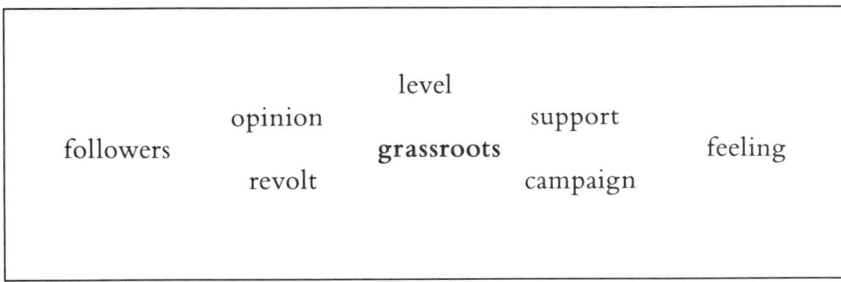

1 Mr Heseltine has travelled the country, addressing hundreds of local party groups
in an effort to build up grassroots _____ .

2 Mr Ruhe sees himself as a future chancellor who has a good feel for grassroots
_____ .

3 Mrs Thatcher fell when her cabinets minister and influential groups of MPs
decided they had had enough of her: the strong support of her grassroots
_____ did not count at all.

4 The ANC will not want to underestimate grassroots _____ that too may
radical political principles are being compromised.

5 Throughout its history, the Soviet Communist Party worked at grassroots
_____ through its network of cells in factories, offices and army units.

6 Webb, the underdog in this race, launched an aggressive grassroots
_____ , walking more that 300 miles in Denver neighborhoods and
sleeping overnight in the homes of residents.

7 Without economic improvements, his country could face a grassroots _____ .

Undemocratic regimes

regime
  authoritarian
  autocratic
  hard-line
  totalitarian

hardliner

one-party rule

dictator
dictatorship

strongman

junta

Undemocratic forms of rule, or **regimes**, are **authoritarian** or **autocratic**. **Hardline** regimes refuse to allow any change in the political system. **Hardliners** are members of such regimes who are particularly resistant to change.

A country may be ruled by:

a **totalitarian** regime controlling all aspects of life and not allowing any opposition;

one-party rule, allowing only the political party in power to operate;

a military **junta**: a group of army officers;

dictatorship: rule by a small group of people, or by one person alone, a **dictator**.

A dictator, or someone else with autocratic powers and methods, may be referred to in the media as a **strongman**.

◆ **LANGUAGE NOTE**

Hardline and **hardliner** are also spelt with a hyphen or as two words.
Regime is also spelt **régime**.

The initial liberal reaction to the break-up of former Communist regimes was to cheer the emergence of national identity. This enthusiasm soon gave way to ambivalence. The removal of an <u>authoritarian regime</u> was one thing, the removal of all central authority was another.

…the intransigence of the <u>hardline</u> regime in Pyongyang, where President Kim Il Sung has been president since 1948.

No event could possibly highlight the fundamental difference between democratic and <u>autocratic</u> government so vividly as her departure, by due democratic process, at this time.

For 70 years, a <u>totalitarian</u> regime forced people to work and distributed the products of their labor through a highly centralized government bureaucracy.

Although Cameroon's constitution provides for a multi-party system, the country has been a de facto <u>one-party</u> state since 1966.

Some elected leaders of Latin America would be happy to offer an example of a military <u>junta</u> reaching a bad end.

But their meeting in 1940, at Hendaye, on the French-Spanish border, was not a success. Franco kept Hitler waiting: not all <u>dictators</u> make the trains run on time.

Referring to Mr Mugabe's plan for a one-party state, the paper says they may be Africa's way forward, but they are often one-way routes to <u>dictatorship</u>.

…Enva Hodja, the Albanian <u>strongman</u> who ruled the country with an iron hand, using Stalin as his role model.

19 **A return to dictatorship?** Read this extract from *The Times* and answer the questions.

Bianca eyes the Nicaraguan presidency

After Bianca Jagger's divorce in 1979, she returned to Nicaragua within days of the Sandinistas taking power and celebrated the end of Somoza's hated dictatorship and what promised to be a revolution bringing equality for all. 'But the Sandinistas betrayed their ideals. They became corrupted by power,' she said. 'They ran the country on the basis of extended patronage so that it was unprepared for democracy when it finally came.'

But Jagger reserves her most bitter scorn for the country's present government. 'Violeta Chamorro was voted into power as something of a Virgin Mary figure. But she has ceded power to her son-in-law, Antonio Lacayo, who now runs the country as an autocracy.'

Leaders of 12 of the 14 parties in Chamorro's coalition have accused her government of forging a 'new dictatorship' in Nicaragua. Critics claim that Chamorro is being manipulated by the Sandinistas, who still form the largest party and control the army, police, trade unions, banking system and businesses nationalised during their decade in power.

An American aid package of $116 million (£58.6 million) has been blocked in protest at Sandinista control of the security forces and failure to investigate a post-election free-for-all in which Sandinistas helped themselves to houses, guns and government property before ceding limited power to Chamorro.

Peasants who fought on different sides in the civil war have been uniting in protest at the government's failure to abide by peace accords reached in 1990. 'The clock is being turned back at a tremendous pace in Nicaragua,' says Jagger. 'There is a desperate need for some new political answers before it is too late.'

1 If something promises to be something, does it necessarily happen?

2 If people betray their ideals, do they remain faithful to them?

3 If you have scorn for someone, you have c o n _ _ _ _ _ _ for them and you d e s p _ _ _ _ them.

4 If you cede power to someone, do you hand over power to them?

5 If you forge something new, do you destroy it?

6 If you are manipulated by someone, are you free to act as you wish?

7 If people fail to do something, do they do it?

8 Are people and events under control in a free-for-all?

9 If you abide by an accord or an agreement, do you break it?

10 If you turn back the clock, you go back to a situation that existed previously, in this case, according to Bianca Jagger, d i c _ _ _ _ _ _ _ _ _ _ . This is happening at a tremendous pace, or very f _ _ _ _ .

accord *164* ⇓

65

Toppling governments

seize power
overthrow
depose
topple
revolution
putsch
military takeover
coup
coup d'état
bloodless coup
bloody coup
martial law
civilian rule
return to civilian
rule

The military may **seize power** in a **coup**, **coup d'etat**, **putsch** or **military takeover** and impose **martial law**, or military control, on the country.

In a **revolution**, there is a sudden, often violent, change of regime involving ordinary people, political parties and usually the military.

In revolutions and military takeovers, the previous government is **overthrown**, **deposed**, or in media terms, **toppled**. A revolution or coup is **bloodless** if there is no fighting, and **bloody** if there is.

The military may promise a **return** or **handover to civilian rule**, or rule by non-military politicians, after a time.

◆ **LANGUAGE NOTE**

Coup d'etat is also spelt **coup d'état**.
The plural of **coup d'etat** is **coups d'etat**.
Overthrow can be a noun and a verb.

For Chilean President Patricio Aylwin, it was a chance to heal old wounds. Aylwin who's a center-right Christian Democrat, once supported Allende's <u>overthrow</u>. But for General Augusto Pinochet, who <u>toppled</u> Allende and then <u>seized power</u> for 16 years, the ceremony was an affront.

The <u>coup</u> that <u>deposed</u> President Jean-Bertrand Aristide has left Haitians and their diplomats angry and frustrated with the United Nations.

But who would be the strongmen in a coup? Yakolev himself thinks admits an army <u>putsch</u> is unlikely.

About every ten years, something sensational happens in Turkish politics. On the past three occasions that something has been a <u>military takeover</u>. This time change may come through the ballot box.

This so called <u>coup d'état</u> was like a bad play with a second-rate cast. Some say it turned into a second Russian <u>revolution</u>, but I say history repeats itself – the first time as tragedy, the second as farce.

cast 187 ⇓

It is unclear what has happened to the president, although reports from the area indicate that it was a <u>bloodless coup</u>.

But in fact <u>martial law</u> seems to have been replaced by equally severe laws limiting political and religious freedom.

The <u>return to civilian rule</u>, which begins with local government elections in December, is being carefully monitored by the current military government.

The League won a sweeping majority in elections two months ago, but the authorities have set no timetable for a <u>handover to civilian rule</u>.

20 **Broken promises?** This BBC broadcast was made at the time of the elections referred to in the last example above. Read it, complete the gaps with the expressions listed (one of them is used four times, one three times and the rest once each), and answer the questions.

a booth	c elections	e seats	g martial law
b voting	d electoral	f exit polls	h coup

Burmese elections pass off peacefully

In one of the most closely watched _____ (1) processes in recent years, Burmese people have gone to the polls in the first multi-party _____ (2) for 30 years. Although there was a great deal of intimidation and arrest of opposition figures by the military government in the run-up to today's _____ (3), the polling is reported to have passed off smoothly and peacefully.

The _____ (4) had been promised by the military junta shortly after it seized power in the bloody _____ (5) of 1988, and the Burmese military leader, General Saw Maung, said at a voting _____ (6) in Rangoon today, 'I have kept my promise.'

Although the general kept his word to hold _____ (7), the military government resorted to all sorts of repressive and restrictive methods in order to curb opposition campaigning and activities. Today's _____ (8) trend, however, suggests that those measures have failed to prevent the Burmese from exercising their right and expressing their view. According to reports from Rangoon, the turnout in today's _____ (9) was heavy, and there were no visible signs of military presence on the streets.

1 If someone intimidates you, they try to prevent you from doing what you want to do by t _ r _ t _ _ i n g you.

2 Is it possible for events such as elections to 'pass off' violently?

3 If you curb someone's activities, do you encourage them?

Although _____ (10) has been lifted, the curfew remains in place. Informal _____ (11) taken by journalists, diplomats, and other observers suggest strong support for the opposition National League for Democracy, whose secretary general, Aung San Suu Kyi, along with two main opposition leaders are all under detention.

A total of 93 parties with more than 2,000 candidates took part in today's _____ (12), contending for 485 parliamentary _____ (13). Election results for Rangoon are expected to be announced in a few hours, but the official national tally will be announced in three weeks.

4 People under, or in, detention are in p _ _ _ _ n or under house arrest.

5 The tally is another word for the c _ _ _ _ _ .

Unrest

social unrest civil unrest protest demonstration protester demonstrator chant slogan	Where opposition to a regime is widespread, there may be periods of **civil** or **social unrest** with **protests** or **demonstrations**: groups of **protesters** and **demonstrators** marching through the streets perhaps silently, or perhaps **chanting**, or rhythmically shouting, **slogans**.

Mugabe is taking no chances. With the threats of industrial and social unrest real, new water cannon and riot gear have been ordered for the police.

The star's entourage were said to be shocked that they had arrived in the West African country in the middle of a period of civil unrest, with student groups trying to overthrow the government. Mr Jones said he did not know how the plans for the making of 'A Return to Africa' video would be affected.

In Romania, a relatively quiet day of demonstration erupted into noisy protest by hundreds of people chanting anti-government slogans in Bucharest's University Square.

21 **Missing item.** The same word or expression from this section is missing from all these extracts. What is it?

occasions might rekindle the anti-government . . .	that ended with the violent government crack-
The summit was called to discuss the wave of . . .	in the south with clashes between demonstrators
would act more firmly against incidents of . . .	. He said that there'd be a greater visible presence
all considered to be at the root of the violent . . .	. In the predominantly black working-class London
the economy; it became more tolerant of labour . . .	, allowing demands for big wage rises; and it
powers of the province in an effort to quash the . . .	. Explaining his decision to resign as Prime
Did the police over-react? And is social . . .	simmering just below the surface?

Rioting and looting

clash

security forces

water cannon
rubber bullets
tear gas
baton
  baton charge

disperse
  break up a
    demonstration

riot
rioting
looting

curfew

state of
  emergency

If there are violent confrontations or **clashes** with the **security forces**, the police and / or army, they may try to **break up** the demonstration with:

batons, short heavy sticks used to beat people back in a **baton charge**,
rubber bullets: bullets made of rubber designed to hurt demonstrators,
water cannon: machines that produce high-powered jets of water, and **tear gas**: an unpleasant gas that causes irritation to the eyes and skin and forces people to go elsewhere, or **disperse**.

A violent demonstration may turn into a **riot** with fighting, stone-throwing, damage to vehicles and buildings and so on. **Rioting** may be accompanied by **looting**: breaking into shops or houses during a riot to steal things.

The government may impose a **curfew**, a period at night when people must stay indoors and keep off the streets. They may also declare a **state of emergency**, where normal laws are suspended and martial law imposed.

◆ **LANGUAGE NOTE**
The plural of **water cannon** can be **water cannon** or **water cannons**. All these forms can be spelt with hyphens.

Algeria's military-backed rulers declared a <u>state of emergency</u> last night. the move followed two days of fighting between <u>security forces</u> and <u>Moslem fundamentalists</u>. All public demonstrations are banned and wide-raging powers are even likely to be used to close mosques.

In the Nepalese capital Kathmandu, a huge public meeting demanding immediate party-based elections is continuing despite one <u>clash</u> between riot police and demonstrators. Tear-gas was fired and <u>riot police</u> used <u>batons</u> to <u>beat back</u> two groups of demonstrators who seemed intent on heading towards the palace of King Birendra.

I saw the police using, first of all, <u>tear gas</u> and a <u>water cannon</u> and later <u>rubber bullets</u> to try to <u>break up</u> the <u>demonstration</u>.

A <u>curfew</u> has been imposed in the Nicaraguan coastal town of Puerto Cabezas after widespread <u>rioting</u> and <u>looting</u> broke out on Thursday. Police and army units are patrolling the streets to prevent further violence.

22 **Familiar scenarios.** Put these sections from two BBC reports into the correct order for each report. (One report consists of two parts and the other of four. The first parts of each are d and e respectively.)

VIOLENT DEMONSTRATION IN JOHANNESBURG
VIOLENT DEMONSTRATIONS IN KOREA

a   The demonstrators are protesting against President Roh Tae-Woo's newly formed Liberal Democratic Party which they have announced as dictatorial and undemocratic. A group of about 50 workers has come down from a crane at South Korea's largest shipyard at Ulsan, ending a thirteen day protest which brought work there to a standstill.

b   When they ignored an order to disperse, the police opened fire with plastic bullets, and the demonstrators replied with stones and bottles. At least 20 people were injured, some of them seriously.

c   Riot police fired tear gas to disperse about 2000 students in the capital, Seoul, who were throwing firebombs and stones. Other clashes took place on university campuses in Seoul, and in at least two other cities.

d   There have been violent clashes between police and demonstrators in the South African city of Johannesburg. A crowd of about 1,000 gathered for a protest march which had been declared illegal.

e   There have been more anti-government demonstrations by students and dissidents in South Korea despite a warning by the government that it would act immediately and decisively to crush protests.

f   The Justice Minister Mr Lee Jong Nam earlier said the authorities would no longer hesitate to send in police to university campuses to disperse illegal demonstrations. He accused students of fanning social unrest.

Repressive measures

dissident

sedition
subversion

crush opposition

repression

clampdown
crackdown

human rights
  abuses

death squads
hit squads

exile
  self-imposed exile

Opponents to undemocratic regimes are **dissidents**.

Autocratic governments accuse opponents of **sedition** and **subversion** and may try to ruthlessly stop or **crush opposition** by various means in a **clampdown** or **crackdown**. This **repression** may involve **human rights abuses** such as censorship, house arrest, imprisonment without trial and torture.

clampdown *26* ⇑, *126* ⇓
crackdown *26* ⇑, *126* ⇓
censorship *26* ⇑

Some regimes use **death squads** or **hit squads**, groups of professional assassins, perhaps from the army or police, to murder opponents.

Opponents may be ordered to leave the country, or **exiled**. Others may themselves choose to leave in **self-imposed exile**.

◆ **LANGUAGE NOTE**

The adjective corresponding to **repression** is **repressive**.

A few brave magazines continue to take the government to task. A few brave lawyers continue to represent the imprisoned <u>dissidents</u>, and to speak of <u>human rights abuses</u>.

lawyer *141* ⇓
imprisoned *149* ⇓

Four other men who had been detained were charged with <u>sedition</u> allegedly aimed at procuring the overthrow of the government, and also charges of possessing banned literature.

detain *138* ⇓
charge *140* ⇓

The government has dropped charges against thirteen students who were arrested and accused of <u>subversion</u> after publishing a document critical of government policy.

arrest *138* ⇓

An opposition leader has claimed that the country's president has no intention of moving away from one party rule and is preparing for a political <u>clampdown</u>.

After the massacres, widespread <u>repression</u> and military <u>crackdown</u> in the country two years ago, most western countries suspended aid and strongly criticised its rulers.

Protests have been called later today by human rights groups and relatives of 9,000 people who disappeared during the wave of <u>repression</u> known as the dirty war.

At the start of the civil war, when thousands of civilians were killed by military and rightist <u>death squads</u>, he went into exile forming an <u>exile</u> with leftist rebels. The exile ended three years ago when Ungo and other Social Democrat leaders returned to try to stimulate a negotiated settlement to El Salvador's civil war.

..two former policemen who say they were members of <u>hit squads</u> which murdered anti-apartheid campaigners.

Karamanlis is the architect of modern Greece. He returned home in 1974 after 11 years of <u>self-imposed exile</u> to pick up the pieces after the collapse of the seven-year military regime.

23 **Forms of exile.** Complete the words below describing the types of exile given in these definitions.

Exile that is:

1   not temporary
2   not in a foreign country
3   self-imposed
4   not self-imposed (three words)

a   <u>v_l_nt_ry</u>
b   <u>f_rc_d</u>
c   <u>_nf_rc_d</u>
d   <u>p_rm_n_nt</u>
e   <u>_nt_rn_l</u>
f   <u>_nv_l_nt_ry</u>

Crossword

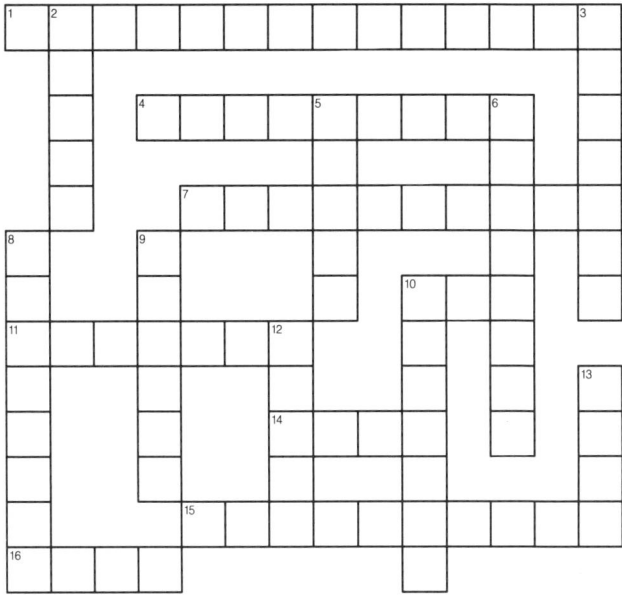

Across

1 Vote-catching activity (14)

4 No one killed in this coup (9)

7 See 13 down

10 Where British politicians stand, Americans do this (3)

11 Concealment of wrongdoing leading to a gate (5-2)

14 A party's PR selection of candidates (4)

15 A low turnout means a high rate of this (10)

16 Candidates stand on this box and speak from it (4)

Down

2 What a rioter does when stealing something (5)

3 What a junta, dictatorship or ruling party does (7)

5 A military takeover, not necessarily in a French-speaking country, is a coup _____ (1'4)

6 This group may form its own party (8)

8 Rival groups within a party (8)

9 Political dirt made to stick (5)

10 What demonstrations may degenerate into (7)

12 There are two types of these, but only one changes governments (5)

13 and 7 across Expert in damage limitation and image improvement (4, 10)

Headlines

Headlines and articles about a company often use language relating to the type of business the company is in.

Pirelli en route to puncture rival: competition in the tyre industry
Turning rags into riches: clothes hire shops
Kick-off for Spurs shares: Tottenham Hotspur football club
Airtours flies highest in a turbulent year: holiday company
Westland prepares for take-off: helicopter manufacturer.

1 **Headline humour 1.** What business activities do these headlines refer to? Match the headlines and the activities.

1 **Bass goes down smoothly**

2 **Capital sounds a quieter £5 million**

3 **Sketchley clean-out brings back profits**

4 **Bodyshop in good shape**

5 **Silentnight bounces in with £11.5 million**

6 **Tootal sews up Chinese link**

a radio
b dry cleaning
c textiles
d beds
e healthcare
f beer

2 **Headline humour 2.** Complete each headline with one of the words below.

a Airbus	c Defence	e computer	g Private medicine
b Spurs	d Airfares	f Car makers	h Ford's

1 Post-boom virus hits _____ services

2 Takeoff for _____ operating profits

3 _____ £1.6 billion blowout

4 _____ firms fight to survive by beating swords into tube trains

5 _____ fire on all cylinders in fight against taxes

6 _____ dogfight

7 _____ shareholders ruled offside

8 _____ runs a temperature

Shares and the stock market

shares
  blue chip shares
stocks
  blue chip stocks
equities

stock exchange
stock market
bourse

listed
quoted

brokers
dealers
traders

invest
investment
investors

shareholders

Company **shares** are **listed** or **quoted** on the **stock market** or **stock exchange**. (**Bourse** is also used, usually to refer to a European stock exchange.) Shares are also called **stock** or **equities**.

Traders, dealers and **brokers** buy and sell shares on behalf of **shareholders**, the **investors** who **invest in** them or make **investments** in them.

Blue chip shares or **stocks** or **blue chips** are the safest share investments in leading companies.

shareholder *217* ⇓

FACE IT — STOCK ANALYSIS IS NOT AN EXACT SCIENCE

BUY... NO, SELL.. ER, WELL, MAYBE BUY A FEW....

Roger Beale, UK – Financial Times

Despite the nervousness in <u>shares</u>, <u>dealers</u> feel the British Telecom offer will be a success.

The Eighties saw an unprecedented rise in the number of healthcare companies <u>listed</u> on the world's <u>stock exchanges</u>.

<u>Equities</u> surged higher, enjoying their biggest rise since the end of October.

<u>Investors</u> were once again subjected to another volatile day.

Pensioners have challenged the fund's <u>investments</u>, which they claim are 'unorthodox'.

It may not be wise to <u>invest</u> all your eggs in one basket.

Individual investors account for 42 per cent of <u>brokers'</u> revenue.

City <u>traders</u> are still worried by the economic situation.

Christmas week is notorious for company announcements and <u>shareholders'</u> meetings that can no longer be put off.

Dealers reported some demand for <u>blue-chip stocks,</u> especially those <u>quoted</u> in New York. Glaxo rose 18p to 795p, Reuters 21p to 964p, ICI 7p to £11.26, Rothmans International 22p to £10.21.

City Wall Street bonds commodities currencies foreign exchange	Other things traded in financial centres such as **Wall Street** (in New York) and the **City** (the financial district of London) include **commodities** (like cereals and precious metals), **currencies** (like dollars, pounds and francs) on the **foreign exchange** markets and **bonds** (investment certificates with a fixed rate of interest).

Panic selling across the Atlantic came hours after the <u>City</u> had shut down for the weekend just as in 1987, when the hurricane that swept Britain sent traders home before the <u>Wall Street</u> collapse.

After oil and corn, sugar must rank as one of the most political of all <u>commodities.</u>

The near-panic conditions on the <u>foreign exchange</u> markets on Friday have made restoring calm over <u>currencies</u> a priority.

The <u>bond</u> market, initially cautious, has now reacted enthusiastically.

gilt-edged securities gilt-edged stocks gilts	Bonds issued by the British government are known as **gilt-edged stocks** or **gilt-edged securities**, or **gilts**.

The government, which repaid £18 billion in 1989, will ask institutions for a similar sum in 1992 to fund its deficit with <u>gilt-edged stocks.</u>

play the stock market speculate speculation speculator	Someone who **plays the stockmarket** is usually a private individual who tries to make money by buying and selling shares, often as much for amusement as for serious investment. **Speculators** are people who make a living and sometimes become rich by **speculating** in shares, currencies and commodities. **Speculation**, especially in currencies, often gets a bad press.

The reclusive woman built up her fortune by cannily <u>playing the stock market</u> with cash she had inherited from her father.

As far as savings, she has none. Instead Chris <u>speculated</u> in the financial markets, but it hasn't gone well.

The two dealers tried to make up for their losses by doubling their investment in further <u>speculation</u>, which the bank now says was unauthorised.

The recent sterling crisis has shown that our economy – and therefore the fate or our nation – is not controlled by governments but by a handful of rich currency <u>speculators</u>.

3 **Key investment words.** Complete the examples with key words from this section.

1 …the Business Council, an exclusive club that admits only the bosses of America's biggest and bluest of _ _ _ _ – _c_ _ _ companies.

2 And there was growing criticism of the market for _ _i_ _ – _ _ _ _ _ government _ _ _ _ _ _ _ _ _ _ _ .

3 Elsewhere in Europe, German, French and Italian _u_ _ _ _ _ _ _ _ _ also closed lower.

4 Here, if a businessman started suggesting to his _ _ _ _ _ _ _ _ _ _ _ r _ _ that he read poetry, everyone would rush out and sell his shares.

5 If those who make the big i _ _ _ _ _ _ _ _ _ _ decisions are right, the outlook for _ h _ _ _ _ on the stock market is particularly gloomy.

6 Most of the shares _ _ s _ _ _ in New York and Tokyo are still domestically based firms.

7 On _ _ _ _ _ _ r _ _ _ _ , stocks closed higher today. The Dow gained more than 29 points to close at 2918.6.

8 'Never again should the lives and livelihoods and the destinies of national economies be directed by a handful of shirt-sleeved _ _ _ _ _ _ _ _ _ r _ _ ,' Mr Brown said.

9 Tea is one of India's major export _ _ _ _ _ d _ _ _ _ _ .

10 The dollar was also strong against other major c _ _ _ _ _ _ _ _ _ _ on the Tokyo market.

11 Three quarters of MPS investments are in _ _ _ _ _ t _ _ _ .

12 He was someone who _ l _ _ _ _ the _ _ _ _ k _ _ _ r _ _ _ _ and needed money for that.

Bull markets and bear markets

bear market
bearish
bears

bull market
bullish
bulls

gain ground
make gains

lose ground

rally
recover
regain ground
regain lost
  ground

recovery

When market prices are rising, or **making gains** or **gaining ground**, journalists, traders and investors talk about a **bull market**, and if they think prices will continue to rise, people are **bulls** or **bullish**.

When prices are falling, or **losing ground**, traders talk about a **bear market**, and if they think prices will continue to fall, they are **bearish**.

If prices rise after a period when they have been falling, they **rally, recover**, or **regain ground** or **regain (lost) ground** in a **recovery**.

Simonds, UK – The Economist

Oil shares were making strong gains in fears of a Gulf War.

Jim O'Neill, international strategist with the Swiss Bank Corp, said the mood in the markets about the pound has swung 'from crazily bullish to crazily bearish'.

It looks like we're going to have a significantly down day. It certainly is a battle between the bulls and the bears right here, and I think we've got an indication that the bears have got the upper hand.

Shares lost ground again yesterday, with the 100 constituent FT-SE share index closing 23 points down at 2,036.2.

After an initial fall of 30p, however, the shares rallied to show a drop of only 13p to £10.

The news hit the Allied share price, although the shares recovered to end only 3p lower at 602p.

4 **Bulls and bears.** Match the two parts of these extracts.

1. The bulls were stampeding. By the end of trading,
2. The bear market which followed the crash of October 1987 was the shortest on record.
3. Fisons continued to lose ground,
4. Since the property collapse,
5. By late afternoon yesterday, bonds were little changed,
6. Precious metals regained lost ground
7. At the 9 a.m. opening in London, the pound traded at $1.9250, 2.15 cents up on Wednesday's close, before ending at $1.9245.

a. with London gold $2.25 higher at $377.25 an ounce and silver 4 cents up at $3.85 an ounce.
b. David Fuller believes we may now have had the opposite: the shortest bull market on record.
c. records lay broken from Austria to New Zealand
d. imminent recovery has been sighted as many times as the Loch Ness monster, and with as much effect.
e. although a rally on the stock market helped the Dow Jones industrial average close up 42.33 points at 2,930.2.
f. It regained some ground in New York, where it ended at $1.9330.
g. finishing 32p down at 423p as brokers continued to take a bearish view of the group's prospects.

Trading on the stock exchange

trade
trading
  active trading
  moderate trading

change hands

turnover

Trading is the buying and selling of goods, services, or, as in these examples, shares, bonds, commodities or currencies. Shares **change hands** when they are **traded**. When a lot of shares change hands, share **turnover** is high. Trading is most often described as being **moderate** or **active**.

Robinson, USA – Cartoonists & Writers Syndicate

Heavy demand saw over four million of the new shares <u>changing hands</u> in the first hour of <u>trading</u>.

The Basle exchange, with a <u>turnover</u> only a seventh that of Zurich, may not survive in the longer term.

In advance of the Thanksgiving holiday, there was only <u>moderate trading</u> on Wall Street as the Dow Jones industrials moved lower.

Gold responded to fresh dollar weakness and worldwide share market nerves, rising $4.75 an ounce in <u>active trading</u>.

dull
hesitant
lacklustre
light
negligible
quiet
slow
sluggish
thin
weak
bumpy
choppy
hesitant
mixed
uncertain
brisk
heavy
hectic
frantic
frenetic
frenzied

Trading on the stock exchange and on other markets can also be:

a **dull, hesitant, lacklustre, light, negligible, quiet, slow, sluggish, thin** or **weak** when activity is low.

b **bumpy, choppy, hesitant, mixed** or **uncertain** when the overall direction of prices is not clear.

c **brisk, heavy,** or **hectic** when there is a high volume of trading, in other words high turnover of shares.

d **frantic, frenetic** or **frenzied** when there is a very high volume of trading.

◆ **LANGUAGE NOTE**

Lacklustre is spelt **lackluster** in American English.

5 Frenzied or lacklustre (or something else)? Look closely at these extracts and deduce from which of the above four groups the missing words come. It isn't always possible to find the exact word: put a letter (a, b, c or d) in each gap.

1 The FT index of 30 shares gained 3.6 to 1,947.3. Volume reached only 384.5 million shares in _____ trading.

2 The City's attention, however, was diverted by the _____ trading in Racal's shares. In all, 149 million shares changed hands during the day, almost 11 per cent of the entire company.

3 Shares in America's only super-bike maker collapsed by 30 per cent last week in two days of _____ trading.

4 Fear, swiftly followed by euphoria, gripped the world's markets last week as the Gulf erupted into armed conflict. _____ trading was seen across the globe as foreign-exchange dealers, oil brokers, commodities traders and stockbrokers grappled with volatile markets and _____ trading after weeks of _____ business.

5 The FT-SE index finished another lacklustre day 17.1 points down at 2,523.4 in _____ trading which saw less than 400 million shares change hands.

6 Paris, Dec 26 – This was one of the few European markets to open, and shares held early gains, but trading was _____ .

7 The price touched 19p as 14 million shares changed hands in _____ trading. But despite the high level of turnover, the price ended the session 1p lower at 16p.

Market movements 1

This section looks at key verbs used to talk about rising and falling market prices.

Going up

| advance increase rise | These key words are used to talk about prices going up. They do not in themselves indicate by how much the prices have gone up. |

Shares advanced across a wide front with many blue chips scoring double figure gains.

Smith Kline Beecham has just announced its third quarter results. The price of its shares increased by 2.5 per cent in London; on Wall Street, by 6 per cent.

The TOPIX index of all first-section shares rose 10 points as winners outpaced losers better than 3:2.

Going down

| decline drop fall retreat slide | These words are used to talk about prices going down. They do not in themselves indicate by how much the prices have gone down. |

The TOPIX index of all first-section shares declined more than 40 points on 680 million shares.

Japanese shares dropped to their lowest level in three months in Tokyo.

But 1000 more jobs are to go and shares fell 7p to 112p.

As Germany's inflation rate rises and its economy slows, share prices will retreat again.

Shares slid in a show of investor disappointment over the outcome of France's referendum.

81

Going up by small or moderate amounts

edge higher
edge up
firm

These words are used to talk about prices when they rise by a small or moderate amount.

◆ **LANGUAGE NOTE**

Edge cannot be used by itself in this context. It must be followed by **higher** or **up**.

ICI was unchanged at £12.86, while Hanson firmed 1½p to 206½p.

Blue Chips, especially Microsoft, edged higher in late trading.

The shares edged up 2p to 145p. Hang on to them if you have any.

Going up by large amounts

climb (higher)
jump
leap
roar ahead
roar up
rocket
shoot up
skyrocket
soar
surge

These words are used to talk about prices when they rise by larger amounts, or when they increase quickly or sharply.

Airtours gravity-defying performance has seen its shares climb throughout the year from 168p to 894p, a gain of 432 per cent.

When Sir Alistair revealed a 10 per cent rise in interim profits, Wellcome stock jumped 12 per cent.

British Steel's share price leapt 34.2 per cent this week to 64p.

Banks, builders, stores, insurance, food and leisure stocks roared ahead.

Within weeks of the signing of the Wimbledon deal, Craven venture shares rocketed from 15 cents each to $2.50.

Wells Fargo's shares shot up when the rest of the market slumped.

The Nikkei average of 225 Japanese shares skyrocketed 2676 points overnight.

In the City shares soared to their highest level in a month.

The group delighted the market with a superb set of results. The shares surged 17p to 465p.

Going down by small or moderate amounts

dip
drift (lower)
ease
edge down
edge lower
slip (lower)

These words are used to talk about prices when they fall by a small or moderate amount.

◆ **LANGUAGE NOTE**

Edge cannot be used by itself in this context. It must be followed by **lower** or **down**.

J Sainsbury, Britain's largest food retailer, <u>dipped</u> 6p to 348p in spite of a better than expected advance in full-year profits.

Disney shares, down almost 14 per cent this year from a peak of $129.75, <u>eased</u> 12.5 cents to $111.75.

A 30-point rise overnight in New York helped the FT-SE initially, but share prices in London <u>drifted lower</u>.

Oil prices could probably <u>edge down</u> from their recent $28-odd a barrel.

Shares in British Aerospace continued to <u>edge lower</u>, with a fall of 8p to 547p, a loss of 26p in the last week as talk persisted that the group may soon be asking shareholders for more money.

GEC <u>slipped</u> 3p to 130p after revealing an expected dip in pre-tax profits of 6 per cent

Shares in New York <u>slipped lower</u> near the end of thin trading

Going down by large amounts

dive
nosedive
plunge
plummet
tumble

These words are used to talk about prices when they fall by large amounts.

The profit-takers were out in force and the leading FT-SE 100 Index <u>dived</u> over 5 points to 2546.5.

No buyers could be found for roughly half the stocks traded on the floor of the exchange. Share prices <u>nosedived</u> 5¾ per cent in just two hours.

It would be impossible for the New York market to repeat its performance during the 1987 market crash when it <u>plunged</u> 508 points in a few hours.

In one spectacular fall in February, the shares <u>plummeted</u> by more than a third.

…figures today that are expected to show pre-tax profits <u>tumbling</u> from £226 million to £110 million.

Going down fast by very large amounts

| crash |
| collapse |
| crumble |
| slump |

These words are used to talk about prices if they fall by very large amounts, especially if they fall very quickly.

collapse *60* ⇑, *163* ⇓

...CH Industrials Group, the former stock market high-flier that <u>crashed</u> in March.

Borland shares <u>collapsed</u> recently when a legal battle erupted between Borland and Lotus, which claimed its product had been copied.

Shares in Mrs Fields, the cookie company, <u>crumbled</u> from 15½p to 11p as the company gave warning that it expected to report a net loss.

When investors concluded that the Retrovir drug was not going to make a lot of money, the firm's shares <u>slumped</u>.

6 **Rising and falling prices: verbs.** Choose the correct alternative for each sentence.

1 Although best levels were not held, shares _____ .
   declined   plummeted   advanced

2 The pound _____ against the dollar, to close up .15 cents at $1.68.
   dived   fell   edged higher

3 Sainsbury's share price has _____ relative to its sector, underlining its position as the ultimate defensive stock in times of trouble.
   shot up   fallen   declined

4 The FT-SE share index _____ below 2,100 points yesterday but an afternoon rally left it just above 2,100, at 2,100.4, down 1.8:
   drifted   rose   rocketed

5 Pre-tax profits have collapsed from £4.57 million in 1989 to just £250,000 in the last financial year. Not surprisingly, the shares have _____ .
   risen   dived   edged higher

6 In London the dollar _____ by a tiny margin at the outset.
   edged up   rocketed   shot up

7 NHL shares have _____ from 157p to 16½p after the collapse of the Bank of Credit and Commerce International.
   crashed   slid   risen

8 GEC _____ 3p to 190p after revealing the expected dip in pre-tax profits for the full year of 6 per cent to £818 million.
   slipped   collapsed   crashed

9 The US dollar fell and Japanese shares _____ to their lowest level in three months in Tokyo trading today.
    leapt   dropped   rose

10 Shares in Henlys _____ 22p to 55p after the coach-builder warned it would report a loss for the half-year ending this month.
    crashed   dipped   edged lower

Market movements 2

This section looks at nouns used to talk about rising and falling share prices.

Going up

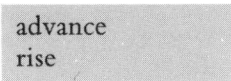

These key words are used to talk about prices going up. They do not in themselves indicate by how much the prices have gone up.

Declines led <u>advances</u> by a margin of 8:7.

Shareholders benefit by the <u>rise</u> in value of their shares.

Going down

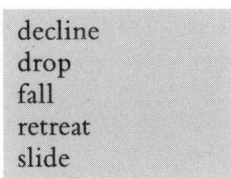

These words are used to talk about prices going down. They do not in themselves indicate by how much the prices have gone down.

Soon after opening the main index showed a drop of over 100 points. This was later halved but then another <u>decline</u> set in.

Insiders described the <u>drop</u> as 'naked panic' as shares slumped 56 points.

The FT-SE index of leading shares recorded a 16 per cent <u>fall</u>.

The sale of a line of stock, probably a million shares started the <u>retreat</u>.

But does this mark the end of this year's <u>slide</u> in Japan's share prices?

Going up by large amounts

climb
jump
leap
surge

These words are used to talk about prices when they rise by large amounts, or when they increase quickly or sharply.

North Sea Brent crude was trading at $38.55 a barrel after a recent steady <u>climb</u> in prices.

Second-section demand remained stable, however; prices there posted a better than 64-point <u>jump</u> on 8 million shares traded.

The Japanese economy is growing at four times the rate of America's, and its prices at less than half. Yet shares have taken a <u>leap</u> off the highest tower in Marunouchi.

William Gates is worth more than £4 million thanks to a <u>surge</u> in the price of shares in his company Microsoft.

Going down by small or moderate amounts

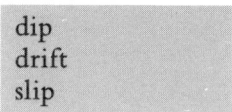

These words are used to talk about prices when they fall by a small or moderate amount.

Many economists reckon the downward <u>drift</u> will continue.

…with the Pound's trade-weighted index closing unchanged at 90.8 on a 0.24 pfennig rise to DM 2.9323, but a 0.5 <u>cent</u> slip to $1.6940 against the dollar.

The matter has split the Australian investment community and been partly to blame for the <u>dip</u> in News Corp shares.

Going down by large amounts

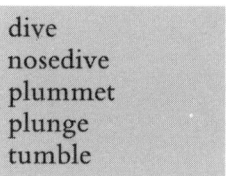

These words are used to talk about prices when they fall by large amounts.

In-Shops itself lost 3p to 81p after a profits <u>dive</u>.

It would also have a catastrophic effect on property values, sending the market into a terrifying <u>nosedive</u>.

After an overnight fall on Wall Street and a 500-point <u>plunge</u> in Japan, the FT-SE index fell 22 points by mid-morning.

The shares jumped 7p to 90p after their abrupt <u>plummet</u> from approaching 300p a year ago.

And shares in Britain take a <u>tumble</u> as concern grows for an international trading group.

Going down fast by very large amounts

crash
collapse
slump

These words are used to talk about prices if they fall by large amounts, especially if they fall very quickly.

collapse *60* ⇑, *163* ⇓

The City's love affair with Wellcome is over, as yesterday's 15 per cent <u>collapse</u> in its share price showed.

Despite the <u>crash</u> in Japanese share prices last year, the Nikkei-225 has risen by 600 per cent in dollar terms <u>since</u> 1979.

The <u>slump</u> in Thorn's share price leaves no doubt that the Virgin acquisition is the most high-risk of the 70 deals struck by Southgate during his five years in charge of Thorn.

7 **Rising and falling prices: nouns.** Choose the correct alternative for each sentence.

1 The Dow Jones industrial average gained 21 points to close at 3007.8. _____ led declines by a margin of 3:2.
Advances   Falls   Drops

2 There's a wide range of forecasts for Natwest Bank, the second of the big four to report. Pessimists expect a _____ into loss.
climb   plunge   rise

3 A bullish statement from the group failed to halt the _____ in the share price.
rise   slump   climb

4 Lord Broackes and Sir Eric Parker are held directly responsible for the _____ in the share price following disappointing results.
rise   climb   collapse

5 The Hong Kong stock exchange celebrated yesterday after a _____ in share prices lifted the Hang Seng index to a record close of 3,997.6.
surge   plunge   nosedive

6 The property company that was one of the first casualties of the property market _____ .
jump   collapse   climb

7 ...as private investors rush to get out of the market in fear of a repeat of the 1987 Black Monday _____ .
crash   surge   leap

8 Wall Street's unexpected _____ on Monday has shaken markets in Asia and Australia.
plunge   rise   climb

9 Following a 52p _____ on Tuesday, the shares lost a further 37p to 563p – a low for this year and half the level reached in July.
slide   rise   advance

10 The wider TOPIX index of all first-section shares gained more than 16 points, but second-section prices posted an 11-point _____ on 3 million shares traded.
drop   rise   crash

Record highs and record lows

| high |
| all-time high |
| record high |

Records are broken: indices like the Dow Jones break new (psychological) barriers to reach **all-time** or **record highs**.

Wall Street surged ahead yesterday and at the close the Dow Jones industrial average was just below its previous all-time high of 3,004, at 3,000.45.

Shares are near to their record high for the year and could go further.

8 **Record lows.** Look at these examples and complete the commentary using the key words in the box.

We believe new lows will be seen. Nomura envisages the Tokyo stock market index falling below 20,000, having once been close to 40,000.

Hanover Druce, the property services company, has become the latest victim of the collapse in the residential and commercial property market.

But the global meltdown failed to materialise. Prices crumbled both in London and Tokyo, but there was little evidence of panic selling.

It would be impossible for the New York market to repeat its performance during the 1987 crash when it plunged 508 points in a few hours.

Wall Street plunged dramatically last night, with the Dow Jones industrial average closing at 2,943.20, a fall of 120 points, the fifth-largest on record. 'It's a free fall right now. People are going off the ski jump,' said Christopher Pedersen, director of trading at Twenty-First Securities Corp.

| collapse |
| crash |
| free fall |
| |
| low |
| all-time low |
| record low |
| |
| meltdown |

But euphoria easily gives way to pessimism. When gains are lost, with prices falling to new _____ , journalists may talk about a _____ or a _____ . If prices fall a very long way and there seems to be no limit to the amount they may drop, they use the parachuting image of _____ . Commentators may even compare events to a nuclear accident like Chernobyl and talk about a market _____ .

Boom, recession and depression

boom

growth

downturn
turn down

slowdown
slow down

weaken

A **boom** on the stock market, with share prices reaching record levels, may or may not reflect what is happening in the economy. An economic boom with high economic **growth** (increasing demand and production), is inevitably followed by a **slowdown** or a **downturn** (periods of slower growth), when the economy **weakens**.

Walt Handelsman, USA – Editors Press Service

◆ **LANGUAGE NOTE**

The verb corresponding to **downturn** is **turn down** and the verb corresponding to **slowdown** is **slow down**.

There is a boom atmosphere. If it continues, share prices could well rise further this year. boom 117 ⇓

Fears that the economy is heading into a fresh downturn will grow with new figures today showing a nosedive in consumer confidence. downturn 217 ⇓

Interest rate increases have undermined confidence again over the past two months, raising the possibility that the economy might even turn down again in the autumn.

The slowdown in economic growth among the industrial countries covered by the latest casts a shadow over British prospects.

As the German economy weakens, it will be forced to cut its interest rates.

recession
slump

recover
recovery

pick up
turn up

pick-up
upturn

A slowdown may be the first sign of a **recession**: a period with little growth, no growth or even negative growth. During a recession, there is a **slump** in many kinds of economic activity and everyone waits for the economy to start expanding quickly again, impatiently looking for signs of a **recovery** or an **upturn**: signs that the economy is **picking up** or **turning up** and that things are getting better. Commentators then talk about a **pick-up** in the economy. recession 217 ⇓

upturn 217 ⇓

◆ **LANGUAGE NOTE**

The noun **pick-up** is also spelt as two words.

Although Japan is likely to avoid a <u>recession</u>, the dramatic slowdown has reduced growth to very low levels by Tokyo's standards.

Indicators supporting <u>recovery</u> were outnumbered 2 to 1 by data suggesting continued <u>recession</u>.

Large percentage increases in unemployment in 1974-76 and 1980-81 were associated with house-buying <u>slumps</u>.

Perhaps investment is really much stronger than industrialists are admitting, and economic growth will now <u>pick up</u> very strongly.

With a <u>pick-up</u> in the economy likely to be hesitant in the months ahead, we are likely to see a continued rising trend in business failures.

Bond traders concluded the economy is <u>turning up</u>.

The government is convinced that Britain is emerging from the <u>recession</u> and will see an economic <u>upturn</u>, possibly as soon as the autumn.

depression Depression	When a recession is extremely severe and prolonged, commentators talk about **depression**. The **Depression**, with a capital D, usually refers to the years following the Wall Street crash of 1929.

America, a straight-talking country where a recession is still called a recession. Unless it is a <u>depression</u>.

'We have nothing to fear but fear itself,' said Franklin D Roosevelt when he took over the management of the Great <u>Depression</u> in 1932.

9 **Growth and recession.** Below are four extracts about growth and recession, each divided into two parts. Match the two parts of each extract.

a   Two surveys have indicated that Britain is headed for an economic slump next year. They refer to a slowdown in orders and the prospect of rising unemployment.

b   At last some people are waking to the reality that British manufacturing industry has been so weakened by the last two recessions that it is simply unable to take advantage of the any upturn in the economy.

c   One of the surveys, by the Confederation of British Industry has forecast a possible recession; the Association of British Chambers of Commerce says there has been a steep decline in business confidence.

d   South Koreans believe their country faces an economic crisis. The rate of growth last year was 6.5 per cent, but South Koreans prefer to think of the double digit growth of the last three years as the norm. And the prophets of doom point to other figures.

e   The US Treasury Secretary, Mr Nicholas Brady, has acknowledged that the United States economy is facing what he called a significant slowdown.

f   These figures indicate a slump in one of the world's most successful economies.

g This was likely to continue into the first quarter of next year, he said, but he predicted that economic growth, jobs and investment would pick up again later in the year.

h As a union with many members in manufacturing we are making every effort to raise the debate on this subject.

People in business

captains of
  industry

magnate
mogul
tycoon

Captains of industry is an expression used to refer to the people who head and run companies, but it sounds rather old-fashioned at a time when some business leaders are media figures like royalty or rock stars. These business leaders may be **tycoons, magnates** or **moguls**: rich and successful people with power and influence who head organisations. These words are often used in combinations like **property tycoon, media magnate** or **publishing mogul**.

magnate *3* ⇑
tycoon *3* ⇑, *210* ⇓
mogul *3* ⇑, *202* ⇓

Peter Morgan, director general of the Institute of Directors, said captains of industry were as entitled to the same sort of pay as 'stars' in any other profession.

Parretti, son of a Sicilian olive merchant, worked as a waiter at the Savoy Hotel and on the QE2 before his sudden appearance as a Hollywood mogul. Where the money for this came from, nobody knows.

John D Rockefeller, the oil magnate who founded Standard Oil and made big oil truly big.

The Hong Kong property tycoon is paying Olympia & York £25 million for a partnership in a 39-storey New York office block through his Concord Property and Finance Group.

entrepreneur

high roller
whizz-kid
yuppy

Hoping to join these business leaders, perhaps, are the **entrepreneurs** who start up new businesses and **whizz-kids**, people with talent, perhaps talent to move up in an organisation quickly.

High rollers are rich, successful people not necessarily at the top of an organisation, and **yuppies** are young middle-class professional people who like to be seen spending money, although they are less visible now than in the boom years of the 1980s, when the word was invented.

The Maxwell brothers see themselves as professional managers rather than buccaneering entrepreneurs.

Grigori Lavlinsky, the whizz-kid economist who collaborates with colleagues from Harvard on multibillion-rouble plans for economic revival.

…the high-rollers of the 1980's: bankers, brokers, admen, property moguls, people who had made their fortune in the boom years.

Scott is painted as a <u>yuppy</u> arriviste flying out to French chateaux in private planes for weekends with French advertising executives.

bean-counter number cruncher nerd techno-nerd	Business organisations need accountants to keep track of the money coming in and going out of the business. Journalists often refer, slightly offensively, to accountants and other numerate specialists as **bean-counters** or **number-crunchers**. The experts who run the computers on which the numbers are crunched are sometimes referred to as **nerds** or **techno-nerds**: very informal words used insultingly, especially by people who don't like or know much about computers.

number-cruncher 11 ⇑

◆ **LANGUAGE NOTE**

Bean-counter and **number-cruncher** are also spelt as two words.
Techno-nerd is also spelt as one word or two words.

The reason for America's robot failure is that we have <u>bean-counters</u> running our companies. The Japanese have engineering and manufacturing people.

…an army of <u>number-crunchers</u> from the accountancy firm Touche Ross.

…although most of the <u>nerds</u> who break unbidden into other people's computers have more in common with Pee Wee Herman than James Bond.

For the ambitious, the true believers and the <u>techno-nerds</u>, the Strategic Defense Initiative was the place to be.

10 **Cast of business characters.** Complete each extract with the most appropriate of these expressions.

a entrepreneurs	c tycoon	e high rollers	g number crunchers
b magnate	d yuppie	f whizz-kids	h bean-counter

1 Caesars traditionally attracts a gold-chained clientele, the kind of wealthy _____ who lay $100,000 on the turn of one card.

2 Even if the recovery is under way, it may be some time before the _____ confirm it.

3 Even when smoking one of his favourite Havana cigars, Benedetti seems a most untycoonish _____ .

4 Now they are an endangered species. For the bold _____ of the Thatcher era are the biggest losers of the Nineties recession.

5 …Silvio Berlusconi, the Italian television and publishing _____ and owner of AC Milan.

6 The absence of a fast-track for _____ explains why Japanese companies find it hard to keep the growing minority of 25-year-olds who have MBAs from western business schools.

7 The myth of the _____ – the Young Urban Professional – was born in the United States in the early 1980s.

8 'He's not an advertising man. He's a _____ who counted the beans wrong.'

Corporate conflict

boardroom
battle
dispute
row
split
coup
reshuffle
shake-up

Journalists, of course, often dramatise disagreements between people, and a disagreement between executives is sometimes described as a **boardroom battle, dispute, row** or **split**.

These differences of opinion may lead to changes in boardroom personnel in a **boardroom coup, reshuffle** or **shake-up**. (A company's board of directors meets in the boardroom even if the events described here do not always take place in it.)

board *11* ⇑

And he will not be back unless the directors end what is a traditional sport at St James' Park: the <u>boardroom battle</u>.

Mr Quinn replaced Mr Plowright, who was forced to resign after a <u>boardroom dispute</u> *over cost-cutting with Gerry Robinson, chief executive of the Granada Group.*

Bruce Ralph takes over from Mr Thatcher. He stressed that Mr Thatcher's parting had been amicable, and that there had been no <u>boardroom row</u>. *'He has gone with our best wishes,' he said.*

The City interpreted the development as the result of a <u>boardroom split</u> *over BP's next dividend payment.*

Robert Malpas yesterday resigned as chairman of Powergen after what appeared to be a <u>boardroom coup</u>.

There is a moment of final ignominy for the sacked executive who loses out in the <u>boardroom reshuffle</u> *when he has to hand back the keys of the company Jaguar.*

There have been widespread whispers of a <u>boardroom shake-up</u> *to bring in new attitudes and fresh ideas.*

compensation

compensation
  payment
compensation
  payoff
compensation
  payout

golden handshake

oust

Boardroom rows are often followed by dramatic departures, sometimes with a **compensation payment, payoff** or **golden handshake**. (These expressions are not to be confused with **compensation**, a technical term used to talk about salaries and benefits in general, especially in American English, as in the cartoon and in the first example below.) There is sometimes uncertainty as to whether the departing executive resigned voluntarily or was **ousted**: forced to leave.

benefits *107* ⇓
golden handshake *109* ⇓

'Management wishes to thank you for our generous compensation. It has been a source of comfort and strength during these stressful times.'

Mr Taylor was paid a fortune to tailor elaborate <u>compensation packages</u> that linked the pay of chief executives to their performance.

Both Mr Hardman and Mr Stow will be entitled to <u>compensation</u> for the loss of office, although Sir Godfrey could not elaborate on the possible size of any <u>golden handshake</u>.

The departure of Mr Smith, the chief executive, and Miss Hignell, the finance director, surprised the City which interpreted the moves as a boardroom coup. Before pension benefits and compensation for share options, Mr Smith's <u>payoff</u> is £1.03 million and Miss Hignell's £770,000.

Mr Smith is the third director to leave the group in 14 months. John James, chief executive, resigned in August last year and Peter Revers, chief executive of the North American division, left in November. They shared a £793,000 <u>compensation payout</u>.

11 Dramatic departures. In this account, from *The Times*, of the ousting of Dave Trott from the GGT agency, explain the use of 'mere' in the second line. If you don't know the word, do you think the article suggests that £175,000 compensation is a) a lot or b) a little. What do you think of the amount in the circumstances?

Limp handshake

Dave Trott, the creative genius behind advertising slogans such as 'Lipsmackinthirstquenchin. . .' received a mere £175,000 in compensation when he was ousted from the Gold Greenlees Trott agency last year.

The amount, revealed in GGT's latest report and accounts, represents only one year's salary with nothing added for loss of office: curious considering Trott was a founder of the company and is the biggest personal shareholder, with 5.7 per cent of the equity.

Word on the street is that he was negotiating for a far bigger golden handshake in return for a promise that he would not set up in direct competition with his old employer. Trott is now running his own advertising agency.

Scandal and wrongdoing

| wrongdoing | Successful business people attract media attention, especially when they are colourful entrepreneurs with unusual lifestyles. But failure is fascinating too, particularly when it is associated with scandal and **wrongdoing**: committing crimes, especially financial ones. |

The proposal, which has yet to win Senate backing, would also tighten the requirement for accountants to report to the Securities and Exchange Commission any financial wrongdoing they find in company reports.

wrongdoing 40 ⇑

12 Types of wrongdoing. Look at the examples and then match each type of wrongdoing to its definition.

Asil Nadir is accused of perpetrating 'the biggest fraud in English commercial history'. A new case for the Serious Fraud Office. Another scandal. All the sums are huge: £550 million is missing from the company.

The London Stock Exchange is investigating several cases of suspected insider dealing in stocks that moved sharply ahead of company announcements.

'This bank would bribe God,' admits one employee. It soon becomes clear that BCCI, already famous as the bank used by drug barons to launder their money, has taken creative accounting to new heights.

There has been growing concern about possible market rigging, the allegations having arisen because of unexplained price surges during August and September. There have been complaints from electricity users who ask why prices did not fall during the summer when demand is at its lowest.

Alan Rosenthal has been charged with 11 counts of conspiracy, fraud and embezzlement. Investigators allege that Mr Rosenthal, conspired to create $1.6 million of false tax losses for David Solomon, a money manager.

The Great Nigerian Letter Scam continues, says the company fraud squad. Letters are still tempting recipients with the offer of millions of dollars if they help transfer money out of Nigeria.

bribery	1 **creative accounting**	a Making or **faking** false documents, banknotes or artworks. These are called **forgeries** or **fakes**.
creative accounting	2 **bribery**	b Illegally giving someone money so that they act in your favour *embezzlement 40* ⇑
embezzlement	3 **embezzlement**	c Accounting that is only just legal or may be illegal
	4 **forgery**	
fake	5 **fraud** or **racket** or **scam**	d Any illegal money-making activity
forgery		e Fixing the price of something illegally *fraud 52* ⇑*, 141* ⇓
forgeries	6 **insider dealing**	
fraud	7 **market rigging**	f Illegally taking money from the organisation you work for
insider dealing		g Disguising the criminal origin of money such as drug money
market rigging	8 **money laundering**	
		h Using knowledge gained illegally to buy and sell shares profitably
money laundering		
racket		
scam		

13 **Spectacular wrongdoing.** Read this article from the *Sunday Times* and put the events listed below into the order they happened.

a She opened a restaurant.

b She worked as a waitress.

c She bought bank bonds.

d Onoue worked in a factory.

e The market crashed.

f The forged certificates of deposit were used to get loans from new lenders so she could pay her debts.

g The banks cut back on her loans.

h She used the bonds to borrow money.

i She invested the money in bank shares.

j She traded up to £1 million pounds of shares every day.

k She is now in prison.

l She started forging certificates of deposit, with the help of some bankers.

Beauty who ran up a beastly debt: Nui Onoue

SHE was the Cinderella of Japan's economic miracle. Born into extreme poverty in Osaka, she traded on her beauty to build a fortune that made her one of Japan's richest billionaires, and the world's biggest individual borrower.

Over the past four years Nui Onoue, 61, an exotic restaurateur, borrowed the staggering sum of 3,200 billion yen (£14 billion) from 12 of Japan's largest and most respected financial institutions.

Now she is in prison awaiting trial for the biggest fraud in Japanese history. Her debts reportedly exceed £1.7 billion and bankers say she is probably bankrupt. So far three bankers have been arrested for allegedly helping her forge certificates of deposit and other instruments to help cover her debts, which soared when the stock market crashed last October.

Yo Kurosawa, the president of Japan's most prestigious and revered private bank, the Industrial Bank of Japan (IBJ), told a parliamentary committee three weeks ago that he had seen nothing wrong in giving her huge loans. The Japanese press has reported that he knew Onoue and that he had dined at her restaurant.

She is the largest individual stockholder of IBJ, Dai-Ichi Kangyo, the world's largest bank, and NTT, which has the largest public listing of any company in the world. Exactly how she managed to borrow so much money has not been adequately explained, but it reflects badly on the banks that lent money to her, particularly on IBJ. 'IBJ's credit approval is the strictest in Japan,' said one banker. 'Anyone who can get a loan from IBJ gets the highest credit rating from other banks. Nobody would question her credentials.'

Onoue started her career as a teenager working in a textile factory. An early marriage soon ended in divorce, and she went to work as a waitress. Eventually she bought her own restaurant and built it into a £4m-a-year business.

She appears to have started her borrowing binge in 1987 by walking into a branch of IBJ and putting down more than £4m for bank bonds. She used the bonds to borrow money from IBJ which she invested in bank shares. The process was repeated with other leading banks, such as Sumitomo and Daiwa, until she was trading 1m shares a day. Onoue insisted she was not a gambler, and invested only in the safest and bluest of chips.

But when the market fell nearly 50 per cent last October, the banks took fright and began cutting back on her loans. At this point, police claim, she and her confederates resorted to 'clumsy' forgeries of £1.5 billion of certificates of deposit. These were used to secure loans from new creditors to help pay off her debts of £4 billion. Most of the fakes were issued by the manager (now under arrest) of an obscure credit union.

The Japanese news agency Kyodo has obtained an informal breakdown of her borrowings from the Osaka prosecutors' office. According to Kyodo she borrowed £61.7m in 1986, £246m in 1987, £986m in 1988, £4.7 billion in 1989 and £5.9 billion in 1990. A further £2.1 billion was borrowed this year.

The bottom line

bottom line

The **bottom line** is the last line of a company's profit
and loss account for a given period. The bottom line
also means the final result or the most important
aspect of something.

bottom line *122* ⇓

*The changes made by Transport Development Group may take a little longer to filter through to
the bottom line of the profit and loss account, but that is a reflection not so much of the revamped
management team as of the economic climate generally.*

*'The bottom line was I had fun out there today.' The other bottom line of general interest to tennis
players is that both finalists will be seriously richer today.*

But the bottom line was unmistakable: build cars on time, of quality, or we don't want them.

14 **Flowing through to the bottom line.** Match the two
parts of these extracts.

1 Finlay has yet to make a contribution
and Guzzler's

2 Analysts estimate that if Virgin
disappeared tomorrow,

3 A Nomura spokesman expressed relief
that this was the end of the
investigation.

4 Julian Budd, Alexandra's finance
director said that the economic climate
is 'having an effect on our top line,

5 Steel companies are like airlines. They
have huge fixed costs.

6 These studies for the first time provide
numerical results from real companies
that have hired older workers.

7 The faster it builds new stores,

a The bottom line speaks for itself: the
case studies prove that hiring older
people makes good business sense.

b which clearly flows through to the
bottom line.'

c 'This is the bottom line. This is a
severe penalty and we are taking it but
the line has been drawn.'

d the higher it pushes its sales, whose
growth promptly drops through to the
bottom line.

e full impact has not come through to
the bottom line.

f British Airways for one would be
£150 better off on its bottom line.

g The moment those costs are covered,
profits start to pour through to the
bottom line.

Sick companies

bleed
haemorrhage
red ink

When the financial bottom line is not healthy, and a company
is losing money, journalists talk about **red ink** (from the days
when negative figures were written in red ink in company
accounts). Companies in financial difficulty are said to
haemorrhage or **bleed red ink**.

Even mighty American Airlines is <u>haemorrhaging</u> so much <u>red ink</u> that last week it said it would ground 11 per cent of its flights.

Michelin and Good Year are <u>bleeding red ink</u>.

lame duck	Organisations and people in trouble and needing outside help are often referred to as **lame ducks**, likening them to birds with difficulty in walking.

lame duck *60* ⇑

In less than two years he has transformed United from <u>lame duck</u> to predator.

Tom Benyon described David Coleridge as a <u>lame duck</u> chairman and called on him to stand down.

15 **Business bestiary.** Lame ducks are not the only animals that troubled organisations are compared to. Look at the following animals and their descriptions. Which is the most appropriate in each of the examples?

a dinosaur: large extinct reptile
b vulture: large bird known for circling in the air over dying animals
c pterodactyl: a type of flying dinosaur

1 Tokyo financiers now brand Mitsubishi Bank a _____ for its failure to explore some of the more risky business projects.

2 The _____ are not yet circling the British Aerospace, the wounded giant of British manufacturing excellence.

3 ...unprofitable national airlines, the _____ of the airline industry.

4 The _____ would surely scent blood if the share issue failed, leaving British Aerospace with a group of involuntary shareholders.

5 Such has been the evolution at Woolworth over the last six years that even Charles Darwin would be surprised at how successfully the _____ of the high street has been transformed into one of the fittest retail businesses around.

Going bust

ailing company doctor turnaround turnround turn round	Companies in financial difficulty are often described as **ailing**, a word used more in this context than to describe people who are ill. Sometimes **company doctors**, people with financial training who specialise in this area, are brought in to **turn round** companies in difficulty and make them successful again. If they succeed in difficult circumstances, the resulting **turnround** or **turnaround** is often described as dramatic or remarkable.

Heavy social security payments have made it hard for governments to balance their budgets. That will make them reluctant to hand over huge sums to <u>ailing</u> companies.

What is one to make of the bedside manner of David James, the <u>company doctor</u> brought into cure such sick animals as Eagle Trust and Dan Air?

More money will enable Treuhandanstalt to increase its staff and employ more western managers to help <u>turn round</u> the ailing companies in the east.

Despite the recession, the engineering company has competed a remarkable <u>turnround</u>, moving from losses into profit.

assets
asset-stripper
 	
bankruptcy
  file for
  bankruptcy
 	
collapse
 	
creditors
 	
debts
 	
go bankrupt
go out of
  business
	Unsuccessful companies may **collapse, go out of business** or **go bankrupt**. **Bankruptcy** is the situation of going or being bankrupt. In America, companies in difficulty may declare their bankruptcy to the authorities or **file for bankruptcy** to get temporary protection from their **creditors,** the people and organisations they owe money to. The **assets** (buildings, machines, unsold goods and so on) of a bankrupt company are sold, so as to pay the company's **debts**, or some of them.
	
	An **asset-stripper** is someone who buys a company, not necessarily a company in trouble, so as to sell its assets for more than they paid for them and close the company down.
		collapse *60* ⇑
		163 ⇓
		
		assets *173* ⇓

The Bath-based company <u>collapsed</u> at the end of July with <u>debts</u> of more than £12 million.

It believes that without the price agreement, many small bookshops would <u>go out of business</u>.

Some companies – many of them old-established sleepy heads – failed to make a decision and <u>went bankrupt</u>.

<u>Bankruptcies</u> are running at about double last year's rate. Four of the 10 largest collapses since the second world war have occurred in the past few months.

Mint & Boxed in its last accounts owed £6 million pounds to various banks, institutions and other creditors. The company has filed for bankruptcy.

When it filed for bankruptcy, it had $16 million more debts than assets to meet them.

Many locals assumed he was an asset-stripper. Not so. Mr Hall has transformed the mills into a thriving industrial park.

fold **go bust** **go to the wall** **salvage** **wreck** **wreckage**	More informal expressions for a company going out of business include **fold**, **go bust** and **go to the wall**. Sometimes the image of corporate **wreckage** is used, likening the state of the company to a car or plane after a serious accident. Journalists often write about people trying to **salvage** something from the **wreck** or wreckage in the same way that shipwrecks are salvaged for anything of value that remains.

Last year the company folded, leaving Gilbey with no choice but to change careers again.

One of the recent winners of the Queen's Awards for Export has not only gone bust, but is now being investigated by the fraud squad.

UBS Phillips & Drew, in a timely study in the growth of creative accounting techniques, not surprisingly find that they were widely used by many of the companies that have recently gone to the wall.

When Rolls-Royce's parent, the aircraft-engine maker, went bust in 1971, it was Plastow who led the car-maker, renamed Rolls-Royce, out of the wreckage.

Another survivor has emerged from the wreck of International Leisure Group, Harry Goodman's fallen holiday empire.

The sheik's assistants are trying to salvage something from the world's largest bank crash.

receivers
  call in the
    receivers
 	
liquidation
  go into
    liquidation
  in liquidation
 	
insolvency
 	
wind up a
  company
	Receivers are specialised accountants who are appointed, or **called in**, perhaps to try to rescue companies in trouble and avoid **insolvency**: the situation where the company is technically bankrupt, and must be **wound up**, with the receivers selling what they can to pay off the debts. A company in this situation **goes into liquidation** and is then **in liquidation**.

In Britain alone, 23,000 companies have filed for bankruptcy in the first half of this year. The number of insolvencies is a clear sign of the current economic recession. Critics of British insolvency law say that many of these liquidations need not have happened.

The decision to call in receivers was taken after Lloyd's Bank, the company's principal banker, rejected refinancing proposals put forward by the Tern board.

The courts later appointed Grant Thornton as liquidator. The latter then sold the remaining assets and produced a surplus over the bank debts. Other parts of Caledonian were simply wound up.

OGC Nice, one of France's oldest clubs, is to go into liquidation with debts of over $10 million.

16 **Calling in the receivers.** Read this article from *The Times* about companies in difficulty and complete these tasks.

1   Find:
   a   two words or expressions relating to illness,
   b   two words or expressions relating to death and
   c   one word relating to blood.

2   Find:
   a   a word meaning the period when receivers are trying to help a company get out of difficulty
   b   a two-word expression meaning a business that can be run normally and profitably
   c   a noun that can be used to mean a period when prices go up after they have been going down and here means an improved state for a previously failing company
   d   a two-word expression meaning a firm of accountants specialising in helping companies in difficulty. What, paradoxically, do they try to help companies avoid?
   e   what happens to companies that do not continue in some form.
       They _____ _____ _____ .

3   The chairmen of failing companies referred to in the last paragraph are overbearingly, or excessively, co-operative with the receivers, often because they have been 'up to no good'. Does this mean:
   a   they have been honest, but have not been good managers of their company
   b   they have been dishonest, perhaps doing some of the creative accounting described earlier?

No sector can feel secure

They used to say the tell-tale signs were personalised car number plates for the chairman and a fountain in the reception area. But these days receivers no longer joke about terminally ill corporations. 'Recession sickness' is afflicting even well-run companies.

Britain's receivers have never had it so good. After their busiest year in living memory, business undertakers predict a further rise in corporate mortalities.

Keith Goodman, a partner at Leonard Curtis, the oldest independent insolvency practice in Britain, sees the business landscape as 'a bloodbath'. He says: 'It's unprecedented. Every phone call I get is a problem call. This year is going to be horrendous, far worse than 1990 in terms of number and size.'

It is a lucrative business for accountants. The early days of a receivership can involve about 100 people, who will pass on the paperwork to a team of maybe three to six working full-time on the project. They will try to sell the business, or parts of it, as a going concern within a month. If this fails, the business goes into liquidation, which can continue for years. The team at Touche Ross has been working on Laker Airways since 1982.

To cope with the demand for receivers, accountants are transferring staff from their inactive merger and acquisition departments and even recruiting from outside.

Corporate-recovery specialists, who invade head offices at a moment's notice, have a glamorous image within large practices. But, says Morris, their colleagues don't think about the human tragedies they have to deal with. 'It's not very pleasant standing in front of 200 people and telling them they are out of a job,' he says. 'Regrettably, the workforce always seems to be the last to know when things are going wrong'

Tim Hayward, head of corporate recovery at KPMG Peat Marwick McLintock, says his staff has doubled to 500 in the past two years. His largest project is the Levitt Group, but he expects bigger fish will float to the top as the year proceeds.

'Much of our work is with companies where we hope to avoid insolvency,' says Hayward. By the end of last year, 24 per cent of the receiverships were in manufacturing.

Christopher Morris says company chairmen are usually relieved to see him arrive at their gates. 'Sometimes they are shocked and depressed,' he says. 'But don't forget we arrive at the end of a period of enormous pressure. The chairmen to watch are the ones who are overbearingly co-operative. They become obsequious. And you often find they've been up to no good.'

Crossword

Across

4 If you kick someone out of the boardroom, you _____ them (4)

5 A share price _____ up, like a gun into the air (6)

7 Insult these people if you like, but they may keep your computer going (5)

8 This specialist does not undress for work, despite appearances (5-8)

11 Pessimistic about market trends (7)

12 A dull day on the markets (10)

14 This share price doesn't just rise in value, it _____ (5)

17 Owners of dirty shirts and drug money do this (7)

18 What this company's shares do when they increase slightly in value (4)

Down

1 These prices go ahead like lions (4)

2 People sometimes expect this to last forever, but it never does (4)

3 When shares are bought and sold, they change _____ (5)

5 These people together own a company (12)

6 This share price increases very fast, too (5)

9 Company event sometimes seen as a miracle (10)

10 What the economy does at the end of a recession (5, 2)

11 Optimistic animals at the stock exchange (5)

13 If a share price increases slightly it _____ up (5)

15 If the Dow, the FT-SE, the Hanseng or whatever rise very fast, they _____ (4)

16 This commodity is extremely sensitive to world events (3)

 **Work, Unemployment and Welfare**

Ways of working

flexible working hours
flexitime
flextime
job-sharing
nine-to-five job
part-time

Working hours are very different in different countries. In the English-speaking world, people who work full-time regular hours are said to have a **nine-to-five job**, even if they don't work exactly from 9 am to 5 pm. People with **flexible working hours** are free, within limits, to work when they want, as long as they do a minimum number of hours. This is known in Britain as **flexitime** and in the US as **flextime**.

Another flexible arrangement is to work **part-time** and share a job with someone else. This is called **job-sharing**.

I've worked in an accounts office, so I know I don't want a boring nine-to-five job.

Many women working long hours on low pay, often with more than one part-time job, naturally resent those who have come to expect the state to provide for them instead of helping themselves.

Employers should encourage programs that give parents time with their children, programs such as parental leave, flextime, shared jobs or work at home.

Flexitime, job-sharing and working from home would be encouraged.

commute
commuter
commuting
teleworker
telecommuter
telecommuting
telecottage

If you **commute** to work, you live outside a city centre and travel to work there everyday. If you do this you are a **commuter** and you take part in the activity known as **commuting**.

Teleworkers are people who work from home using phones, computers and fax machines. This is **teleworking** or **telecommuting**.

A **telecottage** is a building in the country with the equipment necessary for telecommuting, shared by people who work in this way.

It took Julie an hour to commute home and she would come back tired and frustrated.

The report says that 85 per cent of British commuter traffic is by car, 40 per cent of which is devoted to commuter traffic.

Teenagers nowadays dislike the prospect of commuting and would rather go abroad to work, at least for a time.

One of the major difficulties for teleworkers has been the psychological effect of moving from a sociable to an unsociable environment.

If projections are accurate, many more people will be <u>teleworking</u> in the future.

Godfrey Claff, director at the trust, said: 'The centre is based on the highly successful business <u>telecottage</u> concept from Scandinavia. It will bring the benefits of high technology to companies and people in the surrounding rural area and will attract business from commercial centres both nationally and internationally.'

1 **The pros and cons of telecommuting.** Read this article from *The Times* about teleworking and complete the tasks.

1 Find three advantages of teleworking for the worker.
2 Find three advantages for the employer.
3 Find one perceived disadvantage for the employer.
4 Find one possible disadvantage for certain traditional commuters.
5 Find one possible disadvantage for people the teleworker lives with.

WORKING FROM HOME 'COULD SAVE BILLIONS'

Strategic Workstyles 2000, an Oxford forecasting unit, says that industry could make huge financial savings by allowing their staff to work from home. Noel Hodson, the report's author, says that the effects of allowing 15 per cent of Britain's 22 million workforce to work in their own homes using telephones, facsimile machines and computers would be enormous.

London would feel the biggest benefits with 526,000 fewer drivers on the roads. More than 11,000 commuters would not need to enter central London daily. Commuters would benefit from seeing their families more, saving up to four hours a day travelling to work. Companies would have a fresher workforce which did not need to be transported into a central, expensive location daily.

A study for a big financial institution planning to allow 20 people to 'telecommute' calculated that the company would save more than £430,000 per year. The study examines the reasons why telecommuting has not achieved the advantages of time saved and cost cutting. It says the managers are often nervous about leaving staff unattended and out of sight of the office. For the 'teleworker', working from home might bring unforeseen hazards, such as a partner who does not want the house invaded by machinery and office paperwork. 'A number of car commuters thoroughly enjoy the total isolation and privacy available to them in their cars,' the report says.

Benefits and headhunters

benefits package
fringe benefits
perks

headhunt
headhunter

Apart from the salary, employers may offer a **benefits package** containing a number of **fringe benefits**, or, more informally **perks**, such as a company car, or as in the second and third examples below, much more. A lot of people find work by looking at job advertisements in newspapers. A few people are **headhunted. Headhunters** search for executives with specialist skills and try to persuade them to leave their current job to go to work for a new employer, perhaps by offering them better pay and benefits.

benefits 94 ⇑

◆ **LANGUAGE NOTE**

Headhunt and **headhunter** are also spelt with a hyphen.

…*Brian Pearse, the banking expert <u>headhunted</u> by the Bank of England to give it re-direction.*

Local government managers have none of the other commercial <u>fringe benefits</u>: car, bonus schemes, health insurance and so on.

The motoring <u>perk</u> is only one of the special privileges that can provide an MP with a total pay and <u>benefits package</u> worth more than £100,000 this year. Now the MP's are demanding more.

2 **Luxurious packages.** Look at this article from *Today* and put words from below in the spaces. Not all the words are used.

a	benefit	c	handshake	e	headhunting	g	package	i	salary
b	duty	d	headhunted	f	opportunities	h	perks	j	tax

£200,000 to fly smokeless sultan

An oil-rich Sultan is searching for a non-smoking airline captain to become the highest paid chauffeur in the world. The pilot, who will fly the £40 million pound Boeing 747 used by Sultan Qaboos of Oman, can expect a ＿＿＿＿＿＿ (1) worth more than £200,000.

The health-conscious Sultan, who is offering a ＿＿＿＿＿＿ (2) – free ＿＿＿＿＿＿ (3) of at least £60,000, hates cigarettes, and prefers to surround himself with non-smokers.

Exact figures are secret, but ＿＿＿＿＿＿ (4) include an expenses-paid luxury home, medical bills for consultants anywhere in the world, private schools for the children back home, free air tickets and two months leave a year. There would also be a handsome golden ＿＿＿＿＿＿ (5) at the end of the two-year minimum contract.

Though applications are flooding into an exclusive London headhunting agency from all over the world, the Sultan is known to prefer a British pilot. ...

Discrimination at work

discriminate

discrimination
  racial
    discrimination
  sexual
    discrimination
  ageism

sexual harassment
sexually harassed

If someone such as an employer treats someone differently from someone else in the same situation, they **discriminate against** them. People who suffer **discrimination** are **discriminated against**.

People discriminated against on the grounds of their race are victims of **racial discrimination**, people (usually women) discriminated against because of their sex suffer from **sexual discrimination** and those discriminated against because of their age are victims of **ageism**.

In cases of **sexual harassment**, people (again usually women) are victims of unwanted sexual advances by their colleagues or bosses. People in this situation complain of being **sexually harassed**.

The Supreme Court in America has ruled that the ban discriminated against black people.

The tribunal found in favour of PC Surrinder Singh who alleged racial discrimination against his employees, the Nottinghamshire police.

Mrs Preisler had claimed that she was sexually discriminated against by Mrs Buggins who had told her she would not be promoted because she was pregnant.

Even staff as young as 40 are victims of ageism by ambitious newcomers trying to take over their jobs.

Some small businesses have sought expert advice in establishing sexual harassment policies. Other companies say they're removed from the issue and that sexual harassment is not their problem.

Corning employees who think they are being sexually harassed in any way are encouraged to confront the person or persons responsible for causing offence. In most cases, the company says, this puts an immediate end to the misconduct without anybody else getting to hear about it.

3 **Putting on the golden muzzle.** Read this article from *Newsweek* about sexual discrimination on Wall Street and complete the definitions below it, using the correct forms of the key words. (The Great White Way usually refers to Broadway, see page 195, but here it refers to the conservative attitudes of some white males working on Wall Street).

TAKING ON THE GREAT WHITE WAY

... Wall Street businesses have traditionally lagged behind other industries in hiring women and minority executives. Salomon has just five women managing directors compared with 150 men. Kidder has four, compared with 111.

At most firms, grievances are settled quietly in arbitration hearings in arrangements sometimes dubbed 'golden muzzles'. That's why few cases get public attention. Take the case of Kristine Utley, a former Goldman Sachs sales associate who collected a settlement after charging that her work environment was 'hostile' and 'sexist'.

To bolster her point, she submitted memos she said she discovered that heralded the arrival of new female employees with nude pinups. Neither she nor Goldman can comment on the settlement. ...

grievance	Complaints about discrimination and other injustices at work are called _____ . An employee may take or bring their grievance to a tribunal, which during its _____ (sessions),
hearing	
arbitrate	_____ in the case (listens to the arguments of both sides) and proposes a _____ : an agreement that both employer and employee accept. Sometimes the settlement, especially in the US, includes a condition called a _____ _____ that prevents both sides from commenting on it. (A muzzle is usually something you put on a dog to prevent it from barking or biting.) Compare this expression with 'golden handshake'.
settlement	
golden muzzle	

settlement *123, 178* ⇓

golden handshake *94* ⇑

Getting the sack

dismiss
dismissal
  unfair dismissal
 	
fire
 	
sack
  give someone the
  sack
 	
sue
 	
tribunal
	If someone is told to leave their job, especially if their employers say they have done something wrong, they are **dismissed**. More informal ways of talking about a **dismissal** are to say that the person has been **fired** or **sacked** or **given the sack**.
	
	If someone feels that they have lost their job unfairly, they may take their case to a **tribunal** and **sue** or make a claim against their former employers for **unfair dismissal**.

sue *24* ⇧

First I shall be consulting the League Managers' Association and <u>suing the club</u> for <u>unfair dismissal</u>. It will make great listening at an industrial tribunal.

The fact is they haven't been <u>sacked</u> or <u>dismissed</u>. They are still employees.

She was unjustly accused of stealing money and then <u>given the sack</u>.

He is <u>fired</u> from his job because he has been uttering unAmerican thoughts.

4 **Unfair dismissal 1.** Below are sections from two articles: each article contains three sections. Put the articles together, putting the sections in the right order, and match each article to its headline. (One article begins with section a and the other with section b.)

1   *BT MAN DROPS SICK DAYS CASE*
2   **PONYTAIL MAN CLAIMS SEX BIAS**

a   A BT engineer sacked after taking more than 1,100 sick days dropped his claim for unfair dismissal yesterday. BT claimed that Michael Stoneham's complaint had been frivolous and should never have been brought.

b   A ponytailed man who was dismissed from his job for refusing to have his hair cut claimed yesterday that he was the victim of sexual discrimination because women employees were allowed long hair.

c   Mr Stoneham was ordered to pay BT £200 costs. Outside the industrial tribunal hearing in Chelsea, west London, he said: 'They had always wanted to get rid of me. I felt I had a case.'

d   Mr Lloyd of Wapping, East London, said he refused the request on principle. Clients were interested only in his technical knowledge. 'There was no one who said to me, 'You can solve my computer problem, but first get your hair cut.' He is

110

claiming unfair dismissal and sexual discrimination against Computer Associates of Slough, Berkshire.

e Mr Stoneham, 43, of Leytonstone, east London, had claimed that his 1,158 sick days over 16 years had been due to a series of mishaps. However, Michael McDonough, his representative, withdrew the case 'in the light of evidence which has been given'.

f Kevin Lloyd, 36, left his job as computer engineer after being ordered to trim his hair, which reached halfway down his back, or to find a new job. Brian Wizard, customer services director, said that his haircut clashed with the company image.

5 **Unfair dismissal** 2. Below are sections from two more articles: each article contains three sections. Put the articles together, putting the sections in the right order, and match each article to its headline. (One article begins with section a and the other with section b.)

1 # LOVE OF ROBBER COST JOB

2 # A WOMAN'S HANDBAG IS NO PLACE FOR A MAN TO BE LOOKING INSIDE – BY LAW

a Bosses at Woolworth's were yesterday ordered to pay £10,000 to an employee who wanted to keep the contents of her bag private.

b Danish beauty claims she has been sacked by a top fashion house because of her love for Britain's biggest robber.

c Mrs Taylor panicked and rushed out of the shop after acting manager Tony Beazer asked her to open her shoulder bag for a routine search at the store in Lyme Regis, Dorset. The tribunal said Woolworth's had no right to demand the search and ruled Mrs Taylor had been unfairly dismissed.

d She had been manager of a boutique owned by the company in London's West End. But Hella, 28, said yesterday she was fired after it was revealed that she was featured in a book written by Viccei in prison. Hella said: 'For them to fire me can only make me feel that they are afraid of the publicity.'

e The girlfriend of Valerio Viccei, who is serving 22 years in jail for robbing a safe deposit centre of more than £40 million, wants to sue Joseph Ltd for unfair dismissal.

f The store giant sacked cashier Jacky Taylor, 42, for gross misconduct after she refused to have it searched by a male colleague when they were left alone together in the shop.

Redundancy

downsize
rightsize

lay off
let go
make redundant

overstaffed

payroll
workforce

If an organisation gets rid of employees because they are no longer needed, it **lays** them **off** or **makes** them **redundant**.

Companies doing this sometimes talk about **downsizing**, **rightsizing** or **letting** employees **go**. They may say that they are **overstaffed**: they have too many employees and need to make cuts in the **payroll** or the **workforce**, the total number of people they employ.

Signe Wilkinson, USA – Cartoonists & Writers Syndicate

◆ **LANGUAGE NOTE**

Downsize, **rightsize** and **overstaffed** can be spelt with hyphens.
Workforce can be spelt with a hyphen or as two words.

Thousands of federal employees in the United States face the prospect of being <u>laid off</u> because of the budget crisis.

And as more city firms are making their employees <u>redundant</u>, it doesn't look like the situation is getting any better.

The teachers were <u>let go</u> when the school district lost $47 million in state funding.

The core of this agreement is one of looking at ways to <u>downsize</u> GM's workforce in a very turbulent period.

Lockheed Missiles' management says it has to reduce its <u>payroll</u> by 2,000 positions by the end of the year.

…massive <u>overstaffing</u> with trade unions holding out against technological change. Maxwell negotiated a two-third reduction in the <u>workforce</u>.

Lawton Chiles vowed to get Florida out of the mess it was in by <u>right-sizing</u> the government. That's his phrase for making it smaller and smarter.

axe
  get the axe

layoff
  mass layoffs
  massive layoffs

redundancies
  compulsory
    redundancies
  voluntary
    redundancies

natural wastage

When employees have no choice, the **redundancies** are **compulsory**. But where employees can choose to leave, redundancies are **voluntary**. The payroll can also be reduced by **natural wastage**, with employees leaving over a period of time for the usual reasons: retirement, moving to another job, and so on.

When a lot of redundancies are involved, journalists talk about jobs being cut or **axed**, with **mass layoffs** or **massive layoffs**. Employees made redundant **get the axe**.

◆ **LANGUAGE NOTE**
  Layoff can be spelt with a hyphen.
  Axe is spelt **ax** in American English.

Wall Street still employs 220,000 New Yorkers despite 50,000 redundancies since 1987.

National Power has announced that about 5,000 jobs are to go – that's almost a third of the total workforce of 16,700. The job losses will be spread over several years and the company will be hoping to complete the slimdown without any compulsory redundancies but by natural wastage.

The ailing motor manufacturer wanted 820 voluntary redundancies. Now workers will go on a 'last-in, first-out' basis.

British Nuclear Fuels yesterday announced it was axing 750 jobs at its head office and main design centre.

Another major American company has announced massive layoffs and other cost-cutting measures. Allied Signal Incorporated said today that it would cut 5,000 jobs.

The construction industry is laying people off by the thousand.

6 **Is downsizing rightsizing?** Use appropriate forms of key words below to complete this extract from National Public Radio.® One of the words is used three times, one of the words is used twice, two of the words are used once each and two of the words are not used at all.

a downsize   c workforce   e mass
b layoff   d sack   f overstaffing

Getting the ax

_____ (1) used to mean making a smaller version of a product. But these days when companies talk about _____ (2), employees know it's the _____ (3) that's about to shrink. 20,000 jobs are being phased out at IBM. 10,000 have been cut at Digital. The recession is forcing companies to make payroll cuts they should have started years ago. A lot of the companies that are _____ (4) right now may have been _____ (5) during the whole decade of the 80s and only come about to reduce their _____ (6) now. During the 1981 recession most _____ (7) hurt factory or construction workers. But this time business managers, executives and technical staff are getting the ax.

Redundancy pay

redundancy pay
redundancy
 payment
redundancy
 payoff
redundancy
 payout

severance
 payment

People who are laid off may receive compensation in the form of a **redundancy payment, pay-off** or **payout, redundancy pay** or, especially in American English, a **severance payment.**

◆ **LANGUAGE NOTE**

Payout is also spelt with a hyphen.

British Satellite Broadcasting staff will today be given details of their redundancy payoffs, if as expected, widespread job cuts are introduced.

Bosses feel more embarrassed when they sack fellow managers or professionals, whom they may see again at the golf club, than when they do the same to factory workers. They ease their embarrassment by giving these well-paid employees more generous severance payments.

7 **An expensive drink.** Connect the two parts of each sentence in order to put together this article from *The Times*. The numbered parts are in the correct order.

Man loses drink case appeal

appeal 152 ⇓

1 British Rail yesterday rejected an appeal by a man it

2 He will lose £20,000 in

3 Alex Bryson, 63, a clerk, of Kirk Sandall, Doncaster, who had worked for British Rail for 38 years, was dismissed

4 'I am heartbroken that BR could have

5 His union, the Transport Salaried Staffs Association, said that it

a would take the case to an industrial tribunal.

b with three other clerks and an assistant manager for drinking on duty.

c treated me so badly,' he said.

d sacked for drinking half a pint of beer at his leaving party.

e redundancy pay.

Jobless and on the dole

out of work unemployed unemployment

Members of the workforce without a job are **unemployed** or **out of work**. **Unemployment** is the situation of people without work.

Signe wilkinson, USA – Cartoonists & Writers Syndicate

JOB COUNSELOR... WHO COUNSELS UNEMPLOYED... TO BE JOB COUNSELORS... WHO COUNSEL UNEMPLOYED... TO AVOID ASKING THE QUESTION... WHAT JOBS?

The Minister of Labour, Ruan Chong Wu, said 11 million people would be out of work this year. The BBC correspondent said these figures ignored the countryside altogether. He says several million people laid off from rural factories last year are not classified as unemployed because they can return to the family farmland.

A report by the European commission is predicting that <u>unemployment</u> will rise next year to nearly 11 per cent of the workforce. The release of the report coincides with the latest unemployment figures due out today. These are expected to show an increase in the number of people out of work.

<table>
<tr>
<td>

dole
  dole queue
  on the dole

jobless benefit
unemployment
  benefit

</td>
<td>

Unemployment benefit or **jobless benefit** is also called, informally, the **dole**. People receiving it are **on the dole**. If you lose your job you join the **dole queue**.

</td>
</tr>
</table>

◆ **LANGUAGE NOTE**

    Unemployment benefit and **dole queue** are used mainly in British English.
    Unemployment benefit is also called **jobless benefit**, especially in American English.

Only Belgium pays <u>unemployment benefit</u> indefinitely.

Congress is ready to approve extended <u>jobless benefits</u> for the long-term unemployed.

BT workers ought to think again about wanting to be out of work, because it's not easy living <u>on the dole</u>.

Another 29,100 people have joined the <u>dole queue</u>, stretching it to 2,753,400.

<table>
<tr>
<td>

jobless

job-seeker
job-seeker's
  allowance

</td>
<td>

Unemployed people are often referred to in the media as **jobless**. Jobless people looking for work are **job-seekers** or **job-hunters** and, in Britain, receive money from the state called **job-seeker's allowance**.

</td>
</tr>
</table>

Most EC governments simply leave the <u>jobless</u> to rot on the dole.

The eventual <u>jobless</u> total could rise, according to some experts, to 4 million out of a workforce of just under 9 million.

The <u>job-hunter</u> with a carefully chosen fluent language could find it is an additional advantage which may just tip the balance in his favour.

A <u>job-seeker</u> who sent out 8,700 applications may have finally found work. Steve Horvath used to spend five hours a day sending off applications all round the world. But yesterday his luck changed when company boss Peter Hawkins offered him an interview after hearing about his 10-month work hunt.

8 **Jobless combinations.** 'Jobless' is often used in the combinations below. Group the expressions under the three headings on the right.

jobless	a benefits b claims c figures d pay e rate f toll g total

1 the numbers of people out of work

2 money given to unemployed people by the state

3 the requests from people for this money

9 **Unemployment blues.** Match the two parts of the expressions and use them to complete the article from *Newsweek*.

1 industrialized
2 rising
3 rapid
4 unemployment
5 boom
6 unprecedented

a rate
b world
c period
d years
e growth
f productivity

JOBS

... For more than two decades, from the late 1940's to the early 1970's, the _____ (1) world enjoyed an _____ (2) period of _____ (3) growth and _____ (4) productivity that had economies running at full steam. Trade grew, incomes rose, living standards soared and in Europe, the United States and Japan, practically everyone who wanted a job could have one.

Look at us now. Our economies are growing at a snail's pace, if they're growing at all. Governments are running chronic deficits. And most miserable of all, millions of people can no longer find the work they need. In recession-plagued western Europe, more than 20 million workers are idle, an _____ (5) rate of 11 per cent, and it's rising. Nearly half of Europe's unemployed have been out of work for a year or more. Worse, unemployment has stubbornly refused to contract for more than a decade, even in _____ (6) years. ...

boom *89*

Industrial action

strike
call a strike
go on strike
strike ballot
industrial action
stoppage
walkout
walk out
labor union
trade union

If you stop working normally in order to demand better pay, benefits or working conditions, or to protest about something, you take **industrial action**. In a **strike**, workers stop working completely for a time.

Workers are organised in **unions, trade unions,** or in the US **labor unions**. A union may **call a strike**, perhaps after a **strike ballot** in which union members vote to **go on strike** or against going on strike. Strikes are also referred to as **walkouts** or **stoppages**.

◆ **LANGUAGE NOTE**

The plural of trade union is **trade unions** or **trades unions**.
The verb corresponding to the noun **walkout** is **walk out**.

The leaders of Spain's two biggest unions said they would fix a date for <u>industrial action</u> (i.e. inaction) later this month.

Unions <u>called the strike</u> to demand a 38-peso (78 pence) raise in their basic daily wage.

The two <u>trade unions</u> organising the strike are having talks today after negotiations failed on Wednesday evening.

Power workers gave notice of their own strike <u>ballot</u> after employers refused to increase an 8.9 per cent pay offer.

I told them, if they wanted to <u>go on strike</u>, fine. There was not going to be any company when they came back.

In Germany more than 15,000 teachers and school employees took part in a warning strike in the eastern part of the country. The teachers staged a one-day work <u>stoppage</u> demanding higher pay and job protection. But the teachers' <u>walkout</u> was just one part of growing problems for eastern Germany.

Nationwide industrial action began earlier this week when staff at most banks <u>walked out</u> indefinitely.

10 **Types of strike.** A train strike is one involving railway workers, but what is a wildcat strike? Put each type of strike below under one of these four headings:

1 the proportion of workers involved in the country as a whole

2 the services affected

3 the duration of the strike

4 the unexpectedness or otherwise of the strike

a general
b wildcat
c 24-hour
d indefinite

e nationwide
f one-day
g tube
h all-out

i dock
j airline
k full-blown
l lightning

Strike paralysis

cripple
halt
paralyse

halt
standstill
  complete
    standstill
  total standstill
  virtual standstill

When a strike causes a lot of disruption, it **cripples** or **paralyses** the things it affects, such as services, factories, cities or the economy, stopping normal activity and bringing things to a **standstill** or a **halt**. A standstill may be described as **total, complete,** or **virtual**: almost complete.

cripple *195* ⇓

In Bangladesh a 24-hour anti-government general strike which began from this morning has crippled the entire country.

A strike by about 10,000 shipping workers has paralysed traffic along the Romanian section of the River Danube.

A strike called by Sikh separatists in the northern Indian state of Punjab has brought the area to a virtual standstill.

The strike brought public transport to a halt and shops and businesses failed to open.

11 Crippling paralysis. Match the two parts of these
extracts.

1   The latest challenge to President Ratsiraka comes after weeks of massive anti-government protests, and in the midst of a general

2   The country faces paralysis from a strike by public service workers.

3   President Roh Tae-Woo had become personally involved in trying to prevent a repeat of a crippling strike last year

4   The centre of São Paulo was brought to a standstill for several hours today after bus drivers stopped work in protest

5   Supporters of the separatist movement in the Indian state of Jammu and Kashmir have called a general strike in Srinagar, the summer capital, bringing it to a virtual standstill.

6   The strike leaders are threatening to bring the country's freight

a   at the arrest of one of their colleagues for hooting his horn at a policeman.

b   Banks and the telephone service are at a standstill, as are many government offices.

c   Most shops were closed and only heavily guarded official transport was on the streets.

d   rail transport to a complete halt.

e   strike that has crippled the country's economy.

f   which paralysed the shipyard for 109 days.

Strike escalation

12 Stepping it up, giving in and climbing down.
Look at the examples and complete the definitions
using the key words.

Señor Menem is showing no signs that he will give in to union demands. 'They can go ahead and strike for 100 days and we will never give in,' he said.

Rail workers in Poland have warned that they will step up their week-long strike action if the government fails to meet their pay demands.

On June 19, however, the union had decided to escalate the strike and ballot papers had been sent to all members employed by Newham.

The state rail company SNCF said it expected services to get slowly back to normal following the protesting farmers' climbdown.

Local civic leaders encouraged strikers not to back down.

The committee made David Mellor go and forced a backdown over the mines.

give in to demands back down backdown climb down climbdown escalate a strike step up a strike	If governments and organisations say they will not **give in** to strikers' **demands**, they say they will not agree to them. The strikers may respond by intensifying their industrial action: they _____ it or **step** it **up**. If, in a dispute, one side reduces its demands and gives in to some or all of the demands of the other side, commentators talk about a _____ . In this situation, one side **climbs down** or _____ _____ .

escalate 174, 204 ⇓

◆ **LANGUAGE NOTE**

The noun corresponding to the verb **climb down** is **climbdown** and the noun corresponding to the verb **back down** is **backdown**. Both nouns are also spelt with hyphens.

Pickets, scabs and blacklegs

blackleg picket picket line scab strike-breaker	Workers who continue working during a strike may have to face abuse and insults from strikers when they arrive for work each day. The strikers in this situation are **pickets**, forming a **picket line**, and they call the people who continue to work **strike-breakers**, **scabs**, or in British English only, **blacklegs**. Of course, the people who continue working do not describe themselves in these ways.

picket line 23 ⇑

We extended an open invitation to management to come to terms, to bring us back to work, to get rid of the scabs, the replacement workers who took our jobs. And they refused.

Confrontations between strikers and strike breakers have led to 18 arrests, mostly union members. But a couple of weeks ago, strikers adopted new tactics to win supporters. The union members showered those crossing the picket lines with smiles and friendly cheers.

If you can't call someone who goes into work past a picket line a blackleg, what on earth can you call them? Is it acceptable to call a strike breaker a scab?

13 Violent tactics. Read this article from *The Times* about a newspaper strike in the United States and answer the questions as you read. Some of the answers involve reusing words from earlier in this chapter.

Teamster mob in press battle

Readers of the *Pittsburgh Press and Post-Gazette* have been denied a newspaper for the past two months by mobs of up to 5,000 pickets, organised by the Teamsters Union, who have besieged the printing plant. Bundles of stolen papers have been burnt or dumped, while replacement delivery drivers have been hauled from their cabs.

1 A 'mob' is a kind of crowd. Given the context, is it a noisy, violent crowd or an orderly one?
2 The pickets have besieged the printing plant, surrounding it and preventing people getting in or out. They have burnt and thrown away the papers that have been printed. What might the strikers call the replacement delivery drivers?

The dispute, which centres on a management plan to lay off 405 of the 605 drivers represented by the Teamsters and end home delivery by children, has evolved into a challenge over the power of the labour unions to enforce their will with violence and intimidation.

3 If employers make people redundant, they l _ _ _ them o _ _ _ .
4 The dispute has evolved, becoming more intense: it has
   e _ _ _ _ _ _ _ d.

In an attempt to bring out the newspapers last week, the publishers shipped in beds for workers who dared not step outside, ringed the plant with security guards, and arranged for replacement drivers to hide in a motel. The group published two editions before being forced to stop the presses. Scores of demonstrators, their numbers boosted by flying pickets from other unions, were arrested in pitched battles with riot police.

5 A flying picket is a group of union members not directly involved in a dispute who come to assist pickets who are directly involved. These pickets and other demonstrators were arrested in pitched battles with riot police, police specialised in controlling violent crowds. What sort of battle is a pitched battle: a) a fairly controlled one or b) a very violent one?

'The whole thing got out of hand,' said Jimmy Manis, general manager. 'There was violence on the streets, there was violence all over western Pennsylvania. The bottom line,' admitted Manis, when he stopped the presses, 'is that we don't want to further endanger the public.'

bottom
line *98* ⇑

'This is a union town. Always has been, always will be,' said Joe Molinero, one of the Teamster leaders, celebrating the management climbdown.

6 The whole thing got out of hand: out of control. What was the 'whole thing'?
7 What does Manis mean by the bottom line?
8 What was the management's climbdown?

Calling it off

avert a strike	When a union **calls off** the strike, workers return to
call off a strike	work. (A strike may also be **called off** before it starts:
	in this case the strike is **averted**.) A union calls
reach a settlement	off a strike if it **reaches a settlement** with the
	management or the authorities, perhaps with the
arbitrator	help of someone not directly involved: an **arbitrator**
mediator	or **mediator** who **arbitrates** or **mediates** in the
	dispute.
arbitrate	
mediate	

avert *168* ⇓

settlement *109* ⇑, *178* ⇓

arbitrator *178* ⇓

mediator *178* ⇓

Only members of the Machinists Union were walking the picket line. Pilots and flight attendants had called off their strike

The damaging miners' strike in Bulgaria is reported to be nearing its end after nine days. The government and strike organisers have reached a settlement which includes arrangements for the negotiation of wage rises and Bulgarian radio says the strike will be called off once a formal agreement has been signed.

Lineker feels an independent arbitrator could be the solution. Both parties would stand by his decision.

Nine unions have been on strike for four months. A mediator says a settlement must be reached today if the newspaper is to survive.

14 Can it be averted? In which of these examples is it possible to replace the expression 'called off' by the expression 'averted'?

1 BA STRIKE IS *CALLED OFF.* A strike called by British Airways cabin crews for Friday has been cancelled by their union's national executive.

2 Growing divisions within the union earlier this week persuaded leaders to suspend the strike on Monday, and now the strike has been *called off* altogether.

3 In India, leaders of 400,000 telecommunications workers have *called off* a nationwide strike which has lasted for the last 20 days. The stoppage had caused disruption to India's already inefficient telephone service.

4 TUBE STRIKE *CALLED OFF.* The capital was spared the misery of an all-out tube strike yesterday after an 11th hour deal was struck.

5 The drivers will not move their lorries until the pickets, who have damaged dozens of vehicles, have gone. The pickets will not end their vigil until the strike is *called off.*

vigil *18* ⇑

Welfare

welfare
welfare state
from (the) cradle
to (the) grave

Welfare covers things like unemployment benefit, sickness benefits and state pensions. The **welfare state** refers to all the things provided by a government such as the benefits mentioned above, plus things like child day care centres and hospitals.

Welfare is often said to cover people's needs **from (the) cradle to (the) grave**, from the moment they're born to the time they die.

He claimed that the National government, in its aim to 'redesign' New Zealand's <u>welfare state</u> with its generous pensions and other benefits, had become a 'prisoner of the extreme right'.

She'll be remembered for her attack on the whole idea that the state is ultimately responsible for the individual and should, in effect, look after him <u>from the cradle to the grave</u>.

live on welfare
giro
welfare check

If you **live on welfare**, you depend on the welfare system for money to live. People on welfare in the US usually receive their payments in the form of a **welfare check**, and this expression is usually used showing disapproval by politicians and people who want to change or reform the system. The equivalent in Britain is the **giro**.

The number of single mothers <u>living on welfare</u> grew by more than 200 per cent during the Eighties.

They vote for higher taxes for larger <u>welfare checks</u> for people who won't work.

I expect that he uses his <u>giro</u> to pay for the petrol to ferry his children to private school.

15 Welfare combinations. The word 'welfare' is often used before the numbered words to make two-word combinations. The things on the right, indicated by letters, are examples of these expressions. Match the two.

	1	state	a	child day care centres
	2	payments	b	expenditure on hospitals
	3	reform	c	people claiming unemployment benefit
welfare	4	services	d	checks or giros
	5	mothers	e	reducing benefits
	6	dependency	f	Sweden in the 1970s
	7	spending	g	not looking for a job because you get enough money on the dole and becoming used to this situation

Dismantling the welfare state

workfare

dismantle

Many governments are trying to reduce or cut welfare spending. Some are demanding that people on welfare should work in return for their benefits: this is called **workfare**.

Others are trying to limit welfare spending, but some politicians are not satisfied with cutbacks, even deep ones, and want to **dismantle** the welfare state completely.

◆ **LANGUAGE NOTE**

Workfare is also spelt with a hyphen or as two words.

Riddell, UK – The Economist

Wisconsin is already experimenting with two welfare reform programs. Work Fare requires all able welfare recipients to work if they hope to continue receiving their grants.

The coalition partners want to trim the welfare state's excesses, not to dismantle it.

125

16 **Kinds of cuts.** Find three expressions in this article from *Newsweek* relating to cutting welfare spending that do not contain the letters C–U–T.

DISMANTLING THE EUROPEAN WELFARE STATE

... The leaders of Finland, Sweden and Italy are using their electorate's fears to launch radical surgery on their bloated social welfare systems. All of Europe, to be sure, has been trimming at the edges of its social commitment for a decade. This is what Margaret Thatcher's Britain was all about in the 80's. Helmut Kohl's Germany brought government expenditure down from 48 to 46 per cent of its total output before reunification in 1990 forced a temporary new spending spree. But Sweden, Finland and Italy have done little more than fiddle. ...

The kinds of cuts now being proposed by the three governments are ideologically historic. In Finland, final details of the cutbacks won't be decided until after local elections next month. But the finance ministry has proposed $6 billion in deficit reductions through, among other measures, cuts in pension and unemployment benefits and the introduction of fees for medical-center visits. ...

Cracking down on scroungers

crack down

scrounger

Politicians say that another way of cutting back on welfare spending is to **crack down** on **scroungers**, a word used critically to talk about people who are getting unemployment benefit but should not be getting it, because they have a job, or because they are not willing to work.

crack down *26, 71* ⇑

A crackdown on dole scroungers was announced yesterday by Social Security Minister Peter Lilley. 'I'm closing down the something-for-nothing society,' he told cheering delegates. He pledged to claw back £500 million pounds from the fraudsters' pockets.

She lives in affluent Tunbridge Wells, where locals like to sign themselves 'Disgusted' when writing to the newspapers to complain about long-haired layabouts, scroungers, and other concerns of commuterland.

17 **Missing persons and money.** These words have been left out of this extract from *Today*. Indicate where the words should go. They occur in the text in the same order. (Not all the numbered gaps in the text indicate a missing word.)

a colleagues   c claimant   e taxes   g jobless

b benefits   d payments   f politicians   h scroungers

Cutting the dole

... Mr Major's ——————— (1) cabinet ——————— (2) apparently favour cutting ——————— (3) the period of eligibility for unemployment ——————— (4) from 12 to six months.

    With every ——————— (5) costing the government £9,000 ——————— (6) a year in ——————— (7) and lost ——————— (8), the financial attraction ——————— (9) of such a move is clear.

    The idea of making unemployment as ——————— (10) uncomfortable as possible also appeals to some ——————— (11), who think that most ——————— (12) people are lazy and need prodding back into work.

    But already the British benefits ——————— (13) system is one of the most tight-fisted in the Western world. ... Many other developed countries treat ——————— (14) the unemployed not as ——————— (15) but as people whose fall into hard times needs to be softened. ...

Crossword

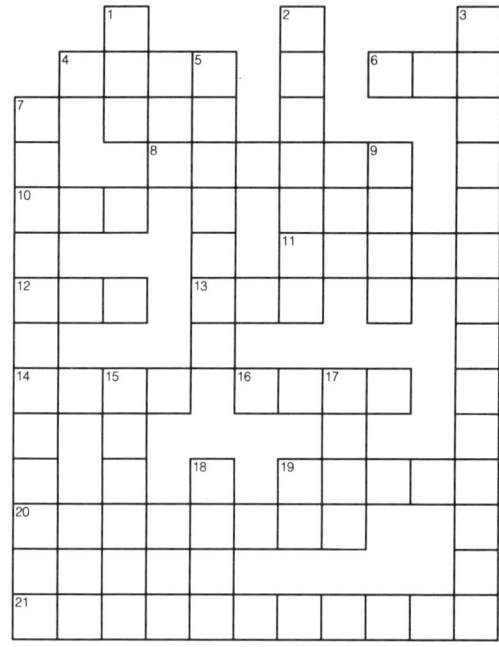

Across

4 The right size for the number of employees in a company is often in this direction. (4)

6 If you lose your 1 down you _____ laid off. (3)

8 Most west European countries are welfare _____ , but for how much longer? (6)

10 _____-offs is another way of talking about redundancies. (3)

11 The end of the welfare state's responsibility for its citizens? (5)

12 Wild animal on spontaneous strike? (3)

13 British cutting tool for trees and jobs. (3)

14 Shorter than massive, but just as big when it comes to redundancies. (4)

16 A series of strikes means a number of walk-_____ . (4)

19 Strike-breakers' legs are this colour (5)

20 21 across may be reached here. (8)

21 Agreements between employers and employees, sometimes subject to golden arrangements. (11)

Down

1 Seekers and hunters look for this. (3)

3 Not popular with strikers: 9 down in the plural (6-8)

5 and 2 Ecological approach to letting people go? (7, 7)

7 Someone working from home does this (12)

9 Not popular with strikers: 3 down in the singular (4)

15 One kind of discrimination (6)

17 Jobless count (4)

18 When almost everyone has a job, there is _____ employment. (4)

19 This university degree is no guarantee of finding a job these days. (2)

5 Crime and Punishment

Robbery

robbery
theft

break in
break-in

burglary
housebreaking

mugging

pickpocketing

shoplifting

Robbery, of course, takes many forms.

Pickpocketing is taking money from someone's pocket or bag in a public place without them noticing.

Shoplifting is stealing goods from the shelves of shops.

Mugging is taking someone's money in the street with threats of violence.

Burglary or **housebreaking** is **breaking in** or breaking into houses or other buildings, entering them by force, in order to steal things in a **break-in**.

These are all types of robbery or **theft**, although robbery is usually used to talk about stealing money from shops, banks, trains and so on, and about stealing artworks from museums.

break in 43 ⇑

burglary 42 ⇑

He began his life of crime pickpocketing at the age of four.

The young Sinead was even taken out by her mother on shoplifting expeditions.

Bank robberies, burglaries and muggings are reported almost daily in the press.

Two-thirds of 11 to 15 year olds admitted crimes from shoplifting to housebreaking.

armed robbery
bullion robbery
street robbery

Robbery is used in combinations like the ones on the left. In **armed robbery**, victims are threatened with a gun. **Bullion robbery** is stealing gold bars. **Street robbery** is another name for mugging.

My son had just been introduced to violence, armed robbery and gun culture all at the same time.

It has been estimated that between £1 billion and £2 billion are stolen from shops every year – equivalent to a Brinks-Mat bullion robbery every two days.

A small number of muggers – perhaps no more than 60 – are responsible for 95 per cent of all street robberies.

hold up
hold-up

at gunpoint
at knifepoint

A **hold-up** is a robbery where a gun or other weapon is used. Robberies like this happen **at gunpoint**, or **at knifepoint**.

◆ **LANGUAGE NOTE**
The verb corresponding to the noun **hold-up** is **hold up**.

129

The police recommend drivers not to stop at red lights, such is the risk of an armed <u>hold-up</u>.

Banks offered a £10,000 reward for information leading to the capture of two armed raiders who <u>held up</u> and kidnapped two female staff.

The driver of the taxi has been robbed at both <u>gunpoint</u> and <u>knifepoint</u>. She loves her job.

heist	Words for a spectacular robbery include **heist** and

heist

raid
  ram-raid
  smash-and-grab
    raid

Words for a spectacular robbery include **heist** and **raid**. A **smash-and-grab raid** involves breaking a shop window or a showcase to steal things and running or driving away with them very fast. A **ram-raid** involves breaking through the front of a building by driving into it with a car, and then stealing things in the building.

Thieves broke into the Gardner museum in Boston and stole about a dozen objects worth an estimated $200 million. It was the biggest art <u>heist</u> in the history of the country.

In the words of a union official, <u>bank raid</u> stress has become a family illness.

Paintings worth £150,000 which were stolen in a <u>smash-and-grab</u> raid from a gallery in London's West End two years ago have been found by police.

...a series of <u>ram-raids</u> in the south-east where high-powered cars were driven into shop windows.

1 **Make the headline fit the crime.** Match the headlines to the first lines of the stories that follow.

1 **SURVEY PINPOINTS BURGLARY BLACKSPOTS**

2 **PC CLINGS FOR HIS LIFE TO JOYRIDER CAR**

3 **CITY MUGGER**   4 **PICKPOCKETS CLEANING UP**

5 **HIT AND RUN ROBBERY**   6 **BOY, 9, IN GUN HOLD-UP**

7 **RAM-RAID ON HOME**

8 **JCB RAIDERS PULL OFF HOLE IN THE WALL HEIST**

9 **COP'S SON RAIDED SHOPS**

10 **FRENCH GANG ROBS BRITONS ON TRAIN**

a Pickpockets 'accidentally' smear visitors with ice-cream or ketchup, then insist on wiping them down.

b A joyrider sped off with a policeman desperately clinging to his windscreen, a court heard yesterday.

c A gang used a bulldozer to steal a hole-in-the-wall cash dispenser yesterday.

d A pedestrian was left badly bruised after he was run over by a car and robbed.

e A schoolboy was robbed at gunpoint by a 9-year old bandit.

f Burglars smashed their way into a family home by driving through the patio windows.

g Fourteen British tourists have been robbed of cash and jewellery worth thousands pounds by a gang of French train thieves who sprayed them with a powerful sleeping gas.

h London's financial centre, the City, has issued an alert to banks and financial institutions around the world after a robbery in which nearly £300 million pounds of financial documents, or bonds, were stolen.

i The son of a top Scotland Yard commander took part in smash-and-grab raids which netted a £20,000 haul.

j You are six times more likely to return from holiday to find your home has been broken into if you live in a top-storey flat in Glasgow than a five-bedroomed detached house in Aberdeen.

Theft

theft
minor theft
petty theft
serious theft

Theft is often used in combinations such as these:

petty theft or **minor theft**, where the things stolen are not very valuable;

serious theft, where the things stolen are valuable.

Theft is also used in combinations like these to indicate the types of things stolen:

art theft: works of art;

vehicle theft, car theft, and, in American English, auto theft;

arms theft, where guns are stolen in a robbery, not used in a robbery.

She can earn more from mugging, shoplifting and petty theft than she ever would from a job.

More women are becoming involved in serious theft and fraud.

The image of art theft as a gentleman's crime is outdated; violence is increasingly common.

The British Crime Survey found that 116,000 of total car thefts and 180,000 thefts from cars occurred in car parks.

Mr Rudolf telephoned a newspaper last week to say his organisation had carried out the arms theft.

2 **Types of theft.** Use these words to complete the
sentences.

a   architectural   c   auto   e   petty   g   art
b   arms   d   bike   f   employee

1   Hoteliers are usually happy to offer you a safe corner to park your machine
    overnight. This is very necessary, particularly in Paris where _____ theft
    is rife.

2   In the area of _____ theft, insiders steal considerably more money and
    merchandise than outsiders.

3   Last year, more than 5,300 vehicles were stolen in El Paso, a city of half a million
    people. That's almost twice the national _____ theft rate for urban areas.

4   Philip Saunders, a former dealer, estimates that works worth about £3.5 billion
    have gone missing this year, putting _____ theft behind only the drugs
    trade and computer fraud in value.

5   South Miami beach is notorious for pickpockets and _____ theft.

6   The organisation behind _____ theft is not as sophisticated as behind
    fine art. Panelling, fireplaces and staircases are being ripped out and sold to dealers
    who do not ask too many questions.

7   Two white men, one of them a policeman, have been arrested in connection with
    an _____ theft last weekend, when a large quantity of weapons was
    taken from an air force base in Pretoria.

Joyriding and carjacking

<table>
<tr><td>carjacking
joyriding</td><td>Car theft includes joyriding: stealing a car for the pleasure of driving it, often at very high speeds, and carjacking, stealing a car, sometimes at gunpoint, when its driver is in it.</td></tr>
</table>

◆ **LANGUAGE NOTE**

   Carjacking and **joyriding** can both be spelt with hyphens.

*A band of youths ran over a policewoman while joy-riding in stolen cars, and police say she was
murdered.*

*The increasing sophistication of car alarms has prompted thieves to take up carjacking, stealing
cars while their owners are still in them.*

3 **Sorting out car crime.** Here are two articles: one about joyriding, consisting of two sections, and the other about carjacking, consisting of four. Complete the gaps with appropriate words and say which sections belong to each article. (The sections are in the correct order for each article.)

a Stop your car at a red light in Detroit and you may find you have lost it for good. Thieves have hit on an easy way of stealing cars: order the driver out at gunpoint, then take his place and drive off. _____ is not limited to Detroit – Houston has reported as many as ten in one day and San Diego, Atlanta and Los Angeles are infected – but it has become a mini-epidemic in the city and some of its suburbs in recent weeks.

b Most teenage _____ are school failures who believe they are very good or exceptional drivers and take cars for excitement, according to a survey on car crime. Although they knew it was wrong to steal a car, most of those interviewed, all under 17, did not consider themselves criminals and had almost no concern for the victims of their crime.

c In the past six weeks more than 300 drivers have been _____ in Detroit. Several people, including an off-duty policeman, have been killed trying to resist.

d Jeff Briggs, who carried out the survey among 200 youths at a car project at Walker, Newcastle upon Tyne, said that while many people complained about the term, _____ was an accurate description of the experience of taking vehicles. 'They get a good time, an enormous amount of joy out of _____ ,' he told a conference on car crime in London yesterday.

e There have been about 200 arrests. _____ may be an easy way to steal a car – and two thirds of the cars have been recovered – but the penalty for being caught is high.

f Armed robbery carries a much bigger penalty than theft. The _____ spree has left Detroit's inner city even emptier than usual.

Making a getaway

haul
loot
escape
get away
make off
escape
make your escape
getaway
make your
getaway
getaway car

After a robbery, the criminals try to **make their getaway** or **make their escape**. Getaway is also often used in the combination **getaway car**. Robbers may **make off** with money or property they have stolen: the **haul** or the **loot**.

◆ **LANGUAGE NOTE**

The verb corresponding to the noun **getaway** is **get away**. **Escape** is a noun and a verb.

On November 8, 1983 a masked gang forced their way into the Brinks-Mat warehouse at Heathrow and coolly <u>made off</u> with 6,800 gold bars worth more than £26 million. The police and the public were stunned at the size of their <u>haul</u>.

The gunmen managed to <u>escape</u>. One hour later, the empty <u>getaway car</u> was found abandoned on the edge of a nearby village.

After collecting the cash, the kidnapper <u>made his escape</u> by disappearing down the disused rail line.

The gunmen <u>got away</u> after a high-speed car chase by German police.

A detective's wife was snatched by a bank robber yesterday after her off-duty husband tried to stop his <u>getaway</u>. The gunman dropped his <u>loot</u> and forced the 42-year-old mother of three into her car.

4 Getaway scenarios. Match the two parts of these extracts.

1 Although the notes may not be marked,

2 The eight men walked out of the bank carrying the money in 25 flour sacks

3 Police believe the gang must have used a lorry to cart off their ripe haul.

4 They forced a rear window then searched through the rooms

5 As one popular joke had it, bank robberies were almost unknown in East Germany

a 'Two tons is a hell of a lot of cheese', said a detective. 'Not your average burglar's loot.'

b and made their getaway in two cars.

c because would-be criminals had to join a ten-year waiting list to buy a getaway car.

d before making off with the engagement ring she was given by the marquis.

e there is still the problem of what to do with such a large haul.

Foiling robberies

foil a robbery	If a robbery is **foiled**, the robbers do not get what

foil a robbery

flee empty-
handed

have a go
have-a-go hero

If a robbery is **foiled**, the robbers do not get what they came for, and they may **flee empty-handed**: they get away, but with no loot. In British English, journalists may refer to passers-by who try to stop thieves making their getaway as **having a go**. The expression is also used in combinations such as **have-a-go hero** or **have-a-go boy**.

He rewarded four 'have-a-go heroes' as they became known, who foiled a gang of robbers. One of the four, aged 12, got £25 for calling the police, his father and another man got £200 each and a third £100. They had grabbed a robber and his £7,000 haul, forcing his three accomplices to flee empty-handed.

5 **Successful or unsuccessful?** 'Flee empty-handed' is used in contrast with 'make a getaway', where the thieves are usually successful. Use an appropriate version of one of the expressions to complete these extracts logically.

1 The woman was left unharmed in Epping Forest in Essex after the gang had picked up the money and _____ .

2 The good people of Eltham made a stand against crime yesterday. One have-a-go hero was shot in the back by armed robbers and a man who used his car to ram their getaway vehicle was facing a costly repair bill. But the brave folk from the south-east London suburb won in the end, and the raiders

_____ .

3 A brave police chief foiled an armed robbery on a jewellers by grabbing the raiders' shotgun. As Chief Superintendent Chris Standen, 54, wrestled with the gunman, a shot blasted into the ceiling of the shop in Bath. Despite being hit over the head, he clung to the gun and the raiders _____ .

4 A sub-postmaster has been shot dead during an attempted robbery of a post-office in Clapton in North London. Police say three armed men were waiting in the post office when the postmaster and his wife arrived to open up. When he refused to hand over any money he was shot. The gunmen _____ .

5 Mr Culling was forced to drive to his bank and hand over the cash. His younger brother Philip was tied up and locked in the boot of a car for three hours while the gang _____ .

Shootings, stabbings and murder

murder
homicide

firearm
handgun
Saturday Night
 special

pack a piece

shooting
 drive-by

knifing
stabbing

Killing someone intentionally is **murder**, often referred to in law, especially in the United States, as **homicide**.

Victims may die as the result of a **knifing** or **stabbing**, where a knife is used, or a **shooting**, when a gun is used. Guns are also called **firearms**. Guns such as pistols and revolvers are called **handguns**. Being armed with a handgun is known, very informally, as **packing a piece**.

Cheap, easily available handguns are called **Saturday Night Specials**, even if people do not always use them at that time of the week.

Where people are shot from a moving car, they are victims of a **drive-by shooting**, or a **drive-by**.

© 1993 Engelhardt, USA – St. Louis Post & Dispatch/Reprinted with permission

'It's not like the kind of monument we used to put up.'

A spokesman said, 'We are treating the attack as attempted murder. We are now waiting to speak to the victim in hospital.' Last year FBI statistics found that Washington had a homicide rate of almost 78 per 100,000 residents, the highest of any city in the United States. Almost every day reports of shootings and stabbings, even of young children, read like a casualty report from a war zone.

That had followed a knifing incident in which a Romanian was killed.

Exactly what kind of protection was being provided is hard to tell, from the picture. If the officers have firearms at the ready, the handguns are well-hidden.

Not that any old Saturday Night Special will do. Packing the right piece matters as much as wearing the right athletic shoes. Semi-automatics are the guns of choice now.

Eight shots were fired from an automatic pistol in a drive-by attack in Birmingham.

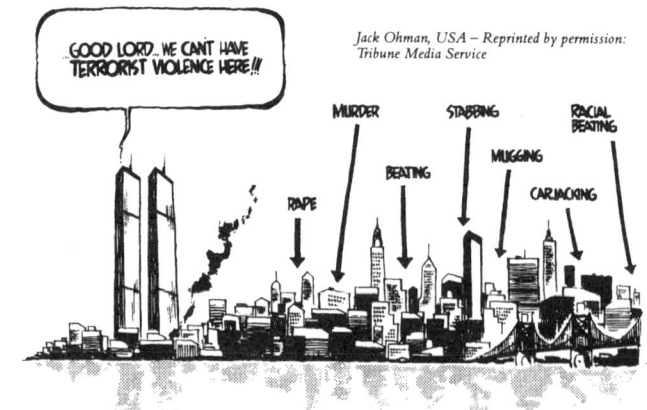

Jack Ohman, USA – Reprinted by permission: Tribune Media Service

GOOD LORD.. WE CAN'T HAVE TERRORIST VIOLENCE HERE!!!

RAPE MURDER BEATING STABBING MUGGING CARJACKING RACIAL BEATING

6 **Gun culture.** The transcript below is from National Public Radio.® The program presenter speaks twice, introducing contributions from two outside specialists, who each speak once. At what two points of the transcript, indicated by numbers, does the presenter start speaking and at what points do each of the two specialists start speaking? (Not all the numbers indicate a change of speaker.)

PACKING A PIECE

(1) The popular image of urban homicide is one of urban gang battles and drive-by shootings. But half the people who kill each other also know one another. Many are members of the same family. Jerry Gliden is director of the Chicago Crime Commission, a non-profit organization that monitors why people commit violent crimes.

(2) They have a lot of pressure on them, put on them by various agencies – whether it's probation or social work or the landlord or the police or whoever.

(3) And if the wife goes out and does something, or if the husband goes out and gets drunk and there's a big argument, and then sometimes one of them will wait till the other one goes to sleep and shoot them or stab them.

(4) The gangs – it's over street turf or to show just how tough they are. (5) Sometimes they'll shoot a group on the corner just to see if – see how the gun works. Makes no sense at all. The availability of a gun often makes a big difference between a mere argument and a shooting. And the deadlier the weapon, the more likely it is that someone will die.

(6) Gwen Fitzgerald, of Handgun Control, says criminals know this and they're looking for the most powerful guns they can find. (7) One veteran law enforcement officer said, you know, 20 years ago when he started, all criminals were not armed.

(8) And then, you know, in the 60's and 70's, yeah, they were armed with the Saturday Night Special handguns – very small, easily concealable handguns, usually a few rounds, maybe six or eight rounds. Now not only all the criminals carry guns, but they've got semi-automatic technology.

Being arrested

arrest	
suspect	
charge a suspect	
detain a suspect	
hold a suspect (in	
custody)	
try a suspect	
crime	
offence	
alleged crime	
alleged offence	
commit a crime	
commit an	
offence	
allegation	

Suspects are people who the police think may have carried out or **committed** a **crime**. A more formal word for a crime is an **offence**.

suspect *53* ⇑

If suspects are **arrested** by the police they may be **held** (**in custody**) or **detained** by them and may be **charged** with an offence.

arrest *72* ⇑
detain *71* ⇑

Until the person charged is **tried** in a court, and the crime or offence is proved to have happened, it is an **alleged** offence.

Alleged offences are **allegations**.

allegations *28, 39* ⇑

◆ **LANGUAGE NOTE**

  Offence is spelt offense in American English.

Police arrested the 13-year-old 23 times last year for theft, burglary and robbery. This year the youngster has been detained six times. Chief Superintendent John Nesbit said: 'He's like a boomerang. He just keeps coming back to commit more offences.'

Last night a man was being held in custody charged with attempted murder, drugs offences and burglary.

The former boss of missing British accountant Simon Law has been arrested in South Africa and charged with fraud and foreign exchange offences worth £10 million.

The latest controversy concerns the attempt by military courts to try a total of 18 journalists for alleged offences against the armed forces.

A police enquiry was launched yesterday after a man facing allegations of drink-driving and other motoring offences was found dead in his cell.

7 **Arresting combinations.** Make meaningful definitions by combining items from the each column in the table. (The nouns at the end of each sentence in the exercise are related to the verbs in the examples in this section.)

Someone...

1	forbidden by the authorities from leaving their home or going anywhere is under	arbitrary	allegation
2	accused of killing someone faces a	damaging	arrest
3	who commits a lot of crimes and goes on committing them is a	fair	charge

4	in prison for political reasons is a	house	detainee
5	held in prison without being charged or tried is in	murder	detention
6	who is accused of doing something seriously wrong faces a	persistent	trial
7	whose case has been discussed a lot in the media may not get a	political	offender

Awaiting trial

jump bail
remand in custody
remand on bail
release on bail

Where an alleged offence is serious, the suspect may be **remanded in custody** and await trial in prison, or they may be **remanded on bail** and then **released on bail**: the judge decides an amount of money that must be paid by, or on behalf of, the defendant so as to ensure that they return to the court for trial later. If someone **jumps bail**, they do not return to court for trial.

Mr Mitchell was remanded on bail until August and ordered to surrender his passport. Dr Christopher Cowley, a scientist from Bristol, appeared separately on a similar charge. In a previous court appearance last week he had been remanded in custody. This morning he was released on bail with the same conditions as Mr Mitchell.

He repeated the promise that Mr Ashwell would not jump bail and flee the country.

8 **Bail logic.** Bail may be a) granted, b) allowed, c) denied or d) refused. Complete these examples logically and grammatically using a phrase containing one of the verbs.

1 John Butcher, Conservative MP for Coventry South West, has campaigned in the Midlands for habitual violent offenders to be _____ bail.
grant   deny

2 Hundreds of supporters shouted 'Free her now' when Kiranjit Ahluwalia was _____ bail.
allow   refuse

3 The fact that he was in custody from day one was incredibly helpful. If he had been _____ bail that would have been horrific.
grant   refuse

4 Brookes, 47, from Peterborough, Cambs, was remanded in custody for seven days after being _____ bail.
allow   refuse

5 Five state Supreme Court judges rejected lawyers' assurances that Tyson, 25, would not try to flee. They upheld the decision to _____ bail made by a lower court.
grant   refuse

The indictment and the charges

indict
indictment

charge

charges
  bring charges
  file charges
  answer charges
  face charges
  admit charges
  deny charges

counts

If someone is formally accused of committing crimes, they are **charged** or **indicted** with these crimes.

An **indictment** may contain a number of **counts** or **charges**. Charges are **brought** or **filed against** people accused of doing something wrong, and they then have to **face** or **answer** the charges in court. They may agree that the charges are true and **admit** them, or they may say that they are not true and **deny** them.

charge 71 ⇑

John Gotti was charged today with ordering the murders of four people, including the head of New York's Gambino crime family. Gotti was indicted on 11 counts, including gambling, obstruction of justice and tax evasion.

The Krill affair is the one count that differs substantially. Here the indictment alleges that Noriega actually met with drug traffickers in 1986 to plan a cocaine deal.

Police, not the victims, should be responsible for bringing charges.

In the Philippines, the authorities have filed charges of arson against the leader of the country's largest left-wing trade union.

The son of a member of parliament appeared in court to answer charges of drug trafficking.

Some of Australia's best-known businessmen are facing criminal charges over the Rothwells collapse.

He admitted charges of forging documents and handling stolen goods.

The rock star Axl Rose, 30, denied charges stemming from a riot at a concert in St Louis last year.

9 **Types of crime.** In the first example above John Gotti faced murder, gambling and tax evasion charges, among others. What sort of charges might be brought against the people below? Match the charges to the criminals.

a rape	c assault	e corruption	g kidnapping	i manslaughter
b drugs	d arson	f murder	h fraud	j extortion

fraud *52, 96* ⇑

1 People accused of dealing in cocaine

blackmail *23* ⇑

2 Someone who is responsible for the accidental death of someone

3 Someone who makes a violent physical attack on someone

4 Dishonest officials who act illegally in their work

5 A businessman who dishonestly takes or uses money

6 Someone who violently forces someone to have sex with them

7 Someone who takes someone away by force and demands money for their release

8 Someone who intentionally kills someone

9 Someone who obtains money from someone by threatening violence

10 Someone who sets fire to buildings intentionally, perhaps because they like watching fires.

Legal eagles

legal eagle
lawyer attorney
barrister solicitor
judge magistrate
courtroom drama

A **lawyer** is someone qualified to advise or act in legal cases. **Legal eagle** is a slightly humorous expression meaning a lawyer, especially a clever one.

lawyer *71* ⇑

Courts are presided over by **judges** or, in lower English courts, by **magistrates**.

In the English system, **solicitors** represent people and prepare their cases before they reach court; **barristers** present and argue the cases in court. Solicitors do not represent people in court except in magistrate's courts.

In the American system, **attorneys**, familiar from a thousand TV and real-life **courtroom dramas**, represent people, prepare cases and present and argue them in court.

Many legal eagles interpret the opinion to imply that nothing short of abolishing the court would satisfy the judges.

The story-telling contest is closed to what the organizers of the event refer to as professional liars — that is lawyers, politicians and real estate agents.

Since the military coup at least one third of Fiji's estimated 130 lawyers, as well as a number of <u>magistrates</u> and judges, have left the country along with thousands of other professionals and academics.

Charles King-Farlow is leading the joint campaign by local <u>solicitors</u> and <u>barristers</u> for the court in his city.

What services can he provide that are worth $600,000? His legal expertise could be gained more for less money from more experienced <u>attorneys</u>.

In another <u>courtroom drama</u>, a man shot a judge during another domestic hearing.

10 **A glamorous profession?** Put together this article from *Today* by rearranging the sections. (The first section is a.)

Where legals dare

a In the TV series LA Law, courtroom drama is all in a day's work. The reality in England is slightly different. Barristers spend many hours in court, but few cases are action-packed. And a solicitor's day is more likely to be spent reading out a will than solving a juicy murder.

b But spokesman for the Bar Council Graham McMillan believes a life in law can be very glamorous. 'In higher courts you can get a lot of courtroom drama, and barristers have to be very quick on their feet.' ...

c Both careers take the same initial route – and only the cream of students need apply.

d It's a fact lost on scores of people who, seduced by LA Law's exciting plots, write into The Law Society's careers officer Jenny Goddard. 'Things are very different here,' ... says Jenny. 'A lot of people, though, do see the Crown Court as very exciting. It's hard to generalise because there are so many different branches of the profession, from personal legal advice to selling your house.'

e Solicitors do, however, present cases in magistrate's courts. Getting into the profession is not easy. There are only 70,000 solicitors in Britain, and 7,000 barristers – just over 1,000 of whom are women. ...

f The main difference between British and American lawyers is that the US legal eagles are all-rounders who both prepare and present cases. Here, solicitors do the litigation (prepare the case) and barristers do the advocacy (present the case) in Crown Court and upwards.

Prosecution and defence

prosecution
bring a
  prosecution
prosecution
  counsel

public prosecutor
district attorney
DA

go on trial
stand trial

defendant
defence counsel

In some countries the **public prosecutor** for each area decides which **prosecutions** should be **brought**: who should be prosecuted by the state, and for what. In the United States, **district attorneys**, or **DAs**, do this.

Someone facing prosecution in a court of law is a **defendant**. When defendants **go on trial** or **stand trial** they answer the charges against them.
A defendant is represented by **defence** lawyers or **counsel**, and the lawyers trying to prove that the offences took place are the **prosecution** lawyers or **prosecution counsel**.

trial 23 ⇑

◆ **LANGUAGE NOTE**

Defence is spelt **defense** in American English.

Paul Gascoigne's favourite restaurant faces prosecution over hygiene.

Mr Bennett issued a formal statement saying, 'The District Attorney's office does not simply want to prosecute Messrs Clifford and Altman, it wants to destroy them.'

In the Jesuit murder case in El Salvador, defense and prosecution lawyers continue to argue their case.

The Democratic Party has claimed that in many cases defendants were not given access to defense lawyers, but Dr Haje said that defense lawyers have worked on every case.

His lawyers have rejected a prosecution claim that he might try to leave the country. They say he wants to stand trial to prove his innocence so that he can return home.

Yesterday, as the trial entered its third week, counsel for the prosecution and defence made their final speeches.

11 **Crime makes the headlines.** The headlines below have been scrambled. Rearrange the words to make them coherent and grammatical.

FOUR UNFIT PROSECUTION FACE OVER WATER COMPANIES

PLOT DEFENDANT ALLEGES MANDELA MURDER

MEN ON SEXUALITY TRIAL NATURAL AND THEIR

OFFICERS EX-COUNCIL FRAUD FACE CHARGES

FACE BERLIN GUARDS TRIAL FOR KILLINGS WALL

CLOSED FOR LEADERS OF PROTESTERS TRIAL CHINESE

Guilty or not guilty

plead
  plead guilty
  plead not-guilty

plea
  guilty
  not guilty
  plea bargaining

Defendants are asked to **plead guilty** or **not guilty**: to say if they committed the offences they are charged with or not.

Guilty and not guilty are **pleas. Plea bargaining** is a system where prosecutors agree to bring less serious charges in return for a **guilty plea**.

◆ **LANGUAGE NOTE**

Pled is a past tense and past participle form of **plead**.

The three journalists pleaded not-guilty and were being released on bail.

She pled guilty to severely beating two of her young children.

More encouraging for the prosecution is the guilty plea on August 28th of a former Panamanian ambassador to Washington.

Mr Staple wants a formal system of plea bargaining on the American model, allowing potential defendants to co-operate with the prosecuting authorities.

12 Guilty! Put together five news stories, each made up of two of these extracts.

a Both men have pleaded not guilty, and the case, which is expected to last at least four weeks, is continuing.

b He lost and received a sentence of 12 years.

c He pleaded guilty to being twice the limit.

d In Anderson, Indiana, a burglary defendant refused a plea bargain agreement that would have given him 90 days in jail. He went to trial.

e Last Friday, Exxon pleaded guilty to four criminal charges in federal court as part of a plea bargain with the justice department.

f Mr Nutting said that Eamonn Wadleigh allowed his premises to be used for the IRA team passing on driving licences and letters in false names.

g Neil, 54, and Michael Taylor, 26, both of London, and Norma Boxall, of Croydon, Surrey, had all denied the charge.

h Seven co-defendants also pleaded not guilty at the Old Bailey and their trial continues.

i Soccer star Kevin Dillon was handed a three-year ban yesterday for drink-driving. The former Newcastle United captain was arrested near his home at Houghton le Spring, Tyne and Wear.

j The judge in this case, however, wants to hear from the victims of the spill before he accepts the plea agreement.

Witnesses and their testimony

appear in court
witness   call a witness
grass   grass on someone supergrass
incriminate
give evidence give testimony testify

The prosecution and defence lawyers **call witnesses**. They require people who know about the alleged crime to **give evidence** or **testimony** or to **testify**: to say what they know in court.

If a criminal tells the police or gives evidence in court about their associates' criminal activities, he or she **incriminates** these associates, or, informally, **grasses on** them. Someone who does this is a **grass**, or, if their evidence is very important, a **supergrass**.

Defendants and witnesses **appear in court** during a trial.

Mr Spence did not <u>call</u> any <u>witnesses</u> as he said the prosecution had failed to prove its case.

They have found that something like 150 charges have been laid against members of the Amasinyora gang, but only 16 have reached court despite the fact that there have been many witnesses prepared to <u>testify</u>.

Mr del Cid, who became a prosecution witness after a plea bargain with the United States government, initially gave <u>testimony</u> that appeared very damaging to Mr Noriega.

The defence was refused permission to produce three last-minute witnesses to <u>give evidence</u> in Tyson's favour.

George Creung incriminated six former gang bosses by telling the Old Bailey they were all members of the Soi Fong Triad. The <u>supergrass</u> said he was instructed to commit crimes which included extortion, protection racketeering, criminal damage and violence.

Mr Enrile was due to <u>appear in court</u> today along with two other defendants on charges connected with last month's coup attempt.

13 Types of witness. Someone called to give evidence by defence counsel is a defence witness. Use these words to make similar combinations to describe the witnesses below.

a	surprise	c	eye	e	expert	g	prosecution
b	federal	d	key	f	star	h	crown

A witness...

1 whose testimony is essential

2 whose testimony is based on scientific or specialised knowledge

3 who was not expected

4 who saw the crime himself or herself

5 who is more important than all the other witnesses

6 who gives evidence against the defendant

7 who gives evidence for the prosecution in Britain

8 who gives evidence for the prosecution in the United States.

Reaching a verdict

jury
juror

deliberate

verdict
  deliver a verdict
  reach a verdict
  majority verdict
  unanimous
    verdict

find a defendant
  guilty
find a defendant
  not guilty

hung jury

In some countries many cases are decided by a **jury**, a group of ordinary people (often 12) called **jurors** who listen to the evidence and then **deliberate** together to decide the case and **reach a verdict** and **deliver a verdict** to the court: the defendant is **found guilty** or **not guilty**.

juror 40 ⇑

In courts in some places, the jury's verdict must be **unanimous**: all the jurors must be in agreement.
In other places only a **majority verdict** is required: for example, only 10 jurors out of 12 may need to agree.
A jury that cannot reach a verdict is a **hung jury**.

jury 23 ⇑, *189* ⇓

Harley Schwadron, USA – Wall Street Journal

'The prison cells are full. Therefore I'm sentencing you to six months of jury duty.'

Boxing champion Terry Marsh has been found not guilty of attempting to murder his former manager, Frank Warren. A jury at the Old Bailey in London reached their verdict after nearly five hours of deliberation. When the verdict was delivered, after more than eight hours of deliberation, three of the jurors were in tears.

Miss Allan, 40, stared hard at the floor as the six men and six women delivered their unanimous verdict at the end of the 12-day court hearing.

Hillier, 49, was found guilty of conspiring to cheat the Inland Revenue by a majority verdict of 10-2.

It was the second time in court for Vento, whose first trial ended in a hung jury.

14 **Guilty or not?** Look at these extracts and decide if the missing expression is 'guilty' or 'not guilty'.

ON DRUG USERS BY AAA. Athletes found	. . .	of taking banned drugs won't be competing in
was charged with racketeering and fraud. His	. . .	plea follows a deal with US prosecutors. Our
A 21-year old computer hacker has been found	. . .	of criminally damaging magnetic computer disks.
juries were acquitting people who were as	. . .	as sin on the merest hint that the rules might have
imprisonment. Eduardo Pardo, a pilot, pleaded	. . .	to a charge of transporting nearly $1 million of
are very serious charges. If she were found	. . .	, it's hard to see how she could escape a prison

Acquittal

acquit
acquittal

clear
  clear someone of
    charges

go free
walk free

get off
get off lightly

If the defendant is found not guilty, there is an **acquittal**, and the defendant is **acquitted** or **cleared** of the charges and **walks free** or **goes free**.

Someone who has committed a crime but is not punished is informally said to **get off**. If they are found guilty, but the punishment is not severe, they are said to **get off lightly**.

The mob was angry over the acquittal of six police officers charged in the beating to death of an alleged Puerto Rican drug dealer.

The jury decided that the jury had not proved its case and therefore acquitted Mr Berkowitz of burglary.

A plumber was cleared yesterday of killing his best friend in a body-in-the-lake murder. Simon James, 26, walked free into the arms of his tearful mother after he was cleared of killing drug addict Alan White.

A jury in Fort Lauderdale, Florida, found the performance by 2 Live Crew to have some art in it, so the rap group went free.

North eventually got off thanks to one of his old bosses.

One former National Security Adviser, Robert McFarlane, got off lightly in exchange to pleading guilty to withholding information from Congress.

15 Terms of acquittal. These words have been left out of the BBC report below. Say where they go. Each word is used once. Not all the numbered gaps in the report indicate a missing word.

a acquittal	c allegations	e charges	g not guilty
b acquitted	d charges	f found	h trial

Imelda Marcos acquitted

A court in New York has _____ (1) Mrs Imelda Marcos – the widow of former President Marcos of the Philippines – _____ (2) of fraud and racketeering. The _____ (3) related _____ (4) to _____ (5) that Mrs Marcos stole more than $200 million from the Philippines treasury and _____ (6) used some of it to buy four buildings in New York, as well as jewellery and works of art.

The Saudi arms dealer and businessman, Mr Adnan Khashoggi, was _____ (7) on _____ (8) of helping her by obstructing justice. In Manila, President Aquino expressed disappointment _____ (9) at the _____ (10) of Mrs Marcos, and said the ban on her return to the country would remain in effect. However, she added that _____ (11) at the appropriate time, Mrs Marcos would have to stand _____ (12) in a Philippines court.

Conviction

convict
conviction

Someone found guilty in a court is **convicted** of an offence. As a result, the person then has a **conviction** for that offence.

The jury at the Central Criminal Court then heard that Berkowitz had 244 previous convictions, 230 of them for burglary. The obvious reason is that no witness dares to testify against the terrorists, and no judge dares to convict them.

…Charlie Wilson, a convicted member of the great train robbery gang.

sentence
  prison sentence
  jail sentence
  pass sentence
  serve a sentence
  suspended
    sentence

jail term

community
  service
fine
imprisonment

probation
  give probation
  place on
    probation
  put on probation

The judge then announces the penalty, or **passes sentence**. Depending on the seriousness of the offence, the defendant might be given one of these penalties:

a **fine**: the defendant is ordered to pay money to the authorities;

fine 40 ⇑

probation: the defendant is not sent to prison but must report to the authorities regularly and not break the law again;

imprisoned 71 ⇑

imprisonment: being sent to prison or **jail** to **serve** a **prison** or jail **sentence**;

community service: organised work to help people in the community.

People who are sentenced to probation are **given probation** or **put** or **placed on probation**.

A **suspended sentence** is one which the defendant does not have to serve on condition that they do not commit another crime within a specified period.

Stayskal, USA – Tampa Tribune

" I'M SENTENCING YOU TO 25 YEARS IN PRISON WITH NO HOPE OF PAROLE UNTIL AFTER 3 P.M. TOMORROW AFTERNOON ! "

◆ **LANGUAGE NOTE**

Jail is also spelt **gaol** in British English.

Four of the policemen went to jail, the longest <u>sentence</u> being three and a half years; the fifth defendant was given a <u>suspended</u> jail sentence. In <u>passing sentence</u>, the judge said the killing had been unintentional. The prosecution had demanded <u>jail terms</u> of up to three years.

He was <u>fined</u> £1,000 and <u>put on probation</u> for breaking into a chemist's in search of drugs.

Rose must now report to a halfway house in Cincinnati to serve 1,000 hours of <u>community service</u> at a boys' center and at five inner city schools.

Judge Pickles also attacked the new rule by which anyone given less than four years' jail is automatically released after <u>serving</u> half the <u>sentence</u>.

do time	Someone who serves a prison sentence **does time**: an informal expression. People in prison are **convicts** or **inmates**.
convict	
inmate	
	Prisoners who are released from prison before the end of their sentence are **parolees**: they are **paroled**, or released **on parole**.
parole	
release on parole	
parolee	
	If someone is sentenced to spend the rest of their life in prison, they are sentenced to **life imprisonment**, even if, in practice, they get out of prison before they die.
life	
imprisonment	

◆ **LANGUAGE NOTE**

Convict is stressed on the first syllable when it is a noun and on the second when a verb.

He makes about $2,000 a week, but can't spend the money for fear of arrest, conviction, doing time.

Spanish police have re-captured three convicts who have escaped from Lannemezan prison in south-west Spain.

Armley was built in 1847 and was meant to house 642 inmates.

The government has also proposed tighter controls on parole, following a number of incidents where parolees have committed serious crimes.

In Argentina, the government has proposed that sentences of up to life imprisonment should be imposed on officials convicted of corruption.

16 **Does the sentence fit the crime?** This article from *The Times* discusses typical sentences for three types of crimes in different places. Complete the table with details of crimes 2 and 3, including details of sentencing in places not mentioned in connection with the first crime.

Lawyers uncover big divide in nations' jail terms

Big disparities in sentencing of criminals between different countries, even within Europe, are revealed in a survey to be published at the biennial conference of the International Bar Conference in Cannes later this month. The survey team put a series of hypothetical cases to legal authorities in more than 20 countries and found penalties in Europe varied by more than 10 years for crimes such as rape and by more than 40 years when countries from different continents are compared.

In one question, a 19-year old man had been found guilty of raiding a bank with four other people, masked and armed with a machinegun. He was unemployed, the youngest member of the gang, and the £800,000 had been recovered. The defendant had several convictions for petty theft. Canada suggested a likely sentence of three to five years. Norway two to three years and Denmark six years. Spain said four years, two months and a day, and Ireland five to six years for a not guilty plea. England said ten to 14 years, or five years in a young offenders' institution, and Texas ten years.

In a case of burglary of a stately home, goods worth £90,000 were taken and later recovered from a man with a substantial record of theft. Canada said it would impose a jail sentence of five to seven years, Kenya three years plus hard labour, Denmark one to two years and the Cook Islands probation of three months. Texas suggested ten years' jail and England suggested from three to seven years.

Likely sentences for a domestic assault case, where the husband broke his wife's nose, where there was a long history of disputes and previous charges of assault, ranged from between six and eighteen months in Canada to 30 or 40 days in Denmark, possibly suspended. Six months' imprisonment was likely in Kenya, a fine in Scotland and ten days' jail in Texas. The likely sentence in England is six months, suspended for two years.

Peter Michael Muller, an attorney in Munich and chairman of the association's criminal law committee which conducted the survey said the findings would help practitioners in transnational criminal law and could lead to sentencing reforms.

	Crime no. 1: Bank robbery	Crime no. 2:	Crime no. 3:
Canada	3–5 years		
Denmark	6 years		
England	10–14 years (or 5 years in a young offenders' institution)		
Ireland	5–6 years		
Norway	2–3 years		
Spain	4 years, 2 months, 1 day		
Texas	10 years		

Appeals

appeal
  appeal against a
    conviction
  appeal against a
    sentence

appeal
  dismiss an appeal
  reject an appeal

extenuating
  circumstances

lenient sentence

conviction
  overturn a
    conviction
  quash a
    conviction
  reverse a
    conviction

Someone convicted of an offence may **appeal against** their **conviction** or against their **sentence**. The offender asks another court to look again at the case and to **overturn, reverse** or **quash** the conviction, or to reduce the sentence.

appeal 115 ⇑

The offender may ask for the sentence to be reduced because of **extenuating circumstances** not taken into consideration at the trial: these are circumstances that partly explain or justify why they committed the crime.

In some places the authorities may have the right to appeal against a sentence if they think it is too **lenient** or light.

If the appeal court refuses to change the original conviction or sentence, it **rejects** or **dismisses** the appeal.

◆ **LANGUAGE NOTE**

In the expression appeal against a conviction or a sentence, against
is sometimes omitted in American English.

*When Peltier <u>appealed</u> his conviction, his lawyers discovered that federal prosecutors had changed
their theory about Peltier's role in the murder.*

*I really believed the jury would find Kevin not guilty. I'm very disappointed, and I'm hopeful on
appeal that his conviction will be <u>overturned</u>.*

*Bruce was convicted by a divided court, sank deeper in drugs and depression and was dead before
an appeal court <u>reversed</u> his conviction.*

*Hundreds of motorists in the north-west of England could have their convictions <u>quashed</u> following
a case in the High Court in London.*

*The legal defence of provocation is failing women who kill their partners in reaction to brutality.
Despite <u>extenuating circumstances</u>, they are sentenced to life imprisonment.*

The right to refer <u>lenient sentences</u> to the Court of Appeal was introduced in 1989.

17 **Crime is not a game.** Read this article from *Today*
and answer the questions after it.

TV Raid Copycat

A masked schoolboy held up a Chinese takeaway to copy raiders on
television's Crimewatch UK, a court heard yesterday. 'I just wanted to be
chased like the villains on the telly,' said the 13-year-old.

Nicholas Gareth Jones, prosecuting, said the youngster terrified the
takeaway staff with a fake gun. The boy, of Rumney, South Glamorgan, was
found guilty of attempted robbery by a juvenile court.

Yesterday he appealed against the conviction at Cardiff Crown Court. 'I
told the woman it was just a toy gun,' he said. 'I wouldn't have taken any
money.' But Judge John Rutter increased his sentence from 12 to 24 hours
at an attendance centre.

1 A copycat crime is one where the criminal copies another crime. In this case,
   the boy copied a crime he had seen on Crimewatch UK, a TV programme that
   shows crimes re-enacted by actors and asks witnesses to the real crimes to
   give information about them to the police. 'Villain' is an informal word for
   _____ and 'telly' is an informal word for _____ .

2 Which two words indicate that the gun used in the robbery was not real?

3 From the boy's point of view, what were the extenuating circumstances?

4 Did the judge q _____ the conviction? No, he d _____
   the appeal and increased the sentence, perhaps because he thought the
   original sentence was too l _____ .

Capital punishment

capital
  punishment
death penalty
death sentence
condemn to
  death

execution
execute
put to death

death row

clemency
  show clemency
  grant clemency

commute a death
  sentence

Punishment for certain crimes in some places is the **death sentence**, also known as the **death penalty**, **capital punishment** or **execution**.

Prisoners who have been **condemned to death** and are waiting for the penalty to be carried out are on **death row**. They may appeal to a court or someone in authority to **show** or **grant clemency** and **commute** their sentence: to change it to one of life imprisonment.

If appeals for clemency are rejected, the prisoner is **put to death** or **executed**.

Since 1976, when the Supreme Court declared that <u>capital punishment</u> was not unconstitutional, more than 100 people have been <u>put to death</u>.

Governor Richard Bird of Ohio has <u>commuted</u> the <u>death sentences</u> of eight out of 102 <u>death row</u> inmates.

It's understood the <u>condemned</u> men will appeal to President Ben Ali for <u>clemency</u>.

A Foreign Office statement urged him to <u>show clemency</u> towards 31 other suspects facing a retrial.

The <u>executions</u>, by firing squad, were carried out shortly after the Armed Forces Council had rejected appeals against the <u>death sentences</u>. Those <u>executed</u> included both military personnel and civilians.

18 Debating the death penalty. This report about a vote in the British House of Commons on restoring or reintroducing the death penalty (in Britain traditionally by hanging) comes from the BBC. Answer the questions as you read.

HANGING VOTE

The last judicial hanging in Britain was back in 1964. But every two years or so, supporters of capital punishment make an attempt to persuade the Commons to bring back the death penalty. The latest, on Monday, saw the most emphatic rejection yet of the arguments for bringing back the hangman. The Commons voted by a ratio of two to one that courts should not be able to sentence convicted murderers to death. Such a decisive vote will settle the matter for some years.

1 Which two words in the instruction above the article mean the same as 'bring back' in this context?
2 Is an emphatic rejection a) a strong rejection, or b) a weak rejection? What two-word expression in this paragraph confirms this? What two-word expression in the last paragraph below also refers to the strength or weakness of the rejection?

But inevitably, sooner or later the hanging lobby will make another attempt to amend the law.

3 If the House of Commons amends the law, does it a) change it, or b) confirm it?

For while MPs have turned their backs on the biblical doctrine of 'an eye for an eye and a tooth for a tooth', among the general public there's strong support for the death penalty. This was one of the main arguments used by supporters of the death penalty during the Commons debate. Not only would the return of the rope reflect public opinion, it was argued, it would also act as a deterrent to criminals and cut down on the number of murders.

4 Two expressions have been used since the beginning of the report meaning the reintroduction of hanging. Neither of them use the word 'hanging'. What are the two expressions?
5 If you deter someone from doing something, do you a) encourage them to do it, or b) discourage them from doing it?

The anti-hanging lobby argues on practical grounds – that there's no evidence that the death penalty functions as a deterrent – and on moral grounds, that the state has no right to deprive its citizens of the right to live.

6 Does a deterrent dissuade people from doing something?

The arguments have been well rehearsed over the years. But the most compelling argument, and the one which most contributed to the enormous majority against hanging in Monday's vote, is the possibility of a miscarriage of justice. The 'Guildford Four' – jailed in the mid-seventies for IRA bombings it later transpired they did not commit – might well have been hanged if the death penalty had still been in force.

7 What can be rehearsed, apart from an argument?
8 If an argument is compelling, is it a) a very strong one, or b) a very weak one?
9 If there is a miscarriage of justice, are the people who are punished guilty?

rehearse 187 ⇓

155

Crossword

Across

4 This happens when the accused is found not guilty (9)

5 Spectacular robbery (5)

7 Takes money with menaces in the street (4)

10 This person is not popular with former criminal colleagues (10)

12 A glamorous profession, or a boring one? (3)

13 This might come in the form of witnesses' testimony (8)

14 and 15   Two types of witness (3, 3)

16 Abbreviation for day of the week when this special gun is used? (3)

19 See 11 down

Down

1 'The judge _____ the appeal, ruling that such issues were not the court's business.' (9)

2 Another word for announce in the context of sentence (4)

3 These criminals like working in crowded places (11)

4 American lawyers, not always in court (9)

5 What a burglar does (11)

6 English lawyers found in court (10)

8 If you try to foil a robbery, you have a _____ (2)

9 'The man has told friends there's no question of him _____ fraud charges in New York. He maintains he's done nothing wrong.' (9)

11 and 19 across   Some people criticise this system, where criminals get shorter sentences in return for giving evidence for the prosecution (4, 10)

17 Not so good for the person paying it (4)

18 Abbreviation for District Attorney (2)

⑥ Diplomacy and War

Talks, and talks about talks

talks
hold talks
round of talks
discussions
negotiations
talks about talks
talking shop

When governments or other bodies wish to reach agreements, they **hold** or have **talks, discussions** or **negotiations**. A meeting or a series of related meetings of this kind is a **round of talks**.

Where preparation is needed before the main talks, for example to decide on the meeting place and the participants, they may first hold **talks about talks**.

An official organisation where representatives meet regularly to give speeches and exchange opinions, but which has no real power, is a **talking shop**.

Agriculture ministers of the European Community are to hold a new round of talks on Friday aimed at reaching agreement on proposals to reduce subsidies to farmers.

He said they had held what he termed very interesting discussions on arms control.

Guatemalan guerrillas and leaders of the country's nine largest parties are holding negotiations near Madrid to try to end Guatemala's long-running civil war.

Japanese diplomats described today's meeting as talks about talks. Japan is seeking no more than to agree the date, venue and level for formal talks on opening diplomatic relations with North Korea.

Governments, especially in the West, which used to dismiss the United Nations as a mere talking shop, now see the possibilities for the body to act more as a world policeman.

1 **Talks combinations.** Use the verbs in the box to complete the extracts.

conclude
attend   break off
resume   **talks**   walk out of
convene   suspend

1 A Brazilian delegation flies to Washington today, Wednesday, to _____ talks with the International Monetary Fund which broke down without agreement last week.

2 It wants to cut interest rates as soon as it has successfully _____ talks on cutting the budget deficit.

3 Mr Alatas has made it clear that he would not _____ talks unless he was convinced of the commitment of all the parties concerned.

4 Mr Hameed is to travel to the northern Jaffna peninsula in an attempt to meet the Tigers, who refused to _____ talks arranged on Thursday in the east of the island.

5 The latest attempt at negotiation broke down on Friday after one of the Mohawk factions _____ talks with the Quebec government.

6 Two of the world's largest tire makers, Germany's Continental and Italy's Pirelli, have decided not to merge. The two companies say they have _____ talks after 15 months.

7 Yesterday Nelson Mandela said the ANC would _____ talks with the government about a new constitution if a set of demands were not met by May 9th.

Delegates, opposite numbers and sherpas

delegate
delegation

counterpart
opposite number

sherpa
summit

communiqué
declaration

A government, party or other entity may be represented by one or more **delegates**. A group of delegates representing one side is a **delegation**.

When the representative of A has the same job or rank as the representative of B, they are **counterparts** or **opposite numbers**.

Talks between heads of government or other very important representatives are **summits**, and the officials who prepare for them may be referred to as **sherpas**: see the example below.

The final statement made to journalists and others at the end of talks is a **communiqué** or **declaration**.

The Palestinians will give him a list of proposed delegates for a joint Jordanian-Palestinian delegation to the conference.

At lunch, the Premier toasted his Russian counterpart, telling him, 'You are turning a new page of history by being here.'

A team of veterinary experts are meeting their British opposite numbers at the Ministry of Agriculture's offices today to discuss the French ban on imports of British beef.

As is the way with these international gatherings, the declarations were largely drafted before the delegations arrived. Each country nominates one official who does much of the groundwork – sherpas, they're called, the traditional term for Himalayan mountain guides, who assist their charges to a rather different kind of summit.

The discussions finally collapsed because of disagreement over the wording of the final communiqué.

2 **Dizzy heights of diplomacy.** Read this article from
The Times and answer the questions.

DIPLOMATIC SHERPAS FEEL THE STRAIN IN SURFEIT OF SUMMITS

Despite the bright Finnish sun and invigorating northern air, many of the delegates in Helsinki have a weary look to them. 'This is my third summit in six days,' said one British official, arriving direct from the G7 meeting in Munich and the European Community-Japan summit in London last weekend.

Only a week earlier he and many others had just finished another gruelling round in Lisbon and Douglas Hurd even managed to squeeze in a few hours in Strasbourg, addressing the European parliament before arriving in Helsinki. Today he has two more summits as well: the Western European Union and Nato, which decided that since everyone else was having a summit, it had better have one as well.

The main burden of this extended talk falls on the sherpas, the men who toil up to the peaks of diplomacy, hacking their way through jungles of verbiage and removing political boulders that stand in the way of agreed communiqués. They work in shifts, and larger countries can put different teams onto different events for the summer summitry season. Foreign Office European specialists for Lisbon, Treasury men for G7, security specialists for CSCE. These latter have had three days to organise this two-day ceremonial speechifying.

But no burden falls as heavily as it does on the political directors, the men who have to agree the communiqués line by line. 'I had a pretty good night yesterday,' said one. 'We were finished by 1 am.'

1 If you are weary, do you feel tired?

2 Are gruelling talks tiring?

3 If you squeeze something in between two other things, you don't have much time for it and you f _ _ it in with difficulty.

4 A burden is a l _ _ d .

5 If you toil up a mountain, do you climb it easily?

6 Is verbiage easy to read or listen to?

7 If you hack through something, do you cut through it easily?

8 A boulder is a large r _ _ k .

9 Does 'speechifying' imply that the speeches were useful?

159

Cordial and friendly, or businesslike and frank?

atmosphere
cordial atmosphere
agreement
broad agreement
exchange of views
frank exchange of views
differences
deep differences
narrowing differences
widening differences
stumbling block

The **atmosphere** at talks is often described in communiqués as **cordial**, and in other ways mentioned in the exercise below.

Communiqués may talk of a **frank exchange of views** and **broad agreement** on a number of issues.

Where there is still disagreement, communiqués may talk of **deep differences** that remain. Differences may be described in other ways, again mentioned in the exercise below.

Commentators may talk of differences **narrowing** (getting smaller) or **widening** (getting bigger).

An obstacle to agreement is often described as a **stumbling block**.

hurdle *220* ⇓

They say although the two sides have reached <u>broad agreement</u> on a number of issues, <u>deep differences remain</u> over the timetable for peace and political change.

Mr Davidow said his two days of talks with the Angolan government had taken place in an exceedingly <u>cordial</u> and open <u>atmosphere</u>. There'd been a very <u>frank exchange of views</u> about the peace talks under way between the MPLA government and Unita rebels.

There's been no <u>narrowing</u> of <u>differences</u> on one of the main <u>stumbling blocks</u>, aircraft.

3 **Atmosphere and differences.** Some of the adjectives below relate to the atmosphere at talks and others to differences between sides at talks. Complete them and say which describe 1) the atmosphere and 2) the differences.

a f r _ _ n d l y

b c _ n s t r _ ct _ v _

c s _ g n _ f _ c _ nt

d _ pt _ m _ st _ c

e m _ j _ r

f r _ l _ x _ d

g f _ nd _ m _ nt _ l

h sh _ r p

i b _ s _ n _ ss - l _ k _

j p _ s _ t _ v _

k f r _ nk

l s _ bst _ nt _ _ l

Compromise and deadlock

stance
  tough stance
  aggressive stance
	A negotiating position, particularly one unlikely to change, is a **stance**. A stance is often described as **tough** or **aggressive**.

concession compromise	Negotiators try to reach agreement by making **concessions**, demanding less than they demanded earlier, hoping to get concessions from the other side, thus reaching agreement through **compromise**.
veto use your veto	If one side refuses a proposal during talks, it **vetoes** it, or **uses** its **veto**.
deadlock deadlocked	Where there is disagreement, the two sides are **at loggerheads**, and where there is no prospect of a change in negotiating positions, commentators talk
impasse loggerheads at loggerheads	about **deadlock**, or an **impasse**. Talks in this state are **deadlocked**.

stalemate *224* ⇓

◆ **LANGUAGE NOTE**

The verbs corresponding to the nouns **concession** and **compromise** are **concede** and **compromise**.
The nouns corresponding to the verbs **break down** and **collapse** are **breakdown** and **collapse**.

Yet while some club chairmen are taking a tough stance, others are now more wary of confrontation – worried about the financial implications to the clubs themselves if suddenly there were no games.

She is either so confident of her strength that she feels she can get away with such an aggressive stance, or so committed to her underlying beliefs about Europe that she feels compelled to speak her mind regardless of the consequences.

Prince Sihanouk has put forward a compromise proposal to break the deadlock in peace talks being held by the Supreme National Council in Bangkok.

The conference is still deadlocked over the Americans' refusal to agree to provide extra money.

Whenever the Democrats have compromised, the White House negotiating team have said, 'Thank you very much. Now let's start over and compromise what's left.'

Gamble, USA – The Florida Times – Union

161

Featherstone rejected two offers from Halifax, and refused to <u>concede</u> any significant price <u>concessions</u> to Leeds.

The Latvians are confident that these talks will continue, thus avoiding the 'no concessions, no talks' <u>impasse</u> that exists between Moscow and Vilnius.

America's decision to re-establish a dialogue with Vietnam might in the long run help resolve the issue, but meanwhile ASEAN and the United States remain at <u>loggerheads</u> with no compromise in sight.

One recent EC rule on air pollution would have cost Spain Ptas 300 billion to enforce, according to Spanish officials – if it had not used its <u>veto</u> to win a let-out for its factories to continue burning dirty brown coal. Spain likes those bits of <u>political union</u> that come free.

4 **Compromise or deadlock?** Match the two parts of these extracts.

1 After Lucas described the character to his collaborator, Steven Spielberg,

2 But after five hours of talks, the British government's political initiative for Northern Ireland

3 If Clintonism were ever to exist, it would describe the art of picking a la carte from his favourite policy menus.

4 Officially there has been no change in Taiwan's standing policy of 'three noes':

5 Talks between El Salvador's leftist rebels and government representatives remain

6 The 55-day budget deadlock in New York State has been broken.

7 The Dalai Lama evidently has little hope of

a remained deadlocked. And neither side appears hopeful of a breakthrough.

b compromise with China's current rulers.

c deadlocked over the thorny problem of reforming El Salvador's US-backed military.

d In Arkansas he has compromised so much that even at 45 he is the longest-serving governor in the country.

e no contact, no compromise, and no negotiation.

f The government and state lawmakers reached a tentative agreement last night.

g the two men compromised on 'someone like Harrison Ford'.

Brinkmanship

talks
  falter
  founder
  break down
  collapse
	Where there are obstacles to agreement, and discussions continue with difficulty, they **falter**. When discussions end because of disagreement, talks **break down, founder** or **collapse**.

brinkmanship	When negotiators behave in a way that may cause talks to collapse, but hope to gain advantage if they continue, they may be accused of **brinkmanship**.
scupper talks torpedo talks	If someone is accused of **torpedoing** or **scuppering** talks, they are accused of intentionally causing them to collapse.

collapse *60, 100* ⇑

scupper *28* ⇑

The Jakarta talks, faltering from the outset, would in all likelihood have collapsed had it not been for Washington's announcement on 5 September.

The talks foundered because most ministers were unable to accept a package of compensatory measures for farmers likely to be hit by proposed cuts.

A great number of speakers at the meeting made it clear that it was pointless to go on with this sort of farce. In spite of what appeared to be total breakdown, talks will continue later today.

The American delegation are speaking of imminent collapse; there is a very real danger of the talks breaking down with serious consequences for the world economy.

The Malaysian Minister of International Trade Rafeta Aziz criticized Europe for toying dangerously with the world economy. 'I'm not sure whether some people are playing the brinkmanship game so that they will try to create some crisis situation, and that makes people get stirred up.'

That move has led left-wing legislators to say Shamir does not intend to negotiate but rather torpedo the talks. It has also caused his foreign minister to withdraw from the delegation.

Jacques Delors was last night accused of sabotaging thousands of British jobs for the sake of personal ambition. He was accused of scuppering crucial trade talks to avert a world trade war by EC negotiator Ray MacSharry.

5 **Key to destruction.** The same key word from this section is missing from all these extracts. Which is it?

battle. The paper says that a game of political	. . .	has begun at Westminster with the political
up to twelve times this limit. In a show of	. . .	, the government says that Mr Collor will veto any
a German negotiator. Behind the emotion is	. . .	. By asking for a lot, Mr Kohl and Mr Delors hope
And there is, it seems to me, a cynical game of	. . .	being played here, possibly by both sides
the realisation that the time for manoeuvre and	. . .	is now running out. Moreover, in his ruthless
it can play one of Yugoslavia's oldest games -	. . .	and bluff – as well as any of the country's
next year, would like to end the farcical	. . .	of the budget-setting process in the state

Breakthroughs, deals, accords and agreements

breakthrough	Sudden progress in talks is a **breakthrough**. Breakthroughs are often described as major, important, significant or dramatic and may lead to a successful **outcome** of the talks.
outcome	

agreement
  reach agreement
  reach an
    agreement
  strike an
    agreement
	When talks are successful, the sides **reach agreement** or **reach** or **strike an agreement**. An agreement may also be referred to as an **accord** or a **deal**.

accord **deal**	Before it comes into effect, an agreement may have to be approved or **ratified** by an elected body such as a parliament, which may refuse **ratification** by vetoing the agreement.
ratify	

accord *65* ⇑

The vital <u>breakthrough</u> *in GATT talks eventually came with concessions on both sides.*

The high-volume propaganda exhange between the United States and the European Community has not only made a successful <u>outcome</u> *to the talks much more difficult to achieve, but has also soured relations generally.*

Vietnam and Britain have <u>reached agreement</u> *on the return of at least 300 Vietnamese boat people to their communist homeland.*

Dresdner Bank and Banque Nationale de Paris have just <u>struck</u> *an* <u>agreement</u> *to collaborate in international markets.*

That's how he came to meet Lenin in 1921 and broke a trade impasse. Hammer <u>struck</u> *a* <u>deal</u> *in which Soviet furs were exchanged for American wheat.*

He still carries weight in White House, especially on Middle East questions, where he supervised the Camp David <u>accord</u> between Israel and Egypt.

In a follow-up to the Earth summit, the declaration called on other nations to join the G7 partners in <u>ratifying</u> the climate change convention.

6 **Trade talks scenario.** Read this article from *Today* and answer the questions.

WE GATT A DEAL

The world pulled back from the brink of an economic war last night as Europe and the US finally reached a deal in the crucial Gatt talks. ... Officials from the two sides reached agreement at the 11th hour after six years of haggling over Gatt: the General Agreement on Tariffs and Trade. The Americans had threatened to impose savage sanctions against EC goods, including a 200 per cent import duty on French wine.

They were due to come into force on December 5. But the deal was sealed by transatlantic telephone after President George Bush gave the US team the go-ahead. ... After two final days of talks in America, EC Agriculture Commissioner Ray MacSharry in Brussels and US Agriculture Secretary Edward Madigan in Washington spoke the historic words: 'That's a deal.'

The EC's Frans Andriessen said: 'When we left Washington, we did not have a deal. Now we do.'

In Downing Street, a jubilant John Major hailed the accord as 'the single most important trade deal the world has seen.'

1 What's the play on words in the title?

2 If you pull back from the brink of something, does it become less likely?

3 Is an eleventh-hour agreement necessarily decided at 11 pm?

4 If you haggle over something, you <u>n e g _ _ _ _ _ _</u> intensely over it.

5 Are savage sanctions punitive?

6 Does 'the deal was sealed' mean that it was a) rejected, or b) agreed?

7 MacSharry is Madigan's European <u>c o u n _ _ _ _ _ _ _</u>.

8 If you hail something, do you welcome it?

A trade battle would have been catastrophic, he said. Mr Major was mainly responsible for getting negotiations re-started after a breakdown that followed an outburst from EC Commission President Jacques Delors. Mr Delors was accused of trying to scupper the talks because the US was demanding cuts in farming subsidies. Last night France was still opposing the deal, which means less cash for its farmers.

'The conditions defined by the French government are not fulfilled,' said agriculture minister Jean-Pierre Soisson. 'At first sight of this accord, I cannot accept it.' But he refused to be drawn on whether his government would veto the deal which will cut subsidised EC farm exports by 21 per cent. ...

A French farmers' union said it was a 'knife in the back' and called for immediate nationwide protests. ... A small group of farmers burned hay and tyres outside government offices in Calais as a foretaste of likely action. ...

9   If you make an outburst, you suddenly react emotionally, usually angrily, to something. This outburst might have scuppered the talks: it might have caused the talks to b _ _ _ k d _ _ _ .

10 If you refuse to be drawn on something, are you willing to talk about it?

11 The French government might veto the deal: it might not r _ _ _ _ _ it.

12 If you get a foretaste of something, do you get an idea of what it will be like?

Strained relations

relations
  establish relations
  break off relations
  restore relations
  normalise
    relations

sour relations

strained relations
tense relations
frosty relations

thaw

Two countries beginning diplomatic **relations** **establish** them. If they had diplomatic relations previously but **broke** them **off**, they **restore** them, **normalising relations** between them.

Bad relations are often described as **strained**, **tense** or **frosty**. Relations are said to be **soured** by something that negatively affects them.

When bad relations between countries improve, commentators talk about a **thaw** between the countries.

diplomatically isolated
sanctions
trade sanctions
embargo
economic embargo

A country having diplomatic relations with very few other countries is **diplomatically isolated**.

When one country wants to put pressure on another, it may limit trade with that country and impose **sanctions**, or it may stop trade and other contacts and impose an **economic embargo**.

◆ **LANGUAGE NOTE**

Thaw is a noun and a verb.

Denmark and Iceland have become the first countries to establish diplomatic relations with the three Baltic republics.

After Indonesia's invasion of East Timor, Portugal broke off diplomatic relations with Indonesia.

Britain's trade with Iran cannot be wholly unrelated to the two countries' history of strained relations. Though diplomatic relations were restored last year, ambassadors have not been exchanged yet.

The trip is being seen as an important step in normalising relations between the two countries. Our correspondent says that the visit undoubtedly marks a thaw in Harare's previously frosty attitude to South Africa.

Japan – fearful of putting further strain on its already tense relations with the United States – has continued to support the economic embargo against Vietnam, albeit unwillingly.

By extending central rule, the government risks souring relations with the Sikhs.

Some Europeans think that, if Serbia were morally and diplomatically isolated, it would think twice about fighting on.

The United States is considering imposing trade sanctions against Thailand, unless Thailand lifts a ban on foreign cigarette imports and advertising.

7 **Diplomatic relations.** Which of the verbs below mean the same as 1) 'break off' and 2) 'restore' in the context of diplomatic relations? Use appropriate forms of the verbs to complete the extracts below.

a	resume	c	re-open	e	break
b	renew	d	cut off	f	re-establish

1   Senegal and Mauritania have agreed in principle to _ _ _ _ _ _ diplomatic relations, broken off two years ago after bloody clashes along the Senegal river which forms their common frontier.

2   The Moscow talks were the first between senior diplomats of the two countries since the Soviet Union _ _ _   _ _ _ diplomatic relations with Israel in 1967.

3   Mexico and the Vatican _ _ _ _ _ diplomatic relations in 1867, when the reformist President Juarez confiscated all church properties and suppressed the religious orders.

4   The visit is taking place just over three months after Argentina and Britain agreed to _ _ _ _ _ diplomatic relations eight years after the two countries broke all links during the Falklands War.

5   In recent years, Albania has _ _ - _ _ _ _ _ _ _ _ _ _ diplomatic relations with most European countries.

6   Table tennis teams were visiting China before Nixon _ _ - _ _ _ _ _ _ diplomatic relations between Communist China and the United States.

War and threats of war

escalating tension	If the differences between two sides increase, there is **escalating tension** between them. A **standoff** is a period of extreme tension that may or may not lead to violence. If two sides are very close to war, they are (**teetering**) **on the brink of war**.

war
  avert a war
  teeter on the
  brink of war	

standoff	If a war is prevented, perhaps by talks, it is **averted**. If not, **hostilities begin** or **break out**. *avert 123* ⇑

hostilities
  hostilities begin
  hostilities break
  out
	A **hot spot** is a place where tension is high and fighting may break out at any moment.

hot spot	

The American ambassador in Delhi has confirmed that his country is urging India and Pakistan to hold talks to try to <u>avert</u> the threat of <u>war</u> over Kashmir.

North Korea often accuses the South of <u>escalating tension</u> to the brink of war by staging joint military manoeuvres known as 'Team Spirit' with the United States.

In 1961, just after the building of the Berlin Wall, this was the scene of a tense <u>standoff</u> between Soviet and American tanks: the world <u>teetered on the brink of war</u>.

Mr Urqhart emphasised the need for a preventive UN force to be dispatched to <u>hot spots</u> before <u>hostilities break out</u>.

'The only acceptable outcome, if, in fact, <u>hostilities begin</u>, is absolute, total victory.'

8 **Types of war.** Find the following types of war in the table.
Then use the expressions to complete the extracts.

A war...

1 that isolated clashes might degenerate into

2 between East and West that lasted from 1945 to 1989

3 where nuclear arms are used

4 where nuclear arms are not used

5 between factions of the same nationality

6 causing an enormous number of deaths and amount of damage

7 fought by irregular forces, perhaps avoiding direct confrontation with the other side.

		civil		
	guerrilla		Cold	
full-scale		**war**		conventional
	nuclear		devastating	

a The Cold War is over. The world is learning to live without the imminent threat of
_____ war that had conditioned our lives for 40 years.

b A grim reminder of the _____ War – the border crossing point between
East and West Berlin known as Checkpoint Charlie – is to go the way of the rest
of the Berlin Wall and be dismantled.

c As the _____ war in Liberia enters its tenth month, thousands of people
continue to stream across the borders into neighbouring countries.

d Because of the intensity of the fighting – what analysts call 'low-intensity
_____ war' – neither side appears strong enough to defeat the other.

e The President himself said he is against withdrawing all Nato nuclear weapons
from Europe and thus making it safe for _____ war.

f The question is whether anything else but a neutral outside force would be strong
enough to persuade them to leave the scene before the current clashes degenerate
into _____ war.

g The two men stressed the importance of averting the catastrophe of a
_____ war and the need to achieve a common Arab stand.

Warring parties

belligerent
combatant
warring party
wage war

Before or during a war, one side may accuse the other of **belligerent** statements, remarks or actions: things that make war more likely, or prolong or intensify a war that has already started.

Belligerents, **combatants** or **warring parties** are countries or factions participating in a war, or **waging war** against each other. Combatants are also people physically doing the fighting.

wage war *199* ⇓

Troops had been mentally prepared for hostilities. Pakistan believes that India's frustration at its inability to control the situation in Kashmir is leading to increasingly <u>belligerent</u> statements from its politicians, alerting the military on both sides.

The foreign ministers of the four main <u>belligerents</u> of World War Two in Europe have signed in Moscow a treaty endorsing German unity.

It is simply a demilitarized zone – 4 km wide – separating two <u>combatants</u> who have not yet reached formal agreement that the Korean War of the early 1950's is formally over.

His remarks came only a few days before the <u>warring parties</u> to the conflict are due to gather in the Indonesian capital, Jakarta, for another round of peace talks.

President Milosevic called on them to be ready to fight to defend themselves, but he added: 'Before we are forced to <u>wage war</u> we will do everything to preserve peace.'

9 **Adversaries and allies.** Look at the extracts and complete the key words below.

The new government will have to bring Lebanon's <u>warring factions</u> together and end the country's 15-year civil war.

There have been renewed clashes in El Salvador between government forces and left-wing <u>rebels</u> of the Farabundo Marti National Liberation Front.

This seems to be the time of uniting: two Germanies are about to merge and two former <u>foes</u> – Iran and Iraq – have become <u>allies</u>.

The Foreign Secretary, Mr Douglas Hurd, has been stressing the importance of Britain's friendship and <u>alliance</u> with Germany and France.

When John F. Kennedy came to Berlin in June of 1963, he paid a tribute that seemed to turn at least West Germans from being occupied <u>adversaries</u> into allies.

During the second world war Burmese and Indonesian nationalists <u>allied themselves</u> with the Japanese, finding them a useful lever against the colonial power.

None has improved on Palmerston's dictum that Britain has no permanent friends or <u>enemies</u>, only permanent interests.

warring faction	The different sides in a civil war are
	_ _ _ _ _ _ _ _ _ _ _ _ _ _ . Factions opposing a
rebels	central government are _ _ _ _ _ _ .
	Countries or factions with the same interests _ _ _ _
ally	themselves with each other and are _ _ _ _ _ _
alliance	forming an _ _ _ _ _ _ _ _ . Opposing sides are
	_ _ _ _ _ _ , _ _ _ _ _ _ _ _ _ _ or _ _ _ _ .
enemy	
adversary	
foe	

◆ **LANGUAGE NOTE**

Ally is pronounced with the stress on the first syllable when a noun and with the stress on the second syllable when a verb.

Fighting

fighting	When **fighting** starts it **breaks out** or **erupts**. If
break out	fighting **flares** or **flares up**, it starts, or starts again
erupt	after a **lull**, a period when it has stopped or been less
flare	intense.
flare up	
	Fighting may be **sporadic**, perhaps taking the form
sporadic fighting	of brief, unplanned encounters or **skirmishes** with
heavy fighting	only small numbers involved. Or it may be **heavy**,
	with large numbers of troops and other forces
lull in fighting	involved.
skirmish	

In Georgia, fierce fighting broke out today between rebel national guardsmen and troops loyal to President Zviad Gamsakhurdia.

But for all the noise, the air base received only minor damage. In comparison to the permanent heavy fighting in the countryside, the attack was more of a skirmish.

People are taking advantage of a lull in the fighting to get out of the immediate war zone.

The most bitter fighting erupted here in eastern Croatia when federal tanks and airforce jets attacked the town of Vukovar.

While fighting has flared in the breakaway north of Yugoslavia, some of Serbia's leading politicians have begun to reassess their views on the future unity of the federation.

Both Libya and Sudan have denied any involvement in the Chadian fighting, which flared up again last month after a period of relative quiet.

10 Types of fighting. The letters of six adjectives describing fighting have been mixed up. Sort them out and use them to complete the extracts below. Every letter from the box is used, including the first letters given for each missing word. (Some of the words occur in the above examples.)

o	p	e	s	a	e	d	i	e	i	i	h	e
r	y	d	e	c	i	a	t	n	b	n	n	e
s	e	v	w	r	t	c	r	e	t	f	r	e

1   Lebanese army units have taken over General Aoun's long-time headquarters in the Presidential Palace in Ba'abda. Only s _ _ _ _ _ _ fighting continues and it looks as if all support for the General has collapsed.

2   Some of the most b _ _ _ _ _ fighting has been against rebels of the Eritrean People's Liberation front.

3   Bougainville, scene of some of the f _ _ _ _ _ s t fighting in the second world war, is a largely untouched museum of wrecked warplanes.

4   They fear an increase in the number of people fleeing h _ _ _ _ fighting in the Thai / Burma border area.

5   Journalists have not been allowed to go near the battle area, but it's clear that i _ _ _ _ _ _ fighting has been going on in the mountains north of Kabul.

6   There are reports from Angola of r _ _ _ _ _ _ fighting between government troops and Unita rebels, this time in the northern province of Uige.

Casualties

casualties
losses
heavy casualties
heavy losses
inflict casualties
inflict losses
civilian casualties
wounded
friendly fire
collateral damage

Casualties are people killed and hurt, or **wounded**, especially those severely wounded. They may include **civilian casualties**, those not in the military.
Military casualties may be referred to as **losses**. Where there are many casualties or losses, they are described as **heavy**.

Casualties and losses are **inflicted** by one side on the other.

Military casualties killed or wounded by members of their own side are victims of **friendly fire**.

Unintended civilian casualties and damage to non-military targets may be referred to by the military, euphemistically, as **collateral damage**.

Rwandan casualties were 14 dead and 30 wounded.

You don't have to be much of a cynic to take military claims that they're being careful of civilian casualties skeptically.

Tigrean rebels say they inflicted heavy losses on government troops in fighting in northern Shewa region last week.

The United States Defense Department says an investigation has shown that about one in every four Americans killed in battle during the Gulf War died as a result of so-called 'friendly fire' – that is, killed by their own side.

Those of us who have been through it know that you're talking about human lives that are cut short. We don't think of words like 'collateral damage' or 'numbers'. We think of friends.

11 **Language damage.** Read this extract of an interview from National Public Radio® between Bob Edwards, the program host, and William Lutz, a language specialist, talking about what he considers to be abuse of the English language by military personnel, and answer the questions.

THE FIRST CASUALTY

Bob Edwards: Now perhaps more than ever before it could be said that the first casualty of war is language. William Lutz plays close attention to the language that comes from the Pentagon. During the war in the Gulf, he's heard plenty of intriguing idioms – collateral damage, for instance.

William Lutz: That's an official term that's been around for some years now and is even in the official Pentagon dictionary.

BE: So collateral damage is...

WL: Civilian casualties caused by incontinent ordnance.

BE: Incontinent ordnance?

WL: Yes, those are bombs, artillery shells, bullets, etc that strike inadvertently civilian targets. Military language is the language of bureaucracy and technology ratcheted up a few levels. For example, we don't attack targets, we visit them and revisit them.

BE: And once we're there, we acquire them.

WL: Oh, yes, and then we acquire the target and deliver the assets, which, by the way, are carried there by weapons systems. We don't fly planes any more, we fly weapons systems. We don't bomb the anti-aircraft missile sites or the anti-aircraft guns. This is a suppression of assets.

1 If something is intriguing, does it arouse people's curiosity?

2 Is it normally possible for objects to be incontinent?

3 If something happens inadvertently, does it happen on purpose?

4 If you ratchet something up, do you intensify it?

5 In normal language, planes attack and d e s _ _ _ _ _ enemy targets.

6 What sort of things are a company's assets? assets *100* ⇑

7 Suppress is another euphemism for d e s _ _ _ _ _ .

BE: I suppose if you're spending many millions per copy of these planes, you want to get a weapons system, not just a plane.

WL: Systems is a very popular term within the military. Everything is a system. You can't move without a system. But weapons are not only weapons systems, they are firepower assets. You see, assets is great. It's a wonderful economic term to apply. These are our assets, and we use our assets effectively. And it sounds less horrible, of course, than it is.

8   What is 'it'?

Victims of war

escalate	If a war intensifies, it **escalates**.	escalate *121* ⇑, *204* ⇓
war-torn	A country devastated by war is, in media terms, **war-torn**.	
atrocities ethnic cleansing genocide	One side may accuse the other of **atrocities**: for example forcing civilians to leave an area for reasons of ethnic origin: **ethnic cleansing**. Or they may accuse them of the mass killing of civilians for racial or political reasons: **genocide**.	
evacuee refugee	People fleeing war-zones are **refugees** or **evacuees**, and the help provided to them by organisations is **relief** or **relief aid**. Organisations such as the Red Cross are **relief organisations**.	

relief
  relief aid
  relief organisation		

Bosnian sources estimate that 50,000 people have so far been killed or are missing. <u>Atrocities</u>: rape, torture and murder, are unquestionably being carried out on a large scale.

'<u>Ethnic cleansing</u>', in which people are forced from their homes at gunpoint, has not stopped.

The Khmer Rouge objected to Vietnam's insistence on including the word '<u>genocide</u>' in reference to the Khmer Rouge's three years in power during which some two million Cambodians died.

… a flood of <u>refugees</u> from Somalia's <u>escalating</u> civil war.

The agreement calls for the return home of the <u>evacuees</u> who fled the fighting.

Refugee organisations say the majority of those arriving in Britain and the rest of Europe are fleeing from genuine persecution and misery in their <u>war-torn</u> countries. They want more resources to care for the refugees.

Britain yesterday pledged a further £18 million in food and <u>relief aid</u> to war-torn Somalia.

Monsieur Kouchner is a co-founder of the French <u>relief organisation</u> Médecins sans Frontières and accustomed to high-profile missions to trouble spots.

12 **Protecting relief organisations.** Rearrange these extracts from the BBC into a complete report. (The report begins with extract a.)

RED CROSS EMBLEM TO GO ELECTRONIC

a The International Committee of the Red Cross has been told that its famous symbol, painted on field hospitals and ambulances since the Austro-Prussian war in 1866, is in need of urgent updating.

b Modern weapons can fire automatically and with a range and velocity that mean it's virtually impossible to identify hospitals or aircraft flying casualties. Tests on the visibility of the Red Cross, using thermal imaging revealed that the signs are invisible at night despite being made from a special kind of paint.

c Other tests using flashing lights on medical aircraft showed that visibility was reduced by distance and bad weather. The only solution, the Red Cross experts concluded, is to fix radar transponders to hospitals and medical aircraft, and to fit underwater acoustic equipment to hospital ships.

d Technical experts commissioned by the Red Cross concluded that with modern missiles capable of destroying targets without seeing them, the painted Red Cross and red crescent must now have an electronic counterpart.

e The famous symbol will of course remain. But in future years, a symbol is all it might be. And the real protection for the war wounded accorded by the Geneva conventions will be secured by a stream of electronic pulses.

f The Red Cross emblem is distinctive enough, and with few exceptions, principally in Afghanistan and Lebanon, it's honoured by the warring factions. But with the increasing mechanisation of weapons, and the widespread use of electronic identification, a painted symbol is now hopelessly out of date.

Ending the bloodshed

bloodshed
end the bloodshed
war-weary
peace-keeping force
peace-keepers
ceasefire
truce
hold
break

During wars, there are calls to **end the bloodshed**, or violence. Military and civilians tired of a war are **war-weary**.

Outside governments may try to end a civil war by sending a **peace-keeping force**, or **peace-keepers**, who try to stop the fighting, or prevent it from starting again.

If the sides say they will stop fighting, at least temporarily, they agree to a **ceasefire** or a **truce**. If a ceasefire or truce continues as agreed, it **holds**. If not, it is **broken**, usually with one side accusing the other of having broken it.

◆ **LANGUAGE NOTE**

Peace-keeping, peace-keeper and cease-fire are also spelt as one or two words.

Everyone accepts the need for negotiations, to break the deadlock and try to end the bloodshed. In this, one of the world's worst examples of intercommunal violence, more than 3,000 people, Protestants and Catholics, have been killed.

People are very increasingly war-weary and disgusted and angry, but it is very hard for them to give expression to this in sectors where there is very strong intimidation and fear.

Over the past few weeks the peace-keeping force has been doing a good enough job that people feel safe to go back out on the streets and so there are markets everywhere.

Yesterday the Security Council passed a resolution warning all warring parties that they must abide by the latest cease-fire before peace-keepers can be sent.

The Phnom Penh government and its three guerrilla rivals unexpectedly agreed to a ceasefire. The truce held.

There were reports of fresh outbreaks of fighting in Rwanda, with the government accusing rebels of breaking the ceasefire agreement.

13 Keeping the peace. Read this article from *The Economist*, written just after the beginning of the war in ex-Yugoslavia, and answer the questions.

THE LIMITS TO INTERVENTION

In divided Europe, America and Russia would never have let a war like Yugoslavia's start, let alone rage this far. Now that the cold war is over, it is up to the Europeans themselves to do what they can to stop the fighting their fellows have been foolish enough to start.

They have four means at their disposal: talk, sanctions, peacekeeping and armed intervention. With Yugoslavia, the last is foolhardy and none of the others is foolproof.

Talk has so far got nowhere. So long as the Serbs and Croats showed a minimum of good faith, the Europeans did what they can to keep them at the bargaining table. After months of fruitless negotiation and countless broken ceasefires, European patience has worn thin.

The EC, having imposed economic sanctions, is now asking the United Nations to add oil to its embargo on arms sales to Yugoslavia. Sanctions alone are unlikely to end the killing. Neither Serbia's nor Croatia's leaders seem unduly troubled by the economic wreckage the war is causing.

There have been proposals for a UN or EC peacekeeping force. Especially in Europe, which has forgotten what bitter civil wars are like, peacekeeping can have a reassuring, almost magical sound. But there is no point in sending peacekeepers where there is no peace to keep. Without a durable truce, peacekeepers, even armed ones, are simply targets.

1 Foolish behaviour is
u n _ _ _ _ _ _ _ a b l e.

2 Foolhardy means f o o l _ _ _ _ _ .

3 If something is foolproof, is it certain to work?

4 If your patience wears thin, are you willing to wait much longer?

5 Economic wreckage is economic
d e s t _ _ _ _ _ _ _ .

6 Do durable things last?

7 Are targets shot at?

The peace process

arbitrator
arbitrate

mediator
mediate

reconciliation

envoy

shuttle diplomacy

peace conference
peace process
peace settlement
peace talks

convention

A dispute may be resolved more easily with the help of someone not directly involved in it.

A **mediator** or **arbitrator** is someone from a third party who helps opposing parties settle their differences and reach an agreement by **mediating** or **arbitrating** in the dispute. This process is **reconciliation**.

arbitrator *123* ⇑
mediator *123* ⇑

An **envoy** is a representative sent by one of the parties, or a mediator sent by a third party, who travels specially in order to take part in negotiations.

Shuttle diplomacy involves a mediator visiting and re-visiting a number of places in a short period to mediate between the parties involved.

Where negotiations are in many stages, and progress is at times very slow, commentators talk about the **peace process**.

settlement *109, 123* ⇑

Discussions between parties trying to reach a **peace settlement** are referred to as **peace talks** or a **peace conference**.

A conference involving many parties may be referred to as a **convention**, and so may the agreement reached at such a conference.

convention *37* ⇑

Bill DeOre, USA – The Dallas Morning News

India says Kashmir is an internal Indian problem which doesn't require <u>mediation</u> by anyone else.

They have chosen their words with great care to describe America's role in the Middle East peacemaking effort. Not 'arbitrator', which would mean dictating an outcome; not 'mediator', which would imply it could suggest a solution.

The four pillars of her government, she said, would be national <u>reconciliation</u>, economic regeneration, social justice and the consolidation of democracy. But the first task, she said, was to end the war.

Mr Primakov, who arrived in Bagdad on Saturday from Cairo, was to leave today for Riyadh on the next leg of his exercise in <u>shuttle diplomacy</u>.

The United Nations Secretary General's personal <u>envoy</u>, Mr Alvaro de Soto, will <u>mediate</u> between the two sides in an attempt to settle El Salvador's ten-year conflict.

He had asked Switzerland to help organise a <u>peace conference</u> to negotiate a <u>settlement</u> to the Afghan conflict.

The African state of Liberia says it will not continue <u>peace talks</u>, describing them as a waste of time.

Mr Boucher says that the absence of a <u>peace process</u> contributes to the spiralling violence in the region.

The agreement is scheduled to be formally signed at a peace <u>convention</u> on September 14th once remaining differences have been resolved.

A draft resolution also proposes a meeting of parties to the Fourth Geneva <u>Convention</u> on protecting civilians in time of war.

Pancho, France – Cartoonists & Writers Syndicate

14 **Peace partners.** Find the following expressions in the table and use them to complete the extracts.

1   efforts to reach peace (two expressions)

2   someone who tries to mediate a peace agreement

3   economic benefit of having reached a peace agreement

4   popular protest against a war

5   peace agreement

6   recognition of peace efforts

	broker	
movement		treaty
move	**peace**	dividend
	prize	initiatives

a   A spokesman for the Nobel committee said Suu Kyi, 47, is one of the foremost examples of civilian courage in Asia. Today's news found the peace _____ winner in exactly the same place she has been for the past two years: under house arrest in Burma's capital, Rangoon.

b   Afghan guerrilla groups based in Pakistan and Iran have rejected the president's latest peace _____. They want nothing short of his removal from power.

c   Camp David in 1978 was the high point of Mr Carter's presidency. He badgered and cajoled Menachem Begin of Israel and Anwar Sadat of Egypt into a peace _____. Twelve years on, he feels he has unfinished business in the region. Now he's a freelance peace _____.

d   German doubts about the fighter plane project make its whole future uncertain. In many countries now there's talk of a 'peace _____' – money to be saved on defence being diverted to other uses.

e   The battle zone, which borders Iraq and Turkey, is populated mostly by Moslem Armenians and is claimed by Armenia. Previous peace _____ have failed and ceasefire declarations have been ignored as each side accuses the other of genocide, massacres and atrocities.

f   Word of the demonstration has been spreading for weeks, and the result could be one of the largest anti-war rallies since Vietnam. While the peace _____ mobilized, those who support military action are also taking their message to the streets.

Crossword

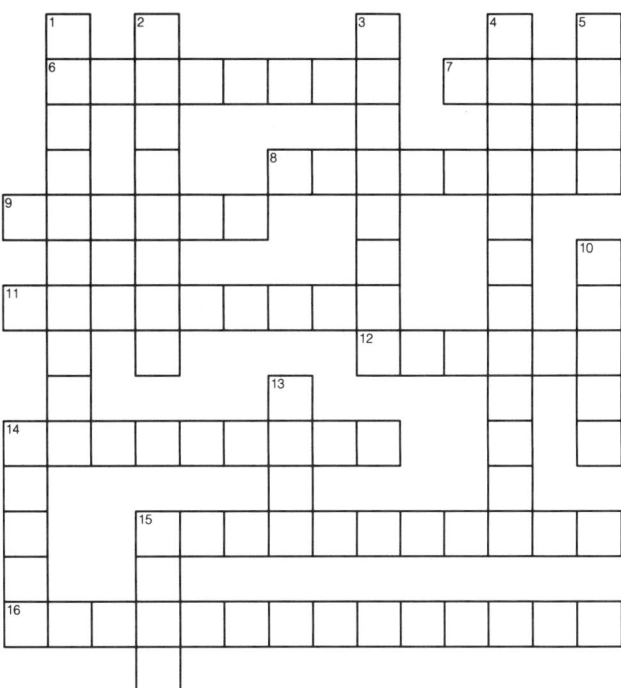

Across

6 Counterpart across the negotiating table with the same number? (8)

7 Good agreement for headline writers? (4)

8 Victim of war or disaster (8)

9 See 1 down

11 Shuttle diplomacy is one form of this (9)

12 Nepalese negotiator? (6)

14 What peace talks try to end (9)

15 What to make to break the deadlock? (11)

16 Countries with few friends are _____ isolated (14)

Down

1 and 9 across   Unintended destruction (10, 6)

2 What off and on fighting is (8)

3 These can lead to war if they escalate (8)

4 War participants (12)

5 One of 4 down on the same side (4)

10 Tired of war (5)

13 Talking place you can't buy things at (4)

14 Agreement: general, but it may not be enough (5)

15 The one that followed WW2 was low temperature (4)

Entertainment

entertainment
pure
  entertainment
sheer
  entertainment
mere
  entertainment
	Entertainment is plays, films, television programmes, music and so on that people watch and <u>listen to for pleasure.</u>

entertainment 8 ⇑

The word is sometimes used to emphasise the <u>enjoyment aspects</u> rather than the <u>thought-provoking aspects</u> of these things, as in the second, third and fourth examples below. In this sense, entertainment is often <u>preceded by</u> **pure** or **sheer** <u>when viewed positively</u> and **mere** <u>when viewed negatively.</u>

Walt Disney believed an <u>informal friendly organisation</u> produces the finest in family <u>entertainment.</u>

Molière was never like this at school. This is <u>pure entertainment</u>. <u>Take it for what it is</u>, and enjoy.

– What is fiction good for, if anything? – Well, we could certainly say entertainment with that big 'E', as broad as possible. P G Wodehouse is <u>sheer entertainment</u> – not so much <u>to ponder on</u> there. Well, there's a little more than people would <u>admit</u>, but in general <u>it's pretty sheer.</u>

The <u>dinosaur exhibition</u> is a great deal more than <u>mere entertainment</u>. <u>The idea is to involve the audience</u>, and, by asking questions, <u>provoke thought.</u>

1 Entertaining combinations. Complete the extracts below with the words listed.

a	sheer	c	light	e	mass
b	mere	d	in-flight	f	popular

1 Maybe the karaoke machine will help to bring unused vocal chords back to life and reverse the passivity of so much modern _____ entertainment.

2 The BBC plans to restore its pre-eminence in drama and re-establish itself as the principle innovator and pioneer in comedy and _____ entertainment.

3 The fact is they're both highly rated shows and Emmy award winners and are taken seriously and thought of as quality shows and more than just _____ entertainment.

4 The middle classes saw what they were missing and built theatres such as the Alhambra to make _____ entertainment respectable and expensive.

5 Virgin Atlantic is more concerned with using technology to improve _____ entertainment. Last year, Virgin became the first airline with individual colour seatback screens for every passenger on its wide-bodied aircraft.

6 Was that the golden age of musicals? Some people feel it's actually from '27 through the thirties and up to Oklahoma and that era. I thought it was a kind of golden age because it was almost all _____ entertainment. And lovely actresses, marvelous dancers, Fred Astaire, Adel Astaire. Marvelous comedians, and the Gershwins of course.

Low-brow to high-brow

| high-brow |
| middle-brow |
| low-brow |

Popular entertainment is sometimes referred to as **low-brow** or **middle-brow**, in contrast to things with more intellectual or thought-provoking ambitions, which are **highbrow**. People interested in these things may be called **highbrows**, though they would probably not describe themselves in this way. All these terms are sometimes used showing disapproval.

◆ **LANGUAGE NOTE**

Highbrow can also be spelt with a hyphen or as two words, especially when an adjective.
Low-brow and **middle-brow** can also be spelt as one or two words.

During the ITV/BBC period, everybody was a public service broadcaster, regulated to provide programming across the range of public tastes from minority to mass, highbrow to lowbrow.

At the highbrow end of the market, mini-series of three or four weeks' duration are now the norm. Longer runs are reserved for such middlebrow fare as Poirot, Sherlock Holmes and Jeeves and Wooster, which provide a different storyline each week.

Chevigny feels that jazz was a victim of the city elite's attitude to 'vernacular' music. 'The people who ran this city didn't conceive of art and entertainment as a group of people coming together in a neighbourhood, maybe for little money. And they're snobs besides, of a very lower-middlebrow sort. If it's not Beethoven, well it's not art.'

2 **Which brow?** Look at these extracts and say whether the missing word in each is

a high-brow   b middle-brow   c low-brow

1 *Coriolanus* is drawing a new audience to Chichester. Not so middle-class, middle-aged and _____ .

2 At a dinner for popular song writers, he was invited to contribute a poem on *The Popular Song*: 'Born just to live for a short space of time, Often without any reason or rhyme, Hated by _____ s who call it a crime, Loved by the masses who buy it...'

3 ...modern theatre, whose audience has seemed increasingly drawn from people in search of a Good Night Out rather than _____ stimulation.

4 While his number of fans in America has grown into a loyal army since *London Fields*, which sold more than 30,000 copies in America and made the *New York Times* best-seller list, his following remains essentially _____ rather than mass-market. Put another way, most people in Hollywood haven't heard of him.

5 He's a popular journalist – so he's not a _____ journalist. He's the equivalent of a small-town gossip columnist.

6 The answer is that poetry is not necessarily a _____ art, nor is it necessarily a middle-brow art.

7 Nobody knows how many people tune into Nuntii Latini, but the station receives between 10 and 50 letters a week, most of them written in Latin, from listeners around the world. The head of Radio Finland, Juhani Niinisto, says the fans tend to be _____ intellectuals and academics.

Entertainers, artists, impresarios and show business

entertainer artiste artist star show show business showbiz impresario	Singers, dancers, comedians and so on are **entertainers**, **artistes** or **artists**. The most popular entertainers are **stars**. Entertainer can be used to refer to someone without thought-provoking ambitions, as in the second and third examples below. Likewise, a **show** is popular entertainment that people watch for pleasure rather than intellectual stimulation. **Show business** refers to entertainers and directors and the **impresarios** who arrange their contracts and promote their productions. Show business is referred to informally as **showbiz**.

show 3 ⇑

◆ **LANGUAGE NOTE**

Show business is also spelt with a hyphen.

I think Elvis gave us so much more than any other <u>entertainer</u> could have.

Louis Armstrong always regarded himself simply as an <u>entertainer</u>. He believed that the so-called 'progressive' generations of jazz musicians were struggling too hard to be original.

And if they say, 'You're just an <u>entertainer</u>, aren't you?' I say, 'Now wait a minute, there are a lot of serious moral concerns here.'

…three hours of open-air entertainment featuring opera <u>stars</u>, more fireworks and flamenco dancing.

Cabaret <u>artiste</u> Monsieur Karah Khavak emerges with one of his 17 crocodiles wrapped in a blanket tucked under his arm.

…dozens of <u>artists</u> representing jazz, blues, country and folk as well as rock and soul.

At London's Savoy Hotel tomorrow, <u>impresario</u> Sir Peter Saunders will host a great <u>show business</u> gathering of 700 guests to celebrate the 40th birthday of 'The Mousetrap'.

The deal I've signed is in telephone numbers but the money isn't important to me. I just want to be up there with the biggest names in <u>showbiz</u>.

3 **Missing item.** The same seven-letter key word from this section is missing from all these extracts. What is it?

teeth, including one in platinum. As with many	...	biographies, you occasionally wonder if
And backing the week are dozens of	...	celebrities, including Paul and Linda McCartney
died later in Charing Cross Hospital.	...	colleagues last night paid tribute to Frankie
Latsis gave the Tories a £2 million boost.	...	and sport stars also do their party piece
whose main interests were booze, girls and	...	gossip, he saw himself as a political leader.
lacquered hair. Even in New York, even in	...	, do people really say, 'Power is the big hit, right?'
what was once thought to be the perfect	...	marriage. Cazenove, 46, has moved out of the

The arts

the arts
performing arts
visual arts

artist

The arts is often used when discussing government policy towards cultural matters.

The **performing arts** include stage presentations such as plays, ballet and opera. The **visual arts** include painting and sculpture.

Artist in this context refers to someone performing or doing creative work in the arts.

There are several hundred theatres in Britain whose survival hangs on funding from the Arts Council, regional arts associations or local authorities. Most are now in difficulties.

There is no justification for government support of the arts at all because what this amounts to is taking away money from all taxpayers, including those who never set foot in a museum or theatre, to help pay for the leisure activities of the privileged classes.

Psychologist Dr Glen Wilson, author of 'The Psychology of Performing Arts' believes an evening of song and dance can actually change people for the better. 'Musicals give a direct emotional lift,' he says.

We already have a European common currency and it's music, dance, theatre, the visual arts, not the Common Agricultural Policy or pesticide control orders.

...Jack Vettriano, a one-time mineworker, who had been earning a living as a graphic artist in Edinburgh and having a go at oil-painting in his spare time.

4 A government of philistines? Read this extract from *the Independent* about arts funding in Britain and answer the questions.

Playing to the gallery: not addressing the issue

The British government's attitude to the arts is in many ways lamentable. Public expenditure on the arts is woefully inadequate compared with our European neighbours (£9.80 per person per annum in Britain against £27.80 in Sweden, £24 in Germany, £21.40 in France and £20.50 in the Netherlands). The arts minister is not in the Cabinet; great national projects such as the Royal Opera House development and the National Gallery extension have to rely totally on private money: museums can barely afford to maintain their buildings; and the government rarely expresses pride in the arts as a central part of Britain's achievements.

Yet, despite such legitimate causes for complaint, the arts lobby will achieve nothing by accusing the government of Philistinism. It would do much better to produce a concrete and realistic manifesto for adequte arts funding

1 An actor who plays to the gallery uses the most extreme dramatic effects. Read the whole extract and say if this term is used showing approval.

2 If something is lamentable, is it a good thing?

3 If something is woefully inadequate, is it a) slightly inadequate or b) extremely inadequate?

4 If you can barely afford to do something, you can h _ _ _ _ y afford to do it

5 Is a legitimate cause justifiable?

6 Do philistines like and understand the arts?

manifesto 33 ⇑

'It's an interesting play, Will, but I'm afraid Senator Helms might consider it immoral trash.'

Gerberg, USA – Cartoonists & Writers Syndicate

Performance and performers

perform
performer
performance
cast
role
rehearse
rehearsal
dress rehearsal

Performers such as singers, musicians and actors **rehearse** or practise together before they **perform** in a **performance**. In the theatre, the final **rehearsal** is the **dress rehearsal**.

rehearse 155 ⇑

The **cast** is all the performers in a production. If someone is cast in a **role** or part, they play that role.

cast 66 ⇑

At 50 years of age, this extraordinary performer retains the power to enthrall audiences with her raw, seemingly inexhaustible energy.

The 'Daily Express' says Pavarotti defied the rain to give the performance of his life. 'The Times' says that for someone who likes to rehearse his arias in the shower, conditions were just about perfect.

Franco's censors would turn up at the rehearsal and follow the whole thing word for word, checking whether those controversial words, had, in fact, been removed.

'Tanzabend II' has more dance 'proper' in it than some of Bausch's previous pieces. Many of the cast perform solos. There is a rehearsal theme which shows us dancers exhaustively repeating their sequences.

'The Public Eye' will cast him in a more dramatic role as a New York tabloid crime photographer.

stage fright
backstage
wings

Stage fright is the nervousness that some performers feel before performances, perhaps when they are **backstage**: the area behind the stage containing dressing rooms and so on, or in the **wings**, the area just to each side of the stage where actors wait to come on to it.

- Do you find many artists coming down with stage fright? - Yes, I've known many artists that have become frightened and nervous. They're shaking.

Not for Cole Porter that last-minute panic backstage, scribbling last minute changes on the backs of chorus girls.

5 **Partners in performance.** Complete these words used to describe the quality of performances. The first seven show approval and the rest disapproval.

1 v _ r t u _ s _

2 d a z z _ _ n g

3 e _ e c t r _ f y _ n g

4 s t _ n n _ n g

5 s c _ n t _ _ _ a t _ n g

6 r _ v e t _ n g

7 d e _ _ g h t f u _

8 _ f f - f _ _ r m

9 m e d _ _ c r e

10 _ a c k _ u s t r e

Premieres, debuts and revivals

preview
  sneak preview

first night
opening night
premiere

debut

revival

The first performances of a play or opera or showings of a film are often **previews**. **Sneak preview** suggests that the audience does not really have the right to see the play, film or whatever before its official opening, but the term is used even when there is no suggestion that the audience is not really allowed to see the preview.

The first 'official' performance, or the first performance in a particular place, is the **first night**, **opening night** or **premiere**. A **debut** is normally a performer's first public performance, again perhaps in a particular place, but a show's first performance may also be referred to as its debut.

A play or opera, or an opera production, may be new, or it may be a **revival**.

◆ **LANGUAGE NOTE**

Premiere and debut are also spelt **première** and **début**, specially in British English.
The nouns **premiere** and **debut** are also verbs, specially in American English.

Gory scenes are being cut from a new Dracula movie because they left an audience feeling sick and faint. Several filmgoers were ill after a <u>sneak preview</u> of Bram Stoker's Dracula.   gory 14 ⇑

Laurence Olivier said on his <u>opening night</u> as Richard III he had a spider, not butterflies, in his stomach.

When the hugely successful musical 'Les Misérables' opened in Manchester, the <u>first night</u> was brought to a halt in mid-performance when a massive section of the scenery, electrically operated, would not move into place.

The original crew <u>premiered</u> the play in London. For the New York premiere, Caryl Churchill devised a kind of mini-version.

Channel Four's new early morning show 'The Big Breakfast' came under fire from critics and advertising agencies after its <u>debut</u> yesterday.

The <u>revival</u> of Frederick Ashton's 1968 'Jazz Calendar' is neatly timed given the current recycling of Sixties fashions.

6 **Dangerous debuts.** Read this extract of an interview from National Public Radio.® At what points do a) the interviewer, and b) the interviewee, start speaking? Not all the numbers indicate a change of speaker.

AVOIDING THE BUTCHER OF BROADWAY

(1) Let me ask you a couple of theater questions to wind up with if I can. (2) Yeah. (3) You've written this new play, *The Ride down Mount Morgan* and it's an American play. Why is it debuting in London?

(4) Well, to put it in a nutshell, it becomes very difficult to cast a play in New York now if the actors required are mature people. (5) You can get a lot of very young actors quite easily, and we have some marvelous ones – people, well, even into their high 30s. But if you want people who look like they're into their mid-40s and, God forbid, 50, they don't exist.

(6) Either they went into the movies and have vanished or they're waiting for a pilot and they don't want to engage four, six months or a year. And the other problem is that you've got a jury of effectively one person judging your work which is totally undemocratic. (7) This is Frank Rich, the *New York Times* theater critic. (8) Yeah, whoever it is.

(9) In London you've got about – I don't know what, nine, ten, eleven newspapers. There are two more this last couple of years that have been established. (10) What's *The Ride Down Mount Morgan* about? (11) Oh, it's about men and women and this mad relationship we have with one another. (12) But I'm not going to tell you any more than that because it will spill the beans.

jury 23, 146 ⇑

Sell-outs and empty houses

sell out
sell-out

packed house
  play to packed
    houses
  play to empty
    houses

run

A show may be a **sell-out**, with tickets **sold out** for weeks or months ahead, **playing to full** or **packed houses**, with a long **run** of performances, or it may **play to empty houses** and close after a short run.

◆ **LANGUAGE NOTE**

The noun **sell-out** is also spelt as two words.

In concert, their light show is so elaborate and expensive that they lost £20,000 on a sell-out UK tour last year.

This line-up of stars has meant that Wembley stadium's 72,000 tickets sold out within 24 hours.

When the producer Duncan Weldon put on Shaw's 'Heartbreak House' last March, it played to full houses and the run had to be extended.

'Jump for Joy' played to packed houses for 12 weeks, but with the United States on the verge of entering World War 2, the army drafted many of the young actors.

- Mozart's music has a soothing effect in times of crisis and war. But of course many people who planned to come to Vienna and who had to fly there in times when you don't like to take the plane, there's a big number of cancellations. - So are you playing to empty houses? - No, the tickets are immediately bought by tourists from Germany, Switzerland and France.

7 **That's showbusiness.** Complete the extracts with the expressions below. Each item is used once.

a   run   c   cast   e   entertainer   g   shows
b   full houses d   opening night f   performances   h   sell-out

1   Cher's first New York concert was called off yesterday when she developed bronchitis. The _____ of her _____ of three _____ at the city's Paramount Theatre was postponed until tomorrow.

2   The commercialism of theatre on Broadway had reached such depths, he said, that it was dependent not only on tried and tested material but on appearances by television and pop stars. A David Mamet play that had attracted _____ while Madonna was in the _____ closed as soon as she left.

3   *The One* could, according to industry estimates, make £7 million for the 45-year old _____ next year. Last weekend, more than 200,000 people paid £22.50 each to watch Elton John and Eric Clapton on stage at Wembley. Then Elton was off to _____ _____ in Birmingham and continental Europe.

Audience reaction

clapping

applause
  tumultuous
    applause
  rapturous
    applause
  thunderous
    applause

ovation
  standing ovation

encore

cheer

heckle
heckler

boo

Audiences traditionally show their appreciation at the end of a performance (and sometimes during it) by **clapping**. Clapping is also referred to as **applause**, which if loud may be described as **tumultuous**, **rapturous** or **thunderous**. In a **standing ovation**, an audience stands up to applaud, perhaps shouting its appreciation, or **cheering**, at the same time.

An audience wanting to hear more at the end of a performance demands an **encore**.

Members of an audience who disapprove of a production or performance may shout out their criticisms, or **heckle**. People who do this are **hecklers**.

heckle *33* ⇑
heckler *33* ⇑

Disapproval is also shown by **booing**, and similar noises.

(Rhythmic clapping, curiously, indicates disapproval in some cultures, such as English-speaking ones, and approval in others.)

There is clapping when one of the characters, a teacher, beats up a government agent, and loud applause, too, when another actor says woefully: 'I love my country, but it does not give a damn about me.'

He came offstage bouncing, ebullient to thunderous applause announcing that, 'Man, this time I really hit it.'

The full-capacity London audience, no doubt overwhelmed by Liepa's artistry and fine physical presence, gave it rapturous applause.

And then in the third act, there is a jailer who is drunk. I came on – 6,000 people, tumultuous applause – I came on with a bottle in my hand and I was, you know, like a drunken jailer, and my first line was [belches].

The concert was a sell-out; and when the work was completed, the audience demanded a series of encores and then gave the orchestra a 15-minute standing ovation.

The first night of Messiaen's Saint François d'Assise in the Felsenreitschule on Monday was the perfect Skandal: bags of booing, bags of cheers, and in the end the cheers had it.

The Irish singer, who was booed at a weekend tribute to Bob Dylan, said the hecklers were 'brainwashed'.

8 Audience displeasure. Two articles from *The Times* about booing audiences have been mixed up. Put together the two articles by rearranging the sections. Each article contains three sections.

HOT UNDER THE COLLAR /
DUCHESS OF YORK AT DUTCH NATIONAL BALLET

a A royal gala with an empty royal box and not even a note of the national anthem? It happened at the Coliseum on Tuesday night when the Duchess of York turned up spectacularly late for the Dutch National Ballet's production of Romeo and Juliet.

b The fans allege that the hotel deliberately delayed the concert to maximise its drinks sales before it began. The hotel vigorously denies this.

c When the singer, Julio Iglesias, finally appeared on stage at 9.30 pm, his first song was drowned out by the fans' jeers and boos. No explanation was given for the delay and, according to the American National Law Journal, 2,000 of the disappointed fans are suing Iglesias and the owners of the Hyatt Grand Champion Hotel for the refund of their money.

d 'But it was still a royal gala,' insists a spokesman. 'She was in the audience.' Some of the time.

e It does not pay to be late in America, especially when the people waiting for you have paid $100 (£60) for the pleasure of hearing you sing. It is a big mistake when those fans are Californians and are kept waiting in the sweltering desert heat for over two hours.

f The house management proposed awaiting her arrival, but a storm of hissing and booing persuaded them to start without the royal guest. Eventually the Duchess slipped into a box at the back of the house and the theatre tactfully decided not to risk the ire of its audience further by playing the national anthem at either the interval or the performance's end.

sue 24, 110 ⇑

Critical reaction

critic critical acclaim	A **critic** is a writer or broadcaster who gives their opinion of a production, performance, record or book in a **review**, or, more formally, a **notice**.
hit	If critics like something a lot, it attracts, draws, earns, gathers, gets, receives or wins **rave reviews** and

review
  bad reviews
  mixed reviews
  rave reviews
	critical acclaim. **Hit** is an informal word for a success.

notice	If some critics like something and others don't, it gets **mixed reviews**, even if this expression is often used when the reviews are mainly, or even only, bad.

| savaged by the critics | Something that gets very **bad reviews** is **panned** or **savaged** by the critics. |
| panned by the critics | |

◆ **LANGUAGE NOTE**

Review is a noun and a verb.

...the critic Frank Rich, known in theater circles as the 'butcher of Broadway'. While the New York Times does have other <u>critics</u>, Rich has earned a reputation as a man who can close a show with a bad <u>review</u>.

When Ibsen's 'Rosmersholm' opened in February, the <u>notices</u> were almost as bad as those 'Ghosts' was to receive in March. 'Impossible people do wild things for no apparent reason,' said The Observer.

Jazz critic Neal Tesser has <u>reviewed</u> the Either orchestra for the 'Chicago Reader'.

And as well as attracting <u>rave reviews</u> from the critics, it's even got psychologists talking about it.

...Gibson, 35, who won <u>critical acclaim</u> for his portrayal of Hamlet in Franco Zeffirelli's film.

Antonia played Agammemnon's scheming wife to <u>mixed reviews</u> – with one critic likening her to a lost member of the Addams family.

'I don't put shows on or take them off just because of a couple of <u>bad reviews</u>.'

American TV films 'Women of Windsor' and 'A Royal Romance' were <u>panned</u> for scenes like the one in which Princess Diana attacks the Queen verbally, forcing Prince Charles to beg: 'Oh please don't speak to mummy like that. She was only trying to help.'

Tatum O'Neal's attempt to relaunch her career ended in disaster because of a dead dog. Her new play in New York closed when one of the main actors pulled out after his pet died. The show, 'Terrible Beauty', had already been <u>savaged</u> by the critics.

9 **Good and bad reviews.** Look at these extracts and say whether each of the words in the box is favourable or unfavourable in the context of reviews.

	ecstatic	
unflattering		rapturous
	review	
stinking		scathing

1 Louie Jordan's music is all set for a major comeback. Ecstatic reviews have already pushed the ticket sales as far ahead as the summer months.

2 *The Golden Gate* met with rapturous reviews in America, Britain and elsewhere and attracted improbable numbers of readers.

193

3   I played *Love Is,* the new album from Kim Wilde, and marvelled at the nothingness of it all. Then I played it again, still shaking my head and planning my most scathing review. Then I played it again and realised with shame that I was forgetting to be critical and actually enjoying the damn thing.

4   There are those among my fellow critics who think I am showing severe emotional disturbance for having thoroughly enjoyed *Batman Returns.* This movie has garnered some truly stinking reviews.

5   Lowri Turner of the London *Evening Standard* was banned by Lacroix and Versace for writing unflattering reviews.

The Great White Way

Broadway
  Off-Broadway
  Off-off-Broadway
Great White Way
West End

mainstream

fringe

Broadway is New York's main theatre district, even if all its theatres are not actually on the street of that name. Broadway is used to refer to **mainstream** productions: commercial, non-experimental ones, increasingly of musicals. Broadway is also referred to, sometimes affectionately and sometimes derisively, as the **Great White Way**.

Likewise, the **West End** is used to refer to a style of production usually found in the West End of London, even if some West End theatres are geographically elsewhere.

More experimental, unusual work is referred to as **Off-Broadway** in New York. Something even more experimental may be referred to as **off-off-Broadway**, or as the **fringe** elsewhere. (The term fringe originated at the Edinburgh festival in Scotland to indicate productions that were not part of the main programme.)

◆ **LANGUAGE NOTE**

Off-Broadway and Off-Off-Broadway are also written off-Broadway and off-off-Broadway.

Mackintosh currently has eight shows playing in more than a dozen languages in 44 countries. Five of his productions are running on Broadway and in the West End simultaneously.

In Britain, it is impossible to make any money except in the commercial theatre. It's a shame London doesn't have an off-Broadway circuit, where you could play a 200–300 seat theatre for eight weeks. Here you leave it at four weeks on the fringe – or you plunge into the West End.

'The Mystery of Irma Vep' is the master-work of Charles Ludlam and was first produced off-off Broadway by his own ridiculous theater Company. In his day the enfant terrible of New York theatre, Ludlam died in 1987, and 'Irma' has been inching closer to the Great White Way ever since.

Impresarios are not blind to the importance of the fringe as an experimental laboratory of mainstream theatre.

10 **The Great White Way.** Read this article from *The Economist* and answer the questions.

BROADWAY PLAYS SAFE

Musical comedies have fascinated New York ever since the supposed inception 100 years ago of 'Broadway', the theatres on and around the Great White Way. But the theatre district's heyday in the Roaring Twenties, when it staged nearly 50 new musicals in a season, is a distant memory.

Far fewer shows open now. They cost a lot more to stage. Too many are revivals or old hits as producers seek to reduce the risk of backers suffering crippling losses.

As a result, interest centres around the finances of the musical theatre rather than the stars and the writer-composer teams. *Variety*, a show-business weekly, used to be the only source of financial information on the incoming, on-going and out-going musicals.

Today the money troubles of shows are reported in the tabloids, and readers of a gossipy weekly column in the *New York Times* can learn, for instance, that a prize-winning Gershwin pastiche *Crazy for You*, took 725 performances to repay its investors their $8.3 million; that *Miss Saigon* got back its $10 million in less than half that time; and that *The Will*

1 Something's inception is its
b e g _ _ _ _ _ _ .

2 Is something's or someone's heyday a period when they boom?

3 Do a show's backers finance it? cripple *119* ⇑

4 An outgoing show has reached the end of its _ _ _ .

tabloid *18, 42* ⇑
gossip column *21* ⇑

5 Is a pastiche a kind of
a) parody, b) fruit, or c) dessert?

Rogers Follies did not recoup its original cost during its long Broadway run.

Such daunting statistics strike fear into the hearts of producers and investors alike. Courageous impresarios still exist, even on a Broadway strewn with lavish theatre marquees announcing that shows have closed (or which never arrived) and shuttered glass doors that display ticket refund information.

But this season, more money seems to be being invested in revivals or in imports of proven material than in new, original shows.

6 If you recoup the cost of something, do you get back the money you invested?

7 If something is daunting, does it inspire hope and confidence?

8 Courageous means b _ _ _ _ .

9 A marquee in this context is a kind of tent put up in front of a theatre to advertise a show and to sell tickets. If Broadway is 'strewn' with marquees, are there a lot of them?

10 If material is proven, has it been tried and tested?

Tinseltown locations

Hollywood
Tinseltown

studio
  major studios
  majors
  studio system

film
movie
(motion) picture

shoot
  shoot a film

set
studio's lot

location
  on location

The American film industry is known, of course, as **Hollywood**. Hollywood is referred to, sometimes derisively, as **Tinseltown**. Important film-making companies are the **major studios**, or **majors**.

Studio system is often used when talking about Hollywood's heyday before the advent of television, or, more recently, the time before most studios became part of large media and electronics groups.

Films are also referred to as **movies**, especially in American English, and as **pictures** or **motion pictures**, especially by people working in the American film industry.

Films are shot on **sets** on a **studio's lot**: its premises, or **on location**: in authentic surroundings.

◆ **LANGUAGE NOTE**

Shoot is a noun and a verb.

Films are now America's second-largest export-earner, after defence, and demand to be taken seriously. Despite its catchpenny title, 'Naked <u>Hollywood</u>' does just that. It packs more home truths about <u>Tinseltown</u> into a comparatively short span than most books twice its length.

196   *The second group of 'minor <u>majors</u>' includes MGM and Orion, which do not own <u>lots</u>.*

That 'Casablanca' hangs together so well is not so much due to considered thought but rather to the smooth professionalism of studio-system Hollywood 50 years ago, where expert skills fused to turn out films with production line efficiency.

Badham is an accomplished director of routine action pictures. As the film moves from one method of transport and one chase to another, Hawn is required to do little more than squeal.

Danziger, USA – LA Times Syndicate

There couldn't have been a worse time to go into the motion picture business than the late 1950s.

Jean Vigo died poetically of tuberculosis after shooting 'L'Atalante' in a hoary Parisian winter.

'A rock is a rock, a tree is a tree: shoot it in Griffith Park.' – Anon.

There is no such animal as an easy film shoot – several nervous breakdowns are de rigueur.

Michael Powell had this remarkable ability to both shoot on location and in the studio.

This beautiful woman, who could enact the most passionate love affairs on the screen was cold and distant off the film set.

11 Hollywood clichés. Make combinations from the table that mean these things relating to Hollywood:

1 someone or something, usually from Hollywood's past, that everyone knows about and talks about

2 failures or 'victims' of Hollywood

3 an attractive male actor

4 publicity not justified by reality

5 films such as *Casablanca, Gone with the Wind* and *High-Noon*

6 superficial glamour

7 the system viewed critically as a place where fantasy is 'produced'

	heart-throb		
casualties		legend	
hype	**Hollywood**		dream factory
glitz		classics	

hype 2 ⇑

Megastars and starlets

megastar
starlet
lead
leading actor
leading actress
leading part
leading role
supporting actor
supporting role
bit-part
extra
cameo role

Stars range from **megastars** and earning enormous amounts of money, to **starlets**: young, ambitious, as yet relatively unknown actresses who are expected to become stars. (Curiously, there is no equivalent word for ambitious male actors, although starlet sometimes refers to young footballers.)

The most important actors in a play or film are the **leading actors**, **actresses** or **leads** playing the **leading parts**, **leading roles** or **leads**.

Other important parts are played by **supporting actors** in **supporting roles**. Very small roles are known as **bit-parts**. People in large crowds are played by **extras**.

A well-known, usually older, actor or actress who plays a small part in a film or play has a **cameo role**.

What is a genius? What is a living legend? What is a megastar? Michael Jackson — that's all.

There will no doubt be more tearful departures, disappointed starlets and furious script sessions.

Sir Alec Guinness, 78, wrote asking if he could play the lead, but instead may have a cameo role as the butler's father.

In 1929 he achieved his first leading role when he played the title part in the New York production of Chekov's 'Uncle Vanya'.

Despite its modern sound, the use of the word star to describe a leading actor can be traced to the early 1700's.

Several of Hollywood's leading actresses, including Demi Moore and 'Pretty Woman' star Julia Roberts are said to be interested in the role.

'Batman' which many feel was stolen by Jack Nicholson in the supporting role of the greatest villain of them all, The Joker.

Columbia dropped Marilyn Monroe and she drifted into bit-parts at other studios.

Hundreds donned their early 1960s gear in the hope of being cast as extras in the film.

12 **Excess in Tinseltown.** Two reports, one from National Public Radio® and the other from *The Times*, have been mixed up. Put together the two reports, complete the missing words and answer the questions. Each report is made up of three sections.

'YOU'LL NEVER EAT LUNCH IN THIS TOWN AGAIN' / TUSSLE IN TINSELTOWN

a *You'll Never Eat Lunch in This Town Again* is brutally frank about Phillips' Hollywood life among the studio m _ _ _ _ _.

b All Hollywood is asking the same questions: are they serious? Who will win?

c 'He cares only about money and his own comfort. He is the epitome of how far the American ideal has come after 200 years in development.' That is one of the milder passages in her book.

d The outcome will affect more than the sumptuous bank accounts of Ovitz and a few stars. The whole c _ _ _ of Tinseltown: the millionaire s _ r _ t - w _ _ _ _ _ s, the Ferrari-driving soap s _ r _, even the wardrobe ladies fear a chill wind.

e The essential m _ _ _ _ owns whatever town he's in, and his name is on everything he owns. He cheats on his taxes, his wife and his partner. Most of all he cheats on the audience.

f The chiefs of Walt Disney Studios, Paramount Pictures and 20th Century Fox are trying to wage war on all that Ovitz has come to represent: high salaries for stars, directors and p _ - d _ _ _ r _ in an era of bloated movie budgets.

1 If someone is brutally frank, do they really say what they think? *mogul 3, 91* ⇑

2 Who is 'who'?

3 Who is 'he'?

4 The epitome of something is the best example of it. If this is one of the milder passages, are other parts of the book even more brutally frank?

5 Which of these things is most often described as sumptuous? a) meals, b) bank accounts, c) people *soap 9* ⇑

6 Do the people mentioned literally fear bad weather?

wage war 170 ⇑

7 If a budget is bloated is it too small?

Blockbusters, turkeys and sleepers

blockbuster
sleeper
turkey
box office
  success
  smash
  hit
  failure
  disaster

flop
bomb

take
gross receipts
gross

A profitable film or play is a **box office success**, **smash** or **hit**. A very successful and profitable film, play or book is a **blockbuster**.

Unsuccessful films are **box office failures** or **box office disasters**. Films like this **flop** or **bomb** and are known as **turkeys**.

A **sleeper** is a film, relatively unknown when it comes out, that does unexpectedly well.

Money taken at the box office is known as the **take**, **receipts** or **gross receipts**. A film is often judged by how much it makes or **grosses** at the box office.

◆ **LANGUAGE NOTE**

  Flop is also a noun.

Dick Locher, USA – Chicago Tribune

It says much for Hollywood values these days that a film can gross $54 million at the American box office in just eight weeks and still be regarded as a turkey.

Whatever the critics say, it is you the cinema-going public who decide whether a film is a blockbuster or a turkey.

This summer had a lot of films that opened strong, then bombed. In just over a year Korda had produced and directed a gigantic box-office success, 'The Private Life of Henry VIII', which was the first British film to conquer the US.

Clint Eastwood has risen like Lazarus from the cinematic dead. After a string of ignominious box-office failures he seemed to be drifting into that limbo of television re-runs and occasional anniversary tributes reserved for those great names that Hollywood supposedly reveres but considers no longer bankable.

The career of this most unpredictable of film directors has been dogged by failure and controversy. A big ambitious project like 'The Cotton Club' was a box-office disaster.

It's another hero, Preston Sturges, whom he is happy to quote with regard to his own directorial career: 'Between my flops, I've had a few hits.'

The American sleeper success 'Ghost' opens tomorrow.

The form really came into its own in 1974 when 'The Exorcist' became the top grossing film of all time. It was so successful that, for the first time in history, horror films accounted for more than 10 per cent of the total American box office take.

13 **Box office partners.** Complete the extracts with words from the list. (Look at all the extracts before completing the gaps. Each word is used once only.)

a power   c receipts   e success
b failure   d records   f disasters

1 After a promising debut in *Desperately Seeking Susan*, she has bombed in a string of box office _____ including *Who's that Girl* and *Shanghai Surprise*.

2 Hollywood studios have yet to experience their first black-directed box office _____ , which will test their willingness to entrust big budgets to black directors.

3 There is still an elite of untouchables who can charge what they like. Top of this list is Arnold Scwarzenegger who is trusted to bring in $100 million in box office _____ with his action movies.

4 The gunfight itself, six minutes long, took 44 hours to film. A substantial box-office _____ , *Gunfight at OK Corral* changed Hollywood's perception of the Western's potential.

5 Peter O'Toole, for example, could fill a theatre by reading his gas bill. The theatre needs such actors because they combine the highest artistic standards with box office _____ .

6 Child star Macaulay Culkin smashed all box office _____ when his film *Home Alone II* took £25 million in its first five days.

Films buffs and cult movies

film buff	A film **buff** is someone who likes films a lot and knows a lot about them.
cult movie cult film	A **cult movie** or **cult film** is one that perhaps not many people know about but that has a devoted band of followers who watch and discuss it repeatedly.

art movie
art film
art house
  art house movie
  art house film
	An **art film**, **art movie**, **art house film** or **art house movie** is one with artistic ambitions, and may be shown in the type of cinema known as an **art house**. These 'art' terms are mainly used by the media, and sometimes show disapproval.

◆ **LANGUAGE NOTE**

    Art house is also spelt with a hyphen.

The novel was filmed as 'Night of the Eagle' in 1962 featuring Peter Wyngarde as a college professor. It was not much regarded at the time, but has since become a cult movie.

There was an implied disdain for film buffs and art movies in Shone's piece: I would remind him that 'La Dolce Vita' was one of the highest-grossing popular films made in Italy at the time, and is still the highest-grossing foreign language film ever released in the US.

'I hope it's an art film in the way that 'Vertigo' is an art film,' he says. 'I'm not afraid of the word 'art'.

You wouldn't see the amounts of money spent on these films lavished on an art movie.

Interscope has specialised in medium-budget commercial movies, avoiding both art house movies and huge blockbusters.

The book teeters on the verge of the overtly pretentious in its art-house movie atmosphere.

14 Film terms. Look at the extracts and match the terms to their definitions.

Despite the noisy gunfire, slick camera work and rock'n'roll sound track, this is in fact little more than the sort of standard shoot-em-up Western that Hollywood appeared to have stopped churning out 30 years ago.

Mr Lynch has produced a 135-minute prequel which shows us all the strange goings-on which led to the murder.

Dickie 'you look fabulous darling' Attenborough has at last given birth to his extensive biopic of Charlie Chaplin with good reports on Robert Downey Jr in the title role.

For Paramount, McCrea played Cooper's old role in a remake of 'The Virginian' (1946), and he concentrated on Westerns thereafter.

It is a pleasure to report that for once the sequel is as good as the original.

'The Kentucky Cycle' is a collection of nine one-act plays, tracing the history of three families over 200 years. The six-and-a-half-hour epic will be presented in two parts and features 20 actors playing 72 different roles.

		a	film on a grand scale with a big budget and a biblical or historical theme
1	shoot-em-up	b	another version of a story told in a film made earlier
2	prequel		
3	biopic	c	film describing events leading up to ones in a film made earlier
4	remake		
5	sequel	d	violent Western
6	epic	e	film recounting someone's life
		f	film describing events following on from one made earlier

Moguls, auteurs and others

mogul	Powerful decision-makers in Hollywood, specially studio bosses, are referred to as **moguls**.	mogul *3, 91* ⇑

| director |
| producer |
| auteur |
| |
| scriptwriter |
| screenplay |
| scenario |

Producers normally control film budgets and personnel, including the **director**, the person who actually makes the film, and the **scriptwriter**, the person who writes the script or **screenplay**: dialogue based on a **scenario**, an outline of the story.

A director with 'artistic' ambitions is an **auteur**.

In the case of the great Hollywood moguls like Zanuck and Thalberg, a grasp of the purse-strings was inseparable from a grip on the audience.

Some actresses try to set up companies to develop roles for themselves because the roles they get offered are terrible. The problem is that actors and actresses may have the power to control a production before they're ever qualified to be producers or directors. By and large, actors do not have the right emotional disposition to judge what is right for them.

'2001's' co-writer and director Stanley Kubrick became terrified that real space exploration might outstrip their scenario. The film took so long in the making that Clarke said they would have to retitle it '2002'.

One of his personal favorites was 'Billy Budd'. Ustinov co-wrote the screenplay, produced, directed and acted in the movie.

If God intended us to believe in the auteur theory, then he had to create Robert Bresson. No other director is so obviously an auteur, leaving a trail of recognisable fingerprints, stylistic and thematic, on all of his 13 mature movies.

15 **Delusions of art.** Read this article from *The Economist* and answer the questions.

AN AUTEUR IN THE JUNGLE

Nowhere has the age-old conflict between high art and commerce been so effectively dissolved as in Hollywood. Few film directors in Tinseltown have any pretensions to being artists (except popular ones), and virtually all of those who do are deluded.

Francis Ford Coppola is an exception. With *The Godfather*, Mr Coppola produced that Hollywood rarity: an aesthetically ambitious highbrow movie that also earned stacks of cash. Then he did it again – in a sequel, no less.

But Hollywood cares little for auteurs, even profitable ones: especially when they start to make demands of its tolerance, patience and

1 If you have pretensions, you try to make people think you have qualities you don't really have. If you are deluded about something, are you mistaken?

2 If something is a rarity, do many of them exist?

money. Struggles between obsessive film-makers and controlling studio bosses have, at times, escalated to mythic proportions. Orson Welles, who battled furiously with the studio system (and lost) after his early triumph, *Citizen Kane*, is one legendary example.

Another is Mr Coppola and his ordeal over the making of *Apocalypse Now*, a Vietnamised version of Joseph Conrad's *Heart of Darkness*. That ordeal is the subject of a new documentary called *Hearts of Darkness: a Film-maker's Apocalypse.*

After considerable acclaim at the Cannes and London film festivals and a successful run on an American pay-tv channel, the film has recently been released in cinemas. Even casual fans of *Apocalypse Now* will find it engrossing. It is sharp, funny, and full of revealing amateur footage shot by Mr Coppola's wife, Eleanor. More than that, it is critically acute, presenting Mr Coppola and his films as object lessons in why Hollywood does not trust visionaries.

Apocalypse Now began filming in the Philippine jungle in 1976. It took 238 days on location to complete, not including time lost to a massive hurricane, which destroyed the film's sets, and a massive heart attack, which nearly destroyed its lead actor, Martin Sheen.

Three years and $35 million (a huge sum at the time) later, when *Apocalypse* won the top award at Cannes, Mr Coppola said of the experience: 'My film is not a movie. My film is not about Vietnam. It is Vietnam. The way we made it is the way Americans were in Vietnam. We had too much money, access to too much equipment, and little by little we went insane.'

Mr Coppola is not exaggerating. Performing one early scene, Mr Sheen is drunk to the point of an emotional breakdown. Mr Coppola rewrites the script each night. The ostensibly liberal film-makers pay Filipino workers a dollar a day to build an elaborate temple brick by brick. And when Marlon Brando arrives, he is a temperamental, corpulent mess – hardly the embodiment of Conrad's 'long gaunt figure of Kurtz.'

3 If something escalates, does it get less intense?   *escalate 121, 171* ⇑

4 Is a triumph a) a major success, or b) a minor one?

5 Do people have an easy time during ordeals?   *ordeal 18* ⇑

6 If you are casual about something, you don't give it a lot of thought. If something is engrossing, it is certainly not b _ _ _ i n g.   *footage 6* ⇑

7 Are acute observations stupid?

8 An informal word for insane is c _ _ _ y.

9 If you exaggerate, do you overstate things?

10 If something is ostensibly true, it looks as if is true, but is it necessarily true?

11 Temperamental people have a lot of different m _ _ _ _ s.

12 Are corpulent people gaunt?

Fiction, faction and other genres

genre

fiction
faction

A genre is a particular type of artistic, musical, cinematic or literary expression.

Fiction refers to stories and books about people and events invented by the author. **Faction** is a genre that uses techniques usually associated with fiction to recount real events, usually ones that have happened quite recently. (Compare this word with infotainment, a combination of information and entertainment, and docudrama, a dramatised documentary.)

infotainment 8 ⇑

docudrama 8 ⇑

Benedictus has been pushing more contemporary <u>fiction</u> into the mix of classics, non-fiction, thrillers and adventure stories.

This is the latest instance of our modern passion for 'true to life' facts. Docudramas, mini-series and the mongrel literary <u>genre</u> named '<u>faction</u>' now issue their versions of history while the participants are still alive and in a position to criticise. We have had a TV version of the ousting of Mrs Thatcher. Already the Charles and Di story is being pored over by Hollywood.

16 Genre quiz. Look at the examples and match the genres to their descriptions.

This is the trick that turned 'The Lawnmower Man' from a low-budget, gimmicky yarn into a minor <u>sci-fi</u> classic. As Jobe's brainpower multiplies and he acquires telekinetic powers, he decides only he knows what's good for the world and goes on the rampage.

We are not talking about Henry James. This is lowbrow <u>pulp fiction</u>.

Finally I managed to forgive myself with this justification: We all read an <u>airport novel</u> now and then. Watch a soap opera. Eat a Big Mac.

It illustrates a design fault that has long lurked in the <u>campus novel</u>: strip away the name-drops and the clever bits in speech marks and what you get is surprisingly old-fashioned.

To sentimentalise Hardy is to do violence to him; Polanski's Tess is like a sentimental <u>bodice-ripper</u>.

Scarlett is supposed to be a <u>page-turner</u> but it's 700 pages long. Anybody who could maintain a high level of excitement at that length would have to be considered a kind of narrative genius.

1	**sci-fi**	a	novel in a university setting
2	**pulp fiction**	b	the sort of novel sold at airports
3	**airport novel**	c	romantic historical novel
4	**campus novel**	d	very readable novel 'you can't put down'
5	**bodice-ripper**	e	low quality fiction
6	**page-turner**	f	short for science fiction

Editors, publishers, agents and ghosts

edit
editor

publish
publisher
publication

literary agent

ghost writer
ghost
ghost-write

An **editor edits** or corrects, changes and perhaps shortens what a writer has written and prepares it to be **published**, or promoted and distributed by a **publisher.** This process is publication. **A publication** is also something that is published, such as a book or newspaper.

editor *19* ⇑

A **literary agent** is someone who manages an author's business dealings with publishers.

A **ghost writer** or **ghost** is someone who **ghost-writes** or **ghosts** a famous person's autobiography for them, perhaps because they are incapable of writing it themselves.

◆ **LANGUAGE NOTE**

Ghost writer and **ghost write** are also written with a hyphen.

The book is poorly edited. There should be no place in the published version of a lecture for sentences like: 'I haven't obviously time to run over what I think would be the right answers here.'

'Obviously,' she said, 'we reject anything that is racist, sexist or stereotypist. Apart from that, I suppose we just choose the books with the most colour. I asked a children's book editor how common this was. 'Quite common,' she said.

The book contained information that might endanger Israel or Israelis. An attempt to prevent publication in the United States has failed and 50,000 copies have already been sold.

It's the first time for more than three years that a publication has been closed by the authorities who under the law have the right to revoke the publishing licence of any publication printing allegedly controversial or damaging material.

'I'm interested in the film deal as it serves the book,' says Virginia Barber, a New York literary agent. She used that strategy for Marti Leimbach, the first-time author of 'Dying Young' (Doubleday) and it worked. The film deal helped Ms Leimbach receive $500,000 for hardback and foreign rights.

The impression is hard to shake that Reagan's publicists or, perhaps his publishers, certainly his ghost-writer Robert Linsey, are saying: 'You lived through the presidency, now read the book.'

Having called a press conference to publicise his new ghosted book, Mansell refused to give out the traditional review copies.

17 Ghostly exercise. Read this extract from *The Times* and answer the questions.

TRICKS OF THE TRADE

I never had a terrible time as a ghost writer, probably because as a ghost you have to subsume your individuality completely. You can't impose yourself in any way. If you stop being transparent, then you're in trouble.

The real test of a good ghost is this. There was one person, I published his autobiography, which was very competently ghosted by a woman journalist from the *Daily Mail*. I heard him later talking about it, saying that he'd enjoyed the experience so much that he was tempted to make a career out of writing.

You could tell he genuinely believed it: somehow in his mind he'd become convinced that he'd written it. The fact that someone else had been involved had somehow been wiped. I think that's the sign of a job really well done: the ghost does not exist any more.

1 If you subsume X to Y, you make X less important than Y. Whose individuality does a ghost writer have to subsume their own individuality to? a) their editor's, b) their subject's, or c) their publisher's

2 If you do something very competently, do you do it well?

3 What does 'experience' refer to? a) talking to the journalist, b) writing, or c) reading what had been written

4 Wiped from what?

Reviewers and literary critics

review
reviewer

literary editor
literary critic

literati

A **reviewer** is a critic who writes book **reviews** in newspapers. A **literary editor** edits the pages of a newspaper where book reviews appear. A **literary critic** may write book reviews in quality dailies or may be someone who teaches and theorises about literature in a university.

Writers, editors, publishers, agents and critics may be referred to in the media, sometimes insultingly, as the **literati**, especially in the context of social occasions they attend.

◆ **LANGUAGE NOTE**

Review is a noun and a verb.
Literati has no singular form.

207

Can anyone explain why, when a novel is <u>reviewed</u>, we get a <u>review</u> of the novel; but when a biography is reviewed, we get an essay on the subject of the biography? Moreover, we can seldom tell when the <u>reviewer</u> is giving his own views on the subject and when he is giving (just occasionally) the biographer's.

A S Byatt has been a university teacher and <u>literary critic</u>, as well as a novelist.

The dream flared up briefly just before the last election when <u>literati</u>, rock stars and modish actors saw themselves replacing the golfers and grocers who currently <u>dine</u> at no. 10 Downing Street.

18 Linking the literati. Match the two parts of these extracts.

1 Over the past two decades a generation of culinary literati has emerged

2 ...Camden High School for Girls, an establishment much favoured

3 That Walter Scott was a Tory

4 The fact is, at the Booker, the glitterati   glitterati 21 ⇑

5 Phillips's scholarly and readable narrative certainly

6 New York's literati are failing to look beyond the glamorous surface.

a 'She is not all mouth and hair. She is clever.'

b are not the literati at all.

c by the quasi-literati of north London.

d that is only too willing to dissect verbally the contents of any given mouthful.

e is something of an embarrassment to the leftist literati.

f rescues Bridges from the sneers of the literati who never achieved half so much.

The glittering prizes

hardback
paperback

bestseller
  bestseller list

blockbuster

literary prize
  prize winner

royalties
  advance

In Britain and America, novels usually appear first in **hardback** or hard covers, and then, if successful, in **paperpack** at a lower price.

Books that sell very well are **bestsellers**. **Bestseller lists** show the top selling books in each category: paperback, hardback, fiction, non-fiction, and so on. Very successful books are, like very successful films, **blockbusters**.

Chances of commercial success are increased by winning a **literary prize**, like the Booker in Britain or the Goncourt in France. **Prize winners** can be sure of increased **royalties**, the money writers earn from each book sold, and a bigger advance, royalties paid in **advance**, for their next book.

◆ **LANGUAGE NOTE**

Bestseller is also spelt with a hyphen and as two words.

In America, the first edition of 50,000 went out with the drawings in all the wrong places. Hawking pointed this out and the publishers attempted to recall copies. It was too late: they had all been sold. In Britain, 'A Brief History of Time' went straight into the <u>bestseller</u> list at No 5 on June 26 and jumped to No 1 the following week. This week the book equals the record of 183 weeks in the top 10 bestseller list.

At Gatwick airport, where most travellers are families, women's <u>blockbusters</u> sell better. But at Terminal 4 in Heathrow, with a third of passengers Americans and Japanese, royal books fill the shelves.

France's most prestigious <u>literary prize</u>, the Prix Goncourt, can only be won once, so Romain Gary, for his second attempt, took his nephew's identity.

The value of the Booker Prize extends beyond its immediate cash pay-out of £2,000; the prize's promoters say that, under the spotlight of publicity, the <u>winner</u> is likely to sell another 50,000 copies in <u>hardback</u> and perhaps 150,000 in <u>paperback</u>.

Burns won a prize in the Jonathan Cape first novel competition, and he was henceforth marked out, by reviewers and the press, for first-class honours. But he was not marked out for huge <u>advances</u> on his <u>royalties</u>, which were undeservedly scant.

19 'It's happened awful fast.' Read this article about literary success from *The Independent on Sunday* and answer the questions.

A ONE-MAN INDUSTRY

'At times it sinks in. At times it's still kinda hard to believe. It's happened awful fast . . .' What has happened is this. Since 1991, Grisham, a 39-year-old former Mississippi lawyer, has sold, in America alone, around 40 million copies of his four novels.

He recently achieved the unprecedented quadruple whammy of having the No 1 hardback and the Nos 1, 2 and 3 paperbacks on the New York Times bestseller list. Last week *The Firm* made its 97th appearance in the paperback chart, *A Time to Kill* its 93rd and *The Pelican Brief* its 49th. Still only in hardback, *The Client* completed 45 weeks on the higher-price list. Grisham has also been a bestseller in 30 other countries.

1 If something is unprecedented, has it been done before?

2 A double whammy is a double success, double blow or double failure. How many events (in this case successes) does a quadruple whammy involve?

3 What name is given earlier in the article for the higher-price list?

The term 'cross-media influence' used to apply only to newspaper tycoons, but Grisham may be on the verge of becoming the first novelist to be referred to the Monopolies Commission. Just as the sales momentum of the books is relenting, the movies give them a new boost. *The Firm* and *The Pelican Brief* were both no 1 box office movies in America. The recent success of the latter returned the paperback to the paperback to the top slot in the book lists.

And so it goes on, a process with more of the feel of an industry than of a writing career. The movie of *The Client* is due later this year. The fifth Grisham novel, *The Chamber*, will be published in Britain and America in May. The film rights to that book were sold, before a word was written, for $3.75 million (£2.5m). Grisham's overall earnings for the year have been estimated at $20 – $25 million.

'The thing is, I never dreamed of being a writer,' Grisham says. 'It wasn't a childhood dream, it wasn't a dream in college. It just hit a few years ago and it hit because I saw something in a courtroom one day that inspired me to write *A Time to Kill*.

4 The Monopolies Commission is an official British organisation that decides whether a company, usually the result of a planned merger, will have an unfair competitive position. Is the reference to the Monopolies Commission here a) serious, or b) a joke?

tycoon *3, 91* ⇑

5 If something relents, does it speed up?

6 What is 'it'?

Art collections and exhibitions

art	**Art** is most often used to refer to painting, drawing and sculpture.
collection	Art in private hands or permanently on display in a museum or gallery is often referred to as a **collection**. **Exhibitions** or **shows** are usually temporary, perhaps touring from place to place. A show that covers part or all of an artist's career is a **retrospective**. Things on display in collections or exhibitions are **exhibits**.
exhibition exhibit	
show	
retrospective	
show	
curator	The person in charge of a museum or gallery or part of one is a **curator**.

◆ **LANGUAGE NOTE**

Exhibit is a noun and a verb.

The Queen's fortune of several thousand million pounds is made up of vast landed estates, large holdings in many commercial companies, and a fabulous art collection which includes hundreds of thousands of drawings by Leonardo da Vinci and many rare paintings from Italy and the Netherlands.

At the end of Munch's life the chief curator of a Paris museum wanted to make a large retrospective show of his paintings, and he went to see Munch, and it was in 1939. And Munch was 76, and Munch told him, 'I'm not ready for Paris yet.'

At the top of the scale, there have been some very high powered exhibitions, including such international names as David Hockney and Francis Bacon. But also there have been several key exhibitions of Scottish artists such as Steven Campbell and Pete Harrison – given solo shows in the city for the first time.

Many exhibits in the collection have never been seen by the public. Important items which have spent decades in museum storerooms include a silver, gold and steel helmet once worn by an eighteenth century Indian ruler and a beautiful nineteenth century red silk sari.

Adolphe-Felix Cals and Stanislas-Henri Rouart exhibited at more of the eight 'Impressionist' exhibitions than Sisley did, but almost nobody now can think of a single painting by either of them.

20 **Art as business.** Read this article from *The Independent* and answer the questions.

IT'S PROFITABLE, BUT IS IT ART?

At the Royal Academy's exhibition in London, Monet merchandise from postcards and address books to champagne and sugared almonds is likely to bring in £1 million.

In New York, $65 million worth of reproductions and publications, from statuettes to art books, are sold annually by the Metropolitan Museum of Art, and an independent chain of up to 100 American museum shops is vying for a market share. Museum shop sales in the West are booming.

In Russia, in spite of the lure of hard currency the Russians have hitherto been inept at mounting exhibitions and marketing artworks abroad. At the Hermitage in St Petersburg, where the works of Rembrandt and Watteau (1684-1721) are particularly well represented, the

1 Merchandise is g _ _ d s .

2 If you vie for something, you c o _ p _ _ e for it.

3 If something has a lure, is it attractive?

4 If you're inept at something, you're not good at it. If you're good at something, are you ept at it?

cramped sales kiosk offers tired postcard views and about 30 books with titles obstinately unrelated to the exhibits.

In fact the Hermitage is the only major Russian museum not to have done a deal that will take seven of the country's top galleries and museums into the world-wide merchandising, licensing and exhibitions market.

David Segal, an academic economist, and his Russian wife Katya, have struck exclusive deals that will thrust Russia's hidden art treasures into the billion dollar museum art market, through their British information technology company, ARS. The company is to handle much of the commercial activity of three of the museums for at least 20 years.

If the Segals have their way, gone are the days when the Metropolitan in New York could give the Russians 25,000 postcards, which cost $1,200 to print, in return for its 1975 blockbusting three-month exhibition of Scythian gold from the Hermitage. Today a 'participation fee' of at least $250,000 would be expected.

The question of how much the commercialisation of Russia's art treasures might eventually be worth is not easy to estimate. The most frequent comment of Western retail buyers, however, is that they are sitting on a gold mine. In Russia, the 3 million Western visitors a year offer a huge potential market. At present they spend less than £25 a head on goods, simply because there are so few to buy.

'High Russian culture has remained almost a state secret in museums there, sections of which are closed to all but their curators,' Dr Segal says. 'We are not interested in the cliché Russian image – the chromium plated samovars, toy balalaikas and nests of dolls that tourists came schlepping back with.'

Instead, headscarves based on the entrancingly intricate and colourful floral patterns that adorned well-heeled Russian ladies' headscarves in the nineteenth century will be printed.

5 Is the opposite of cramped
   a) spacious, b) clean, or
   c) expensive?

6 Merchandising is the selling of
   g _ _ _ s related to things like
   films, museums and theme parks
   such as Disneyland.

7 If something is thrust
   somewhere, does it happen
   slowly?

8 If you have your way, do
   you get what you want?

9 Who are 'they'?

10 Schlep is an informal word for
    come or g _.

11 If something is entrancing, does
    it make people feel delight and
    wonder?

12 Are well-heeled people poor?

The art market

auction
auction house

bid
bidder

go under the
   hammer
come under the
   hammer

reserve price
reserve

When paintings and other artworks are sold at **auction**, with buyers or **bidders bidding** against each other in a series of competitive **bids**, they are said to **go under the hammer** or **come under the hammer**.

The **reserve price** or **reserve** is a minimum price set by the **auctioneer** or **auction house** or by the seller.

Although reserve prices are not normally disclosed to bidders, an auctioneer will usually give a guide price.

Proposed legislation also seeks to require auction houses to disclose the reserve or a minimum price which is now kept secret. It also seeks to limit a museum's ability to sell works from its collections at auction in order to buy other works of art.

The sculptures he brought to light again included a very early Bernini, an 'Allegory of Autumn' and 'Bust of Youth' by Bernini's contemporary, Francesco Mochi. These were bought in a Paris auction in 1988, unattributed and bid for by hardly anyone else.

Christie's is also hoping to attract lovers of Impressionism and the best painting to come under the hammer in a sale at King Street tonight is a view of Charing Cross Bridge by Monet, estimated at £2 to £2.5 million.

A portrait by Dutch master Rembrandt went under the hammer for £4.18 million at Sotheby's yesterday.

YAYO
Montreal
CANADA

Yayo, Canada – Cartoonists & Writers Syndicate

21 **Under the hammer.** Read this BBC report and say where each of the following people starts speaking: they each speak once. Not all the numbers indicate a change of speaker.

a newsreader   b auctioneer   c reporter   d art expert

VAN GOGH BOOST FOR ART MARKET

(1) A world record price for a work of art was set in New York last night when a painting by the Dutch artist Vincent van Gogh was sold at Christie's auction house for $82.5 million (around £50 million.)

(2) Sebastian O'Meara looks at the art market's continuing boom. (3) $73 million, 74 million, $75 million. 75 million, the bid is still in the room, against the telephone. For you sir, $75 million. (Applause)

(4) The hammer comes down at Christie's saleroom in New York on Vincent van Gogh's portrait of Doctor Gachet, a powerful study of the doctor who treated the artist just before van Gogh committed suicide a hundred years ago. (5) The buyer was a dealer from Tokyo, acting on behalf of an unnamed Japanese company.

(6) He was bidding from the auction room floor against an anonymous competitor bidding over the telephone. And to the $75 million price called by the auctioneer, he will have to add 10 per cent commission, bringing the price to $82.5 million. (7) That's almost $20 million more than the previous record for a work of art, set by another van Gogh painting, *Irises*, in 1987.

columnist *19, 36* ⇑

(8) Godfrey Barker, arts columnist with the *Daily Telegraph*, says the astronomical price caught experts by surprise. (9) I am hugely surprised, as everybody is in New York, by $82.5 million for *Doctor Gachet*.
(10) It's an academic picture, hardly anyone knows it. It's a wonderful picture, but good heavens, hardly any of us had looked at it until it came up this month.

(11) It's a big surprise to become the world's most expensive picture.
(12) Christie's experts had expected the painting to fetch between $40 and $50 and even that estimate was far from certain.

Crossword

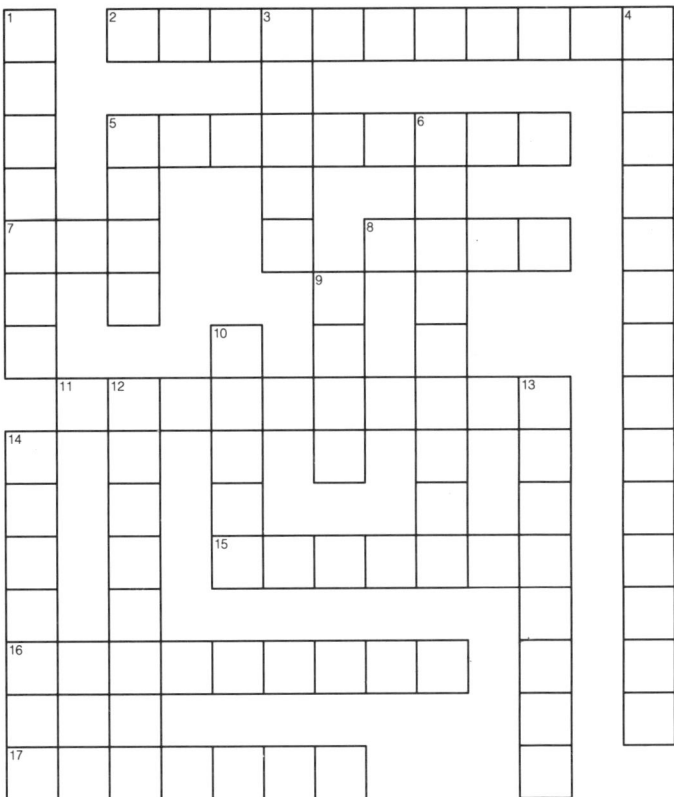

Across

2 Very successful book or film (11)

5 First shown (9)

7 See 14 down

8 Exhibition of entertainment or art? (4)

11 Theatrical deal-maker (10)

15 Hopeful young actress (7)

16 Books, plays and so on with artistic ambitions may do this as well (9)

17 These bad films are birds (7)

Down

1 Performers do these for an audience that wants more (7)

3 Famous actor in a small role (5)

4 Backward-looking art shows (14)

5 What the scathing critic does to a show (4)

6 See 10

9 Often given in order of appearance (4)

10 and 6   Last chance for changes before the show is given 5 across treatment? (5, 9)

12 Roberts, Streep, Nicholson and Schwarzanegger are examples of this (8)

13 Standing ones are particularly good (8)

14 and 7 across   The play with the most performances has this (7, 3)

⟨8⟩ Sport as metaphor

Players, playing fields, goalposts and own goals

key players
level playing field
moving goal posts
own goal

The language of sport is used a lot in the media in non-sporting contexts.

For example, individuals or organisations with a strong influence on events, influential individuals or countries in negotiations, or important companies in a market, are **key players**.

If some participants in a competitive situation feel that others have an unfair advantage, they complain about the lack of a **level playing field**.

If the objective for something changes, people expected to reach that objective complain about **moving goal posts** or the fact that other people are moving the goalposts.

If you make an unforced mistake that gives an advantage to your opponent, you score an **own goal**.

gaffe *35* ⇑

Margulies emerges in the report as a key player in the illegal £25 million share-support operation that enabled Guinness to triumph over Argyll in the £2.7 billion battle for control of Distillers in 1986. But while other leading figures in the affair, including Ernest Saunders, Guinness's former chairman, have been arrested and jailed, Margulies was never charged.

Talks that took place earlier this month between China and Vietnam. If these two key players in the region are sincere about wanting to normalise their relations, Cambodia will be the first to benefit.

Phil Condit, one of Boeing's top executives, says: 'We all need to keep working towards a level playing field. What always worries me is the threat that someone not playing to this set of rules will destroy the whole system of free trade.' That 'someone' is Airbus, the four-nation consortium of French, German, British and Spanish groups, which Boeing claims has received up to $26 billion in direct subsidies, plus billions more through indirect military subsidies and 'privileged access' to commercial research programmes.

Mr de Klerk criticized the ANC for what he said was moving the goal posts. He said that in the past the ANC had said there were obstacles to negotiation. The obstacles were that people were still in prison or exiled for political reasons. De Klerk said now that prisoners are being released and the exiles are coming home, the ANC is setting up new demands.

In the Commons on Thursday, the prime minister asserted that Labour governments 'never have' delivered growth. Not so, as Mr Kinnock swiftly pointed out. Growth under the Labour governments 1964–70 was 2.8% a year; in 1974–79 it was 2%. Since 1979, under the Tories, it has averaged a mere 1.75%. Another own goal by Mr Major.

1 **Self-inflicted injury.** Read this extract from *The Times* and answer the questions.

RATNER ON COURSE FOR COOL RECEPTION

Gerald Ratner, the outspoken chairman of Ratners group, faces his shareholders today for the first time since making his comments about the quality of some of the goods in his shops. If past annual meetings are anything to go by, his shareholders, like Mr Ratner, are unlikely to mince their words.

His speech to the Institute of Directors in April in which he declared his products were 'total crap' was the own goal of the season. Since then he has spent £500,000 on damage limitation advertising and analysts think group sales in Britain are down 5 per cent.

The downturn in sales at the group, which includes Ernest Jones and H Samuel, is due more to recession than to Mr Ratner's remarks. Business in America is believed to have benefited from the upturn in the economy there.

1 Do outspoken people say what they really think?

2 If you go by something, do you use it to predict what will happen in the future?   shareholder *75* ⇑

3 Do outspoken people mince their words?

4 If something is crap, is it good quality?

5 'The downturn in sales is due more to   downturn *89* ⇑
the recession than to   recession *89* ⇑
Mr Ratner's remarks.'   upturn *89* ⇑
Do you believe this?

Professional fouls and the red card

professional foul	Someone trying to gain advantage by doing something unacceptable, knowing it to be unacceptable, commits a **professional foul**.

red card
  shown the red
  card
	An individual or organisation disciplined for unacceptable behaviour is **ruled offside** or **shown the red card**.

offside ruled offside	These expressions come from football (soccer).

He accused Labour of being 'truly sick' and of frightening vulnerable people with its claims that the Conservatives intended to privatise the health service. 'Their scare is what is called in football a professional foul. They know it's wrong and think that it's worth it. What they are doing is setting out quite deliberately to frighten some of the most vulnerable people in our society. They exploit the very people they pretend to care for.'

The terms should establish a series of checks and balances to ensure that incompetent regulators and irregular institutions are <u>ruled offside</u>. The agreement would have called a halt to BCCI's misadventures years ago.

The 'Financial Times', reflecting on the World cup final in which two Argentine players were sent off for fouling Germans, says Mr Ridley seems certain to be <u>shown the ministerial red card</u> for the same offence. The 'Daily Express', however, gives its whole-hearted support to Mr Ridley's speech.

2 **Professional foul or red card?** Complete each extract with one of these two expressions in their appropriate grammatical context.

1 If the bigwigs of Scottish football don't start listening to those in the game with a proven track record of success amid a sea of failure it will be time to _____ _____ _____ _____ to football's has-beens.

2 Not surprisingly, Jones has infuriated doctors convinced that enough is known about heart disease to pin down smoking, diet and lack of exercise as the three main causes. Professor Charles Forbes, a founder of Sharp, the Scottish Heart and Arterial Prevention Group, said: 'I cannot believe what he is saying and I totally and violently disagree with it. For anybody to suggest any such thing is ludicrous. It is so far out that he should be _____ _____ _____ _____ ?

3 Those who dream up the Euro-follies of Brussels and who would stuff their rules and regulations into every crevice of European life must be
_____ _____ _____ _____ .

4 The Association of London Authorities said that the decision not to give the Olympic Games to the capital was a sad indication of the state of London. 'The government deserves a _____ _____ . It is to blame for the crumbling infra-structure in the capital.'

5 But then Crufts Dog Show was never quite what it seemed. There has always been a very fine line between good sportsmanship and the _____ _____ .

Favourites, front runners and stalking horses

race	A competitive situation may be described as a **race**. *race 46* ⇑
stakes raise the stakes odds	The **stakes** are things that participants risk winning or losing as a result of competitive activities such as business or political negotiations. If participants **raise the stakes**, they do something that increases the value of what may be won or lost.
favourite outsider	The **odds** are the probability that someone or something will succeed. The **favourite** is the person or the *favourite 46* ⇑ organisation expected to succeed. An **outsider** is a participant with little chance of succeeding.

| stalking horse candidate | A **stalking horse candidate** in an election, for example to elect a party leader, is one who does not want or expect to win, but who wants to test the popularity of the main candidate or candidates. |

◆ LANGUAGE NOTE

Favourite is spelt **favorite** in American English.

There has been a close <u>race</u> in Sind where no party has emerged with a majority yet.

This debate need never have been held, as the Commons was repeatedly told yesterday. But Mr Major, knowing the risks, insisted on holding it. He <u>raised the stakes</u> by threatening at one stage to call an election if he lost.

Edward Heath was <u>favourite</u>, Margaret Thatcher the 50-1 <u>outsider</u>. 'A gentleman came up to me,' Mr Pollard recalled, 'and said: 'I should be careful of that Thatcher if I were you.' I immediately reduced her <u>odds</u> to 20-1.'

I'm almost sure there'll be a leadership contest and I don't think it's going to be of a <u>stalking horse</u> nature. I think it will be at a significant level and I think we will have a new prime minister before Christmas.

front runner	In competitive situations, the **front runner** is the person or organisation winning or leading before the final result is still decided. Two people or organisations with about the same chances of winning or with about the same amount of support are said to be **neck and neck** or **running neck and neck**. People or organisations losing in a competitive situation are **trailing** or **trailing behind** and those in the weakest position **bring up the rear**.	front runner 46 ⇑
neck and neck run neck and neck		neck and neck 46 ⇑
trail trail behind		trail 46 ⇑
bring up the rear		
dead heat	If it looks as if there will be no clear winner, or if there is no clear winner in the final outcome, commentators talk about a **dead heat**.	

Although negotiations are still in progress with several companies that have access to satellites, the <u>front-runner</u> is Hutchison Whampoa, a Hong Kong-based trading company, which plans to broadcast five channels on its STAR-TV service.

<u>Trailing</u> in these elections and out of the presidential race if these usually reliable projections are confirmed, are the ruling APRA party, suffering from the unpopularity of high inflation and widely accused of corruption, and the divided parties of the Peruvian left.

In the lucrative market for telecommunications switching products, Alcatel is <u>neck and neck</u> with the US giant AT&T with about 15 per cent market share each. Canada's Northern Telecom, Germany's Siemens and Ericsson of Sweden are the other major players, with GPT <u>bringing up the rear</u>.

Thornburgh was the heavy favorite, leading in some polls by 40 points, but that lead has now shrunk to a nearly dead heat with Democrat Harris Wofford.

3 **Key position.** The same expression from this section (containing more than one word) is missing from all these extracts. Which is it?

Lafontaine, the opposition Social Democrat	...	who was stabbed in the neck by a part-time
French-educated former banker who was the	...	before the priest declared his candidacy. Bazan
his present mess, the paper says, should be the	...	for next year's Nobel Prize.
That makes Frankfurt one favourite. Another	...	is Luxembourg, which already hosts the
awaited show of London Fashion Week. A	...	for the Designer of the Year award, Storey
BUTTERFLY ROLE. Actor Jeremy Irons is the	...	for the star role in a film version of controversial
Davies insisted, 'Graham Steadman is the	...	for the full-back position but I'm enjoying

Track records

track record	Someone's history, especially if it's a history of achievement, is their **track record**.
hurdles	If someone overcomes obstacles, these obstacles may be referred to as **hurdles**.
marathon	A competitive or other activity that takes a long time and is very tiring is often described as a **marathon**.

stumbling block *160* ⇑

These expressions come from athletics.

Professor Ogata is regarded by diplomats and UN officials as an exceptional woman, with an impressive track record in diplomatic, human rights and academic fields.

In the GATT talks, the hurdles that have to be negotiated are formidable, and there is a possibility they won't be cleared, or won't be cleared in time. Failure is a real possibility.

And budget negotiators held another budget marathon session that lasted past midnight. There is still no agreement on the deficit reduction plan.

4 **Exhausting activities.** Match the two parts of these 'marathon' expressions.

1 After six days of marathon

2 Atlantis astronauts will hit the halfway mark of their marathon

3 Early this morning, they emerged from a 48-hour marathon

4 Next week, he has another marathon

5 One fun event in London this Saturday is a Poethon, or Poetry Marathon.

6 Platform 2's marathon

7 The BBC's annual television marathon

a bargaining session with an agreement they say provides increased job security.

b concert last week was something of a musical breakthrough.

c for children's charities ended early today with pledges of more than £17 million.

d journey, taking in Brazil, Uruguay, Argentina, Chile and Venezuela.

e military and medical research mission today, charging ahead with a variety of experiments.

f negotiations, he finally reached agreement with the nine striking unions of the New York *Daily News*.

g Some celebrated poets, as well as 120 other reciters, will be moving around the City, speaking memorised poems aloud.

A whole new ball game

ball game

ballpark figure
ball park estimate

softball
hardball

out of left field

singles
doubles
homers

strikes
three strikes and
you're out

A **whole new ball game** is a totally new situation where ideas previously held no longer apply.

A **ballpark figure** or a **ballpark estimate** is a rough estimate.

If you **play hardball** in a business or political situation, you act or negotiate in an aggressive way, and if you play **softball**, you don't.

If something comes **out of left field**, it happens suddenly and unexpectedly.

If you **hit homers**, you have spectacular successes. If you **hit singles and doubles**, you work in an unspectacular but methodical way towards your goal.

Three strikes and you're out is usually used in the context of crime in the United States to mean that criminals who commit three serious crimes should stay in prison for life.

These expressions come from American baseball.

◆ **LANGUAGE NOTE**

Ballpark is also spelt with a hyphen and as two words.
Ball game is also spelt with a hyphen and as one word.

Plainly Geoffrey Howe's resignation this week has totally changed the leadership scene within the party. We are now in a different <u>ball game</u>.

- Margaret, can you estimate how many calls you've been receiving since Magic Johnson's announcement? — Well, I can't give you anything more than just a sort of <u>ballpark figure</u>.

- They're also worried about the question of how a vote in Congress would come out. - I think just in a ball park estimate, about 60 to 40. 60 would support, 40 per cent would be opposed.

Kingsmill is disappointed by the banks' tactics. 'We had hoped for an amicable settlement,' she says. 'But it looks as if they want to play hardball.'

The big firms can't predict what changes Hyatt's announcement may bring. All the firms we've talked to have indicated they don't know. This has really come out of left field to most people.

At Disney, Katzenberg has declared his preference for hitting singles and doubles, rather than homers, and the studio has a reputation for hiring stars whose popularity – and price – is down.

In America's battle against crime, the latest slogan is borrowed from baseball – 'three strikes and you're out' – a rule that locks up repeat offenders for life without parole after their third felony.

5 **The wrong ball game?** Put these sections of an article
from *Today* in the correct order.

ARNIE PLAYS HARDBALL

a But last night Arnie was denying any knowledge of Janice's plight and blamed all the legal actions on his production company. Through his lawyer, Leonard Marangi, he even offered to remove the claim on her home to seize back the debt when she sells up.

b She said, 'Whenever I made an offer through my lawyer he would come back and say, 'His lawyer says Arnold won't go for that,' says Janice, of Los Angeles. 'I just don't understand why a person of his means would play hardball with someone like me who is struggling.'

c Arnold Schwarzenegger has been hounding a penniless widow for £13,000. The actor wanted to recall the cash from Janice Nickerson when her husband died before completing work on his luxury house. Arnie, who is worth £100 million, even slapped a legal claim on her home. Mrs Nickerson says she offered him £6,000 as a settlement – all she had left from her husband's pension – but he turned her down.

d The part-time secretary was left with a string of debts when her husband James died of a heart attack three years ago. He had been paid £40,000 to install a cinema for Arnie who claims in interviews, 'Money's not important. My self-respect is.' The actor won a court judgment against his widow for the return of £10,500. Janice, 46, said she agreed to pay it off a little at a time but that was also refused.

Bodyblows and knockouts

bodyblow
deal a bodyblow
deliver a
bodyblow
on the ropes
knockout
knockout blow
out for the count

If something **deals a bodyblow** or **delivers a bodyblow** to something or someone, it affects them for the worse.

Someone or something **on the ropes** is in a bad situation. If something or someone suffers a **knockout** or a **knockout blow**, or if they are **out for the count**, they are in a very bad situation from which they cannot recover.

These expressions come from boxing.

◆ **LANGUAGE NOTE**

> **Bodyblow** and **knockout** are also spelt with a hyphen and as two words.

Angeli didn't know he was about to take pictures of a little scene that would make him upwards of £1 million for a few rolls of film and bring about the worst <u>body blow</u> the mighty House of Windsor has ever suffered and perhaps damage the entire future of the British monarchy.

Actor Jack Palance was <u>dealt a bodyblow</u> just before he went to pick up his Oscar – his wife Elaine Rogers, 41, told him she wanted a divorce.

Using an analogy from boxing, Mr Wilson said the Poll Tax is already <u>on the ropes</u> and, if people stand firm, it is only a matter of time before it is <u>out for the count</u>.

Nick Faldo is ready to aim a <u>knockout blow</u> at the Americans in the US Professional Golf Association Championship at Bellerive today.

6 **Out for the circulation count.** Read this article from *Today* and answer the questions.

WHO DELIVERED THE KNOCKOUT BLOW FOR 'PUNCH'?

At 11.30 yesterday morning, a man in a black suit stood up to read the last rites over a British magazine that had become an institution.

1 Who normally reads the last rites and when?

223

In a 133-word statement, publisher Michael Sharman brought to an end 150 years of Punch, the humorous magazine variously described as witty and provocative or lame and contrived. ...

The demise of *Punch* was greeted with resignation rather than shock among the 28 advertising and editorial staff who gathered round Sharman and editor David Thomas in the magazine's seventh-floor office in London's Blackfriars.

Nobody needed to ask who had delivered the blow, because they had seen it coming. After all, its circulation, while stabilising, was down to 33,000 last year, compared with the 175,000 it sold in the Forties.

Other graphs were heading down, too. In 1991, according to Graham Wilson, managing director of Punch's publisher United Newspapers, the magazine lost more than £1 million.

'We supported it through its 150th anniversary last year and we spent a not inconsiderable amount on promotion, but circulation has not responded dramatically or enough, and neither has advertising,' he says.

In fact, there were so many bodyblows aimed at 'Punch' that it was small wonder it finally went out for the count. ...

2 Is lame and contrived humour funny?

3 Does something continue to exist after its demise?

4 If you greet something with resignation, do you react hysterically?

5 If a figure stabilises, does it change?   circulation *18* ⇑

6 Is a not inconsiderable amount a lot?

7 If something is small wonder, is it surprising?

Gambits, stalemate and the endgame

gambit

stalemate

If you use a **gambit** in order to achieve your goal, you use subtle means whose purpose may not be immediately clear to others, and which often involve taking a risk.

Where there are no clear winners or losers in a competitive situation, or no apparent solution to a conflict, there is **stalemate** or a stalemate.

stalemate *161* ⇑

endgame	The final stages in a competitive situation or a conflict are the **endgame**, especially when the final outcome is not clear.

These expressions come from chess.

◆ **LANGUAGE NOTE**

Endgame is also spelt with a hyphen and as two words.

The Guadalajara summit may come to seem little more than a smart <u>gambit</u> by President Salinas to massage Latin American apprehension about Mexico's ever-closer integration with the United States.

After 25 days of <u>stalemate</u> with full media coverage, the end of the longest prison protest in British history came almost as an anti-climax.

Because the ground assault is going well for the allied forces, attention is turning to the <u>endgame</u>. Where will the allied forces stop? What are the ultimate goals of this military operation?

7 **Stalemate or endgame?** Match the two parts of each extract and complete them with one of these two words: a) stalemate or b) endgame.

1 As the crisis moves towards _____ , it is clear the president

2 By 1912 the war had reached _____ and both Rome

3 North and South Korea have faced each other across a heavily guarded

4 The Democrats' complaint: that with the budget talks nearing _____ , the president should be back in Washington and

5 There's now something of a _____ with the authorities anxious not to appear too heavy handed ahead of the elections due on 20th May,

6 There remains a _____ both on the battlefield

7 They've been kind of drawing maps of institutions

a all over Europe. But they haven't done it in a way that reveals what their political and philosophical _____ is.

b and Constantinople were ready to talk peace.

c and his advisers have raised the stakes.

d and in the negotiating chambers.

e demilitarized zone ever since the Korean conflict ended in _____ in 1953.

f lending his support to the sensitive negotiations and not playing politics on the campaign trail.

g while at the same time concerned not to be seen as weak in the face of an unauthorized demonstration.

Crossword

Across

2 Avoid being shown this if you want to keep your record clean (3, 4)

3 and 4 down Leader of the pack (5, 6)

5 A foul of this kind is no amateur attack (12)

8 A self-inflicted injury is an own _____ (4)

9 Three of these and you're eliminated (6)

13 Not just a single or a double (5)

14 Talks, sessions, and negotiations of this kind are exhausting (8)

15 Losers may complain that the playing field is not like this (5)

16 See 11 down

17 If you get knocked out, you're out _____ _____ _____ (3, 3, 5)

Down

1 You don't have much chance of succeeding when these are against you (4)

2 An opponent on these is in difficulty (5)

4 see 3 across

6 This may or may not turn out to be the winner (9)

7 There's no way out of a situation like this (9)

10 A history of success is a record like this, but not only in athletics (5)

11 and 16 across Victory comes through this decisive action (5-3, 4)

12 If the goal _____ keep moving, you don't know where you are (5)

Answer key

1 The Media

1 Media partners 1

1 attention, coverage, exposure
2 empire
3 hype
4 campaign
5 circus

2 Media partners 2

1 guru
2 analyst
3 pundit
4 correspondent
5 magnate, mogul, tycoon

a analyst
b pundits
c magnate, mogul, or tycoon
d guru
e correspondent

3 People in the media jungle

N	E	W	S	R	E	A	D	E	R	
	E									
		W								
N	E	W	S	G	A	T	H	E	R	E
	D	I	S	C	J	O	C	K	E	Y
		B	R	O	A	D	C	A	S	T
					S					
	A				T					
	N					E				
	C			R	E	P	O	R	T	E
	H	O	S	T						
	O									
C	O	R	R	E	S	P	O	N	D	E

4 All the news that fits

1g, 2d, 3f, 4a, 5c, 6b, 7e

5 The bland leading the bland?

1a, 2a, 3 Yes, 4 plays (and events in general), 5 one-liner, 6 No, 7 No, 8b.

6 TV diet exercise

1d, 2a, 3f, 4e, 5g, 6c, 7b

7 Decline and fall of the networks

1 Yes. 2b. 3 The broadcasters and the Wall Street dealmakers (finance specialists). 4 Yes. 5 noticing. 6a. 7 No. 8 No. 9 The bagel incident. (A bagel is a kind of pastry that some Americans eat for breakfast.) 10 Yes. 11 ABC, CBS, NBC. 12b. 13a. 14 They are business specialists who work with figures, such as accountants. 15a.

8 Sorting out the channels

1 'Going for the Big Break': a, d, e, f, g, i
   'Shouting at the box': b, c, h, j, k
2 turn over, channel-hop, flip over, change over.

9 TV gore

1 No. 2 Downwards. 3 You admit it, perhaps reluctantly. 4 warning. 5 federally- imposed reforms. 6 protest. 7 Because they would not have to legislate and risk being accused of limiting freedom of speech. 8 No. 9 No. 10 Three. 11 zapping.

10 Primitive exchanges?

'The Promise of Multimedia': a, g, e, d
'A Step through the Looking Glass': b, c, f, i, h

11 Shock Horror Headlines

1, c, ix
2, j, ii
3, f, x
4, a, vi
5, g, vii
6, i, iv
7, d, viii
8, e, iii
9, b, v
10, h, i

12 Naming of parts

1, g, v
2, d, vii
3, a, vi
4, b, iv
5, f, iii
6, e, i
7, c, ii

13 Privacy and the paparazzi 1

1c. 2 police. 3 Yes. 4 No. 5 No. 6 Yes.

14 Privacy and the paparazzi 2

a 10
b 12
c 3, 5, 11
d 7
e 1, 6
f 2, 4
g 8
h 9

15 The last chance saloon

1 *News of the World*: Patsy Chapman, *The People*: editor not named, *Daily Express*: Sir Nicholas Lloyd, *The Sun*: Kelvin Mackenzie, *The Independent*: editor not named. 2b. 3a. 4 tip. 5 Yes. 6 Yes. 7 No. 8 Soldiers, for example. 9 Mellor wanted to limit the freedom of the press to report on people's private lives, but had something to hide himself: his affair with an actress. 10 conceal. 11 Yes. 12 Yes. 13 Yes. 14 Mackenzie scuppered Major's plans to limit the freedom of the press to report on people's private lives.

16 Lexicographically correct or verbally challenged?

1a. 2a. 3 No. 4 Yes. 5 No. 6b. 7 Well, would you? 8 Because its critics say it appears to exclude women. 9 No. 10 Yes.

Crossword solution

2 Politics

1 On the campaign trail

1c, 2f, 3g, 4a, 5d, 6b, 7e

2 Electioneering clichés

1d: tours
2h: rhetoric
3e: promise
4b: clichés
5c: assault
6g: tactics
7f: budget
8a: thuggery

3 Controlling the spin

1 No. 2 No. 3 Yes. 4 Yes. 5 No. 6b. 7 No. 8 Yes. 9 No. 10 Yes. 11 point.

4 The right candidate

3, 5, 7: smoke-filled room
1, 2, 4, 6: smoke-filled rooms

5 Digging for Gold

1 Yes. 2 reveal. 3 No. 4 No.
5 savaged. 6 Yes. 7 counter. 8 Yes.
9 lying. 10 a.

6 Presidential paranoia

1 No. 2 dirt. 3 a. 4 No. 5 bug. 6 No.
7 Yes. 8 plots. 9 No. 10 b. 11 a.
12 paranoia. 13 Yes.

7 Last-minute polls

a: 1, 9, 11, 13
b: 2, 5
c: 8, 12
d: 4
e: 3
f: 10
g: 7
h: 6

8 Ahead in the race, level pegging or trailing behind

1b, 2h, 3f, 4e, 5d, 6c, 7g, 8a

9 The ballot or the bullet?

Voting, polling or balloting takes place at polling stations. In a secret ballot, voters mark their ballot papers in polling booths and place them in a ballot box. The ballot box is often mentioned when contrasting democratic methods with terrorist ones.

10 Legislature quiz

1b, 2e, 3a, 4f, 5d, 6g, 7c, 8h, 9j, 10i

11 A political killing?

a, c, e, b, d

12 Witch way to vote?

1h, 2d, 3b, 4g, 5a, 6c

13 Surprising victory or massive defeat?

A categorical
B comfortable
C convincing
D crushing
E decisive
F devastating
G heavy
H overwhelming
I resounding
J spectacular

14 Throw the rascals out

Reporter: 1, 4; Politician: 2, 6

15 Hung parliaments and splinter parties

If, in a system usually dominated by two parties (usually the British one), neither party gets an overall majority, commentators talk about a hung parliament.
A minority party is a party holding a relatively small number of seats, and a fringe party is one with extreme views and very little support.
A party may be made up of rival groups or factions. A splinter faction may break away to form a separate party, known as a breakaway party or a splinter party.

16 Creaking coalitions

1 Yes. 2 goes. 3 existence. 4 Whoever formed a government. 5 No. 6 Yes.
7 control. 8 No. 9 No. 10 No. 11 Yes.
12 Yes. 13 constituency. 14 No. 15 Yes.
16 important.

17 Political lame ducks

1c, 2e, 3f, 4b, 5a, 6d

18 Grassroots partners

1 support
2 opinion
3 followers
4 feeling
5 level
6 campaign
7 revolt

19 A return to dictatorship?

1 No. 2 No. 3 contempt, despise.
4 Yes. 5 No. 6 No. 7 No. 8 No.
9 No. 10 dictatorship, fast.

20 Broken promises

a: 6
b: 3, 8, 9
c: 2, 4, 7, 12
d: 1
e: 13
f: 11
g: 10
h: 5
1 threatening. 2 No. 3 No. 4 prison.
5 count.

21 Missing item

protest

22 Familiar scenarios

Johannesburg: d, b
Korea: e, c, f, a

23 Forms of exile

1d: permanent
2e: internal
3a: voluntary
4b, c, f: forced, enforced, involuntary

Crossword solution

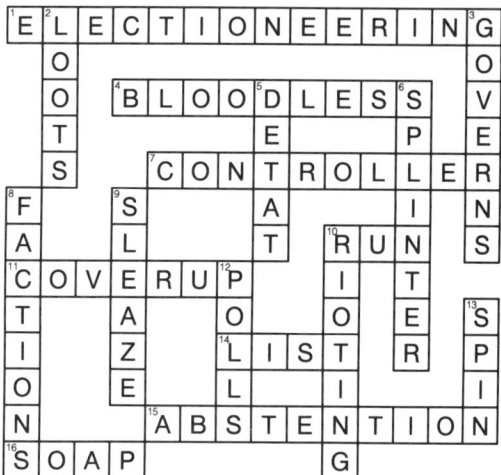

3 The Business pages

1 Headline humour 1

1f, 2a, 3b, 4e, 5d, 6c

2 Headline humour 2

1e, 2a, 3h, 4c, 5f, 6d, 7b, 8g

3 Key investment words

1 blue-chip
2 gilt-edged, securities
3 currencies
4 shareholders
5 investment, shares
6 listed
7 Wall Street
8 speculators
9 commodities
10 currencies
11 equities
12 played, stock market

4 Bulls and bears

1c, 2b, 3g, 4d, 5e, 6a, 7f

5 Frenzied or lacklustre?

The actual word used is given in brackets.
1a (quiet)
2d (frantic)
3c (heavy)
4d (frantic), c (heavy), a (dull)
5a (thin)
6a (negligible)
7d (hectic)

6 Rising and falling prices: verbs

1 advanced
2 edged higher
3 shot up
4 drifted
5 dived
6 edged up
7 crashed
8 slipped
9 dropped
10 crashed

7 Rising and falling prices: nouns

1 Advances
2 plunge
3 slump
4 collapse
5 surge
6 collapse
7 crash
8 plunge
9 slide
10 drop

8 Record lows

But euphoria easily gives way to pessimism. When gains are lost, with prices falling to new lows, journalists may talk about a collapse or a crash. If prices fall a very long way and there seems to be no limit to the amount they may drop, they use the parachuting image of free fall. Commentators may even compare events to a nuclear accident like Chernobyl and talk about a market meltdown.

9 Growth and recession

a, c; b, h; d, f; e, g

10 Cast of business characters

1e, 2g, 3c, 4a, 5b, 6f, 7d, 8h

11 Dramatic departures

'Mere' suggests that £175,000 is not a lot considering Trott was ousted from a company he had founded.

12 Types of wrongdoing

1c, 2b, 3f, 4a, 5d, 6h, 7e, 8g

13 Spectacular wrongdoing

d, b, a, c, h, i, j, e, g, l, f, k

14 Flowing through to the bottom line

1e, 2f, 3c, 4b, 5g, 6a, 7d

15 Business bestiary

1 dinosaur, 2 vultures, 3 pterodactyls, 4 vultures, 5 dinosaur

16 Calling in the receivers

1 a recession sickness, terminally ill;
  b undertakers, mortalities;
  c bloodbath
2 a receivership;
  b going concern;
  c recovery;
  d corporate recovery; insolvency
  e go into liquidation
3 b

Crossword solution

```
      R           B
  H O U S T       O
  A A       S H O O T S
  N E R D S   H M     S O
  D         A     O A
A S S E T S T R I P P E R
        U       E   I   S
  B E A R I S H   C K
  U       N       O K
  L   L A C K L U S T R E
  L   R     D   U     D
  S   O   L E A P S   G
O     U   R     O A   E
I     N   S     A     S
L A U N D E R   F I R M
```

4 Work, Unemployment and Welfare

1 The pros and cons of telecommuting

1 fewer drivers on the roads; better family life; save time by not commuting
2 fresher workforce; no need for expensive, central offices; big savings
3 less control over staff
4 loss of total privacy of the car
5 house invaded by machinery and paperwork

2 Luxurious packages

1g, 2j, 3i, 4h, 5c

3 Putting on the golden muzzle

Complaints about discrimination and other injustices at work are called grievances. An employee may take or bring their grievance to a tribunal, which during its hearings (sessions), arbitrates in the case (listens to the arguments of both sides) and proposes a settlement: an agreement that both employer and employee accept. Sometimes the settlement, especially in the US, includes a condition called a golden muzzle that prevents both sides from commenting on it. (A muzzle is usually something you put on a dog to prevent it from barking or biting.) Compare this expression with 'golden handshake'.

4 Unfair dismissal 1

1a, e, c; 2b, f, d

5 Unfair dismissal 2

1b, e, d; 2a, f, c

6 Is downsizing rightsizing?

1 downsizing, 2 downsizing, 3 workforce, 4 downsizing, 5 overstaffed, 6 workforces, 7 layoffs

7 An expensive drink

1d, 2e, 3b, 4c, 5a

8 Jobless combinations

1c, e, f, g; 2a, d; 3b

9 Unemployment blues

1 industrialized, 2 unprecedented, 3 rapid, 4 rising, 5 unemployment, 6 boom

10 Types of strike

1a, e, h, k; 2g, i, j; 3c, d, f; 4b, l

11 Crippling paralysis

1e, 2b, 3f, 4a, 5c, 6d

12 Stepping it up...

If governments and organisations say they will not give in to strikers' demands, they say they will not agree to them. The strikers may respond by intensifying their industrial action: they escalate it or step it up. If, in a dispute, one side reduces its demands and gives in to some or all of the demands of the other side, commentators talk about a climbdown. In this situation, one side climbs down or gives in.

13 Violent tactics

1 noisy and violent. 2 scabs. 3 they lay them off. 4 escalated. 5 b. 6 The strike and the associated picketing and violence. 7 The main consideration. 8 The management stopped the presses.

14 Can it be averted?

1 and 4

15 Welfare combinations

1f, 2d, 3e, 4a, 5c, 6g, 7b

16 Kinds of cuts

surgery on bloated welfare systems; trimming at the edges of its commitment; Kohl brought expenditure down

17 Missing persons and money

2a, 4b, 5c, 7d, 8e, 11f, 12g, 15h

Crossword solution

```
  J        W           S
D O W N    A      G E T
T    B     S            R
E       S T A T E S     I
L A Y      U      C     K
E          R    G R A V E
C A T    A X E    B     R
O        L        R     E
M A S S    O U T S      A
M    E          O       K
U    X    F    B L A C K
T R I B U N A L         E
E    S    L             R
S E T T L E M E N T S
```

5 Crime and Punishment

1 Making the headline fit the crime

1j, 2b, 3h, 4a, 5d, 6e, 7f, 8c, 9i, 10g

2 Types of theft

1d, 2f, 3c, 4g, 5e, 6a, 7b

3 Sorting out car crime

Joyriding: b, d; joyriders, joyriding, joyriding
Carjacking: a, c, e, f; carjacking, carjacked, Carjacking, carjacking

4 Getaway scenarios

1e, 2b, 3a, 4d, 5c

5 Successful or unsuccessful

1 made their getaway; 2 fled empty-handed; 3 fled empty-handed; 4 fled empty-handed; 5 made their getaway

6 Gun culture

Presenter: 1, 6
Specialist A (Jerry Gliden): 2
Specialist B (Gwen Fitzgerald): 7

7 Arresting combinations

1 house arrest;   2 murder charge;
3 persistent offender;   4 political
detainee;   5 arbitrary detention;
6 damaging allegation;   7 fair trial

8 Bail logic

1 denied;   2 refused;   3 granted;
4 refused;   5 refuse

9 Types of crime

1b, 2i, 3c, 4e, 5h, 6a, 7g, 8f, 9j, 10d

10 A glamorous profession

a, d, f, b, e, c

11 Crime makes the headlines

1 FOUR COMPANIES FACE
   PROSECUTION OVER UNFIT WATER
2 MANDELA DEFENDANT ALLEGES
   MURDER PLOT
3 MEN AND THEIR NATURAL
   SEXUALITY ON TRIAL
4 EX-COUNCIL OFFICERS FACE FRAUD
   CHARGES
5 GUARDS FACE TRIAL FOR BERLIN
   WALL KILLINGS
6 CLOSED TRIAL FOR LEADERS OF
   CHINESE PROTESTERS

12 Guilty!

d, b;   i, c;   e, j;   f, a;   g, h

13 Types of witness

1d, 2e, 3a, 4c, 5f, 6g, 7h, 8b

14 Guilty or not?

guilty

15 Terms of acquittal

1f,   2g,   3d,   5c,   7b,   8d,   10a,   12h

16 Does the sentence fit the crime?

	Crime no. 1: Bank robbery	Crime no. 2: Burglary	Crime no. 3: Domestic Assault
Canada	3–5 years	5–7 years	6 – 18 months
Denmark	6 years	1–2 years	30–40 days, possibly suspended
England	10–14 years (or 5 years in a young offenders' institution)	3–7 years	6 months, suspended for 2 years
Ireland	5–6 years	–	–
Norway	2–3 years	–	–
Spain	4 years, 2 months, 1 day	–	–
Texas	10 years	10 years	10 days
Cook Islands	–	3 months' probation	–
Kenya	–	3 years plus hard labour	6 months
Scotland	–	–	Fine

17 Crime is not a game

1 criminal, television.   2 fake, toy.
3 That he was just copying something
that he had seen on TV.   4 quash,
dismissed, lenient

18 Debating the death penalty

1 restore, reintroduce.   2 strong; decisive
vote; enormous majority. 3a.   4 bringing
back the hangman; the return of the
rope. 5b.   6 Yes.   7 A play. 8a.   9 No.

Crossword solution

```
          ¹D      ²P
    ³P  ⁴A C Q U I T T A L
⁵H E I S T      S    S
O   C T  ⁶B ⁷M U G S  ⁹A
U   K O  A  I    O   N
¹⁰S U P E R G R A S S  ¹¹P   S
E   O N  R  S   ¹²L A W
B   C ¹³E V I D E N C E  E
R  ¹⁴K E Y  S    D    A R
¹⁵E Y E  ¹⁶S A T    ¹⁷F   I
A   T    E  ¹⁸D    I   N
K  S    ¹⁹B A R G A I N I N G
S       S       E
```

6 Diplomacy and war

1 Talks combinations

1 resume
2 concluded
3 convene
4 attend
5 walked out of
6 broken off
7 suspend

2 Dizzy heights of diplomacy

1 Yes. 2 Yes. 3 fit. 4 load. 5 No.
6 No. 7 No. 8 rock. 9 No.

3 Atmosphere and differences

a friendly   atmosphere
b constructive   atmosphere
c significant   difference
d optimistic   atmosphere
e major   difference
f relaxed   atmosphere
g fundamental   difference
h sharp   difference
i business-like atmosphere
j positive   atmosphere
k frank   atmosphere
l substantial   difference

4 Compromise or deadlock?

1g, 2a, 3d, 4e, 5c, 6f, 7b

5 Key to destruction

brinkmanship

6 Trade talks scenario

1 It's a play on the American pronunciation of 'got': We've got a deal.
2 Yes. 3 No. 4 negotiate. 5 Yes. 6b.
7 counterpart. 8 Yes. 9 break down.
10 No. 11 ratify. 12 Yes.

7 Diplomatic relations

Break off: d, e; restore: a, b, c, f
1 resume
2 cut off
3 broke
4 renew
5 re-established
6 re-opened

8 Types of war

1f: full-scale
2b: Cold
3a: nuclear
4e: conventional
5c: civil
6g: devastating
7d: guerrilla

9 Adversaries and allies

The different sides in a civil war are warring factions. Factions opposing a central government are rebels. Countries or factions with the same interests ally themselves with each other and are allies forming an alliance. Opposing sides are enemies, adversaries or foes.

10 Types of fighting

1 sporadic
2 bitter
3 fierce
4 heavy
5 intense
6 renewed

11 Language damage

1 Yes. 2 No. 3 No. 4 Yes. 5 destroy.
6 Land, buildings, machinery, and so on.
7 destroy. 8 War and destruction.

12 Protecting relief organisations

a, d, f, b, c, e

13 Keeping the peace

1 unreasonable. 2 foolish. 3 Yes. 4 No.
5 destruction. 6 Yes. 7 Yes.

14 Peace partners

1b: move
1d: initiatives
2c: broker (2nd word)
3d: dividend
4f: movement
5c: treaty (1st word)
6a: prize

Crossword solution

```
C   S       T     B   A
O P P O S I T E   D E A L
L   O       N     L   L
L   R     C A S U A L T Y
D A M A G E   I   I
  T   D     I O   G     W
M E D I A T I O N G   E
  R   C     S H E R P A
  A       S       E     R
B L O O D S H E D N     Y
R           O     T
O       C O M P R O M I S E S
A       O
D I P L O M A T I C A L L Y
        D
```

7 Entertainment and the Arts

1 Entertaining combinations

1e, 2c, 3b, 4f, 5d, 6a

2 Which brow?

1b, 2a, 3a, 4a, 5a, 6a, 7a

3 Missing item

showbiz

4 A government of philistines?

1 No 2 No 3 b 4 hardly 5 No 6 No

5 Partners in performance

1 virtuoso   6 riveting
2 dazzling   7 delightful
3 electrifying   8 off-form
4 stunning   9 mediocre
5 scintillating   10 lacklustre

6 Dangerous debuts

Interviewer: 1, 3, 7, 10;
Interviewee: 2, 4, 8, 11

7 That's showbusiness

1d, a, f; 2b, c; 3e, h, g

8 Audience displeasure

'Duchess of York at Dutch National
Ballet': a, f, d
'Hot under the Collar': e, c, b

9 Good and bad reviews

Favourable: ecstatic, rapturous
Unfavourable: scathing, stinking,
unflattering

10 The Great White Way

1 beginning. 2 Yes. 3 Yes. 4 run. 5a.
6 Yes. 7 No. 8 brave. 9 Yes. 10 Yes.

11 Hollywood clichés

1 legend, 2 casualties, 3 heart-throb,
4 hype, 5 classics, 6 glitz, 7 dream
factory

12 Excess in Tinseltown

'You'll never eat lunch...': a, e, c

'Tussle in Tinseltown': f, b, d

Missing words: a: moguls; d: cast,
script-writers, stars; e: mogul;
f: producers

Answers to questions: 1 Yes. 2 Ovitz
and the Walt Disney chiefs. 3 The
typical mogul. 4 Yes. 5a. 6 No. 7 No.

13 Box office partners

1f, 2b, 3c, 4e, 5a, 6d

14 Film terms

1d, 2c, 3e, 4b, 5f, 6a

15 Delusions of art

1 Yes. 2 No. 3 No. 4a. 5 No.
6 boring. 7 No. 8 crazy. 9 Yes. 10 No.
11 moods. 12 No.

16 Genre quiz

1f, 2e, 3b, 4a, 5c, 6d

17 Ghostly exercise

1b. 2 Yes. 3b. 4 Their memory.

18 Linking the literati

1d, 2c, 3e, 4b, 5f, 6a

19 'It's happened awful fast.'

1 No. 2 Four. 3 hardback. 4b. 5 No.
6 The dream of being a writer.

20 Art as business

1 goods. 2 compete. 3 Yes. 4 No; the
word ept does not exist. 5a. 6 goods.
7 No. 8 Yes. 9 The people running
Russia's museums. 10 go. 11 Yes. 12 No.

21 Under the hammer

Newsreader: 1;   auctioneer: 3;
reporter: 4;   art expert 9

Crossword solution

1	2	3	4	5	6	7	8	9	10	11	12	13	14
E	B	L	O	C	K	B	U	S	T	E	R		R
N		A											E
C		P	R	E	M	I	E	R	E	D			T
O		A		E			R						R
R	U	N		O		S	H	O	W				O
E		S			C		E						S
S			D		A		A						P
I	M	P	R	E	S	A	R	I	O				E
L	E		E	T		S		V					C
O	G		S			A		A					T
N	A			S	T	A	R	L	E	T			I
G	S							I					V
E	N	T	E	R	T	A	I	N					E
S	A							O					S
T	U	R	K	E	Y	S		S					

8 Sport as metaphor

1 Self-inflicted injury

1 Yes. 2 Yes. 3 No. 4 No. 5 Well?

2 Professional foul or red card?

1 show the red card
2 shown the red card
3 shown the red card
4 red card
5 professional foul

3 Key position

front-runner

4 Exhausting activities

1f, 2e, 3a, 4d, 5g, 6b, 7c

5 The wrong ballgame?

c, d, b, a

6 Out for the circulation count

1 A priest when someone dies. 2 No.
3 No. 4 No. 5 No. 6 Yes. 7 No.

7 Stalemate or endgame?

1c: endgame,   2b: stalemate,
3e: stalemate,   4f: endgame,
5g: stalemate,   6d: stalemate,
7a: endgame

Crossword solution

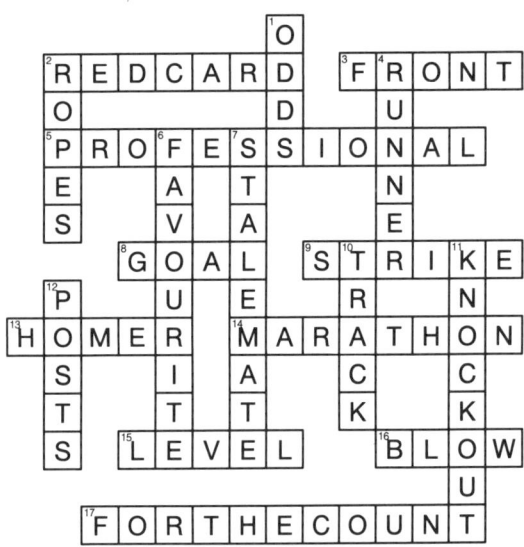

Index of Key Words

The numbers are page numbers for key word entries in the commentaries.

241

Acknowledgements

The author and publisher are grateful to the following for permission to reproduce the extracts and cartoons on the pages indicated:

Extracts:

Page 8, "Blaming the Beltway": ©*Times Newspapers Ltd*, 18.8.92;
Page 11, "Three Blind Mice": *The Economist*, vol 321, issue 7729;
Page 13, "Shouting at the box": © *News (UK) Ltd.* All rights reserved;
Page 13, "Going for the big break; Remote control and TV viewing": © Nicholas Lezard, *Times Newspapers Ltd*, 30.9.92;
Page 14, "US Networks under the Gun": from *Newsweek*, 12.7.93, © 1993, Newsweek Inc. All rights reserved. Reprinted by permission;
Page 17, "The promise of multimedia": *The Economist*, 25.12.93;
Page 17, "A step through the Looking Glass" by Steve Conner & Robin Baker. First published in *The Independent*, 4.11.90;
Page 23, "Mellor: the right to know and the right to stay in office": © Joe Ashton, *Times Newspapers Ltd*, 25.7.92;
Page 25, "Stalking the Stars": from *Newsweek*, 19.10.92, © 1992, Newsweek Inc. All rights reserved. Reprinted by permission;
Page 27, "Was it a hollow press victory?": ©*Times Newspapers Ltd*, 6.7.92;
Page 29, "An All-American Industry": *The Economist*, 25.12.93;
Page 36, "Bight-sized campaigners": © John Miller, *Times Newspapers Ltd*, 4.8.92;
Page 41, "Clinton hires tough Texan to ride Shotgun": ©*Times Newspapers Ltd*, 4.9.92;
Page 43, "What Watergate was all about": ©*National Public Radio*® 1992. Excerpt from National Public Radio's News and Information programs are used with permission of National Public Radio. All rights reserved;
Page 45, "Poll late, poll often": © Bernard Levin, *Times Newspapers Ltd*, 29.7.91;
Page 51, "Brazil's Wild West": from the *BBC World Service*;
Page 53, "Thais cast spells to check poll fraud": ©*Times Newspapers Ltd*, 12.9.92;
Page 55, "Limiting terms of office": ©*National Public Radio*® 1991. Excerpts from National Public Radio's News and Information programs are used with permission of National Public Radio. All rights reserved;
Page 58, "Out of all proportion": from an article first published as "Noughts and Crosses in the Polling Booth" by Kenneth Baker MP in *The Independent*, 6.10.90;
Page 65, "Bianca eyes the Nicaraguan presidency": © Christine Toomey *Times Newspapers Ltd*, 30.8.92;
Page 67, "Burmese elections pass off peacefully": from the *BBC World Service*;
Page 70, "Violent demonstration in Johannesburg": from the *BBC World Service*;
Page 70, "Violent demonstration in S. Korea": from the *BBC World Service*;
Page 95, "Limp handshake": ©*Times Newspapers Ltd*, 15.10.91;
Page 97, "Beauty who ran up a beastly debt", © Garth Alexander, *Times Newspapers Ltd*, 22.9.91;
Page 103, "No sector can feel secure": ©*Times Newspapers Ltd*, 10.2.91;
Page 106, "Working from home 'could save billions' ": ©*Times Newspapers Ltd*, 22.7.92;
Page 107, "£200,000 to fly smokeless Sultan": copyright *News (UK) Ltd.* All rights reserved;
Page 109, "Taking on the Great White Way": from *Newsweek*, 19.7.93. © 1993 Newsweek, Inc. All rights reserved. Reprinted by permission;
Page 114, "Getting the ax": copyright ©*National Public Radio*® 1992. Excerpts from National Public Radio's News and Information programs are used with permission of National Public Radio. All rights reserved;
Page 115, "Man loses drink case appeal": ©*Times Newspapers Ltd*, 25.9.92;
Page 117, "Jobs": from *Newsweek*, 14.6.93, ©1993, *Newsweek Inc.* All rights reserved. Reprinted by permission;
Page 122, "Teamster mob in press battle": © Mike Graham, New York, *The Times Newspapers Ltd*, 2.8.92;
Page 126, "Dismantling the European Welfare State": from *Newsweek*, 5.10.92, © 1992, Newsweek Inc. All rights reserved. Reprinted by permission;
Page 127, "Cutting the dole": copyright *News (UK) Ltd.* All rights reserved;
Page 133, "Your car or your watch/ Hijacking US cars": *The Economist*, 14.9.91;
Page 133, "Joy riders did not see themselves as criminals": © *Times Newspapers Ltd*, 2.9.92;
Page 137, "Packing a piece": copyright ©*National Public Radio*®. Excerpts from National Public Radio's News and Information programs are used with permission of National Public Radio. All rights reserved;
Page 142, "Where legals dare": copyright *News (UK) Ltd.* All rights reserved;
Page 148, "Imelda Marcos acquitted": from the *BBC World Service*;
Page 151, "Lawyers uncover big divide in nations' jail terms": © *Times Newspapers Ltd*, 9.9.92;
Page 153, "TV raid copycat": copyright *News (UK) Ltd.* All rights reserved;
Page 155, "Hanging vote": from the *BBC World Service*;
Page 159, "Diplomatic sherpas feel the strain in surfeit of summits": ©*Times Newspapers Ltd*, 10.7.92;
Page 165, "We Gatt a Deal": copyright *News (UK) Ltd.* All rights reserved;
Page 173, "The First Casualty": copyright ©*National Public Radio*® 1991. Excerpts from National Public Radio's News and Information programs are used with permission of National Public Radio. All rights reserved;
Page 175, "Red Cross emblem to go electronic": from the *BBC World Service*;
Page 177, "The limits to intervention": *The Economist*, 16.11.91;
Page 186, "Playing to the gallery": by David Lister. First published in *The Independent*, 1.11.90;
Page 189, "Avoiding the Butcher of Broadway": copyright ©*National Public Radio*® 1991. Excerpts from National Public Radio's News and Information programs are used with permission of National Public Radio. All rights reserved;
Page 192, "Hot under the collar": ©*Times Newspapers Ltd*, 27.8.91;
Page 192, "Duchess of York at Dutch National Ballet": ©*Times Newspapers Ltd*, 11.7.91;
Page 195, "Broadway plays safe": *The Economist*, 8.1.94;
Page 199, "You'll never eat lunch in this town again": copyright ©*National Public Radio*® 1991. Excerpts from National Public Radio's News and Information programs are used with permission of National Public Radio. All rights reserved;
Page 199, "Tussle in Tinseltown": © Susan Elliott, *Times Newspapers Ltd*, 16.8.92;
Page 203, "An Auteur in the Jungle": *The Economist*, vol. 1321, no. 7737;
Page 207, "Tricks of the Trade": ©*Times Newspapers Ltd*, 6.9.92;
Page 209, "A one-man industry": first published as "Sue, Grabbit & Write", in *The Independent on Sunday*, 6.2.94;
Page 211, "It's profitable, but is it art?": first published as "Capitalising on culture back in the USSR", by John Windsor in *The Independent*, 22.10.90;
Page 214, "Van Gogh boost for art market": from the *BBC World Service*;
Page 217, "Ratner on course for cool reception": ©*Times Newspapers Ltd*, 8.7.91;
Page 222, "Arnie plays hardball": published in *Today*;
Page 223, "Who delivered the knockout blow for 'Punch'?": copyright *News (UK) Ltd.* All rights reserved.

Every effort has been made to contact owners of copyright material. If there are any omissions, the publishers will be glad to rectify these, when the title is reprinted.

Cartoons:

Page 12, Kambiz, originally published in *Courrier International - Paris* © *Cartoonists & Writers Syndicate*;

Page 14, Bill Schorr, *Kansas City Star - United Feature Syndicate;*

Page 16, Stayskal, *Tampa Tribune*;

Page 29, Henry Payne, *United Feature Syndicate*;

Page 38, Peterson, © *Cartoonists & Writers Syndicate*;

Page 40, Wasserman, ©1994, *Christian Science Monitor News Service*. Distributed by Los Angeles Times Syndicate;

Page 48, Mitchell, Originally published in *Courrier International - Paris*. © *Cartoonists & Writers Syndicate*;

Page 60, Cris Riddell, *The Economist*;

Page 75, Roger Beale, *The Financial Times*;

Page 78, David Simonds, *The Economist*;

Page 79, Robinson, Originally published in *Courrier International - Paris*. © *Cartoonists & Writers Syndicate*;

Page 89, Handelsman, *Editors Press Service;*

Page 94, from *The Wall Street Journal*. Permission, *Cartoon Features Syndicate;*

Page 99, Don Wright. ©*The Palm Beach Post*;

Page 112, Signe Wilkinson. © *Cartoonists & Writers Syndicate*;

Page 115, Signe Wilkinson, © *Cartoonists & Writers Syndicate*;

Page 125, Chris Riddell, *The Economist*;

Page 136, ©1993 Engelhardt in the *St. Louis Post & Dispatch*. Reprinted with permission;

Page 136, Jack Ohman, © *Tribune Media Services*. Reprinted by permission;

Page 146, Harley Schwadron, *Wall Street Journal*;

Page 149, Stayskal, *Tampa Tribune*;

Page 161, Gamble 1993, *The Florida Times-Union*;

Page 178, Bill DeOre, Reprinted with permission from *The Dallas Morning News*;

Page 179, Pancho, © *Cartoonists & Writers Syndicate*;

Page 186, Gerberg, © *Cartoonists & Writers Syndicate*;

Page 197. Danzinger, © 1994, *Christian Science Monitor News Service*. Distributed by Los Angeles Times Syndicate;

Page 200, Locher, copyright ©*Tribune Media Services*. Reprinted by permission of Editors Press Service Inc;

Page 213, Yayo, © *Cartoonists & Writers Syndicate*.